BE MY GUEST

FOOTBALL SUPERSTARS
IN AUSTRALIA

BE MY GUEST
FOOTBALL SUPERSTARS
IN AUSTRALIA

Jason Goldsmith and Lucas Gillard

FAIRPLAY
PUBLISHING

First published in 2021 by Fair Play Publishing
PO Box 4101, Balgowlah Heights NSW 2093 Australia

www.fairplaypublishing.com.au

ISBN: 978-1-925914-17-7
ISBN: 978-1-925914-18-4 (ePUB)

Cover design and typesetting by Leslie Priestley.

Front cover: George Best reads Soccer Action with Kisrin Oswin,
Sherril Slamson and Eileen McCarthy.
(Photo: Carlos A Picasso, 3 June 1983, Laurie Schwab Collection with thanks to Dr Roy Hay).
Back cover: Ray Clemence arrives at Sydney Airport with his wife Veronica,
and children Julie (L), Sarah and 8-week-old Stephen.
(Photo: Tim Linsen, 30 May 1978, Fair Play Collection)
Thanks to the following for the use of photographs:
Jim Butterfield, Fair Play Collection, Buddy Farah, Dr Roy Hay, David Jack, Peter Rowney,
Newcastle Jets, Schwab Collection, John Sydenham, Sydney FC.
Other photographs via: Alamy, Shorrock Collection, Wenn.com

All inquiries should be made to the Publisher via sales@fairplaypublishing.com.au

NATIONAL
LIBRARY
OF AUSTRALIA

A catalogue record of this book is available from the National Library of Australia.

Contents

Foreword

Australian pitches have been graced by the greatest footballers the world has ever seen.

The likes of Sir Stanley Matthews, Pele, Franz Beckenbauer, Maradona, Cristiano Ronaldo, Leo Messi, David Beckham and Zinedine Zidane have all played football in Australia, representing either their country or their club.

What's lesser known is that our football clubs have also hosted some of the most legendary players in the world.

We have had World Cup winners, Copa America winners, European Cup and Champions League winners all play minutes in the State and National Leagues of Australia.

Four Ballon d'Or awards have been represented in the former National Soccer League (two of those belonged to Kevin Keegan). Ferenc Puskás, the mightiest of Magyars, won the NSL as South Melbourne coach. Melbourne Olympic Silver Medallist with Yugoslavia, Dragoslav Sekularac, one of the greatest dribblers the world has known, went on to make Melbourne his home—twice winning a NSL Cup with Heidelberg United after a successful spell with Footscray JUST.

There have been gods and rogues, journeymen and gentlemen from across the globe who have suited-up for Australian club sides. From local to state, from the NSL to the A-League, some of the greatest players of all time have left their footprints on Australian football pitches.

Be My Guest presents the many reasons why living legends chose to try their luck in Australia, and why Australian clubs were willing to give them a platform.

Australia has an amazing and at times quirky football history, and *Be My Guest* shows us just how connected we are to the rest of the world and reminds us that Australian club football history is something truly to be cherished.

Craig Foster

Introduction

Football is not Australia's most popular spectator sport.

It is widely played, but it has historically been hidden in sports pages after reams of Australian Rules football or Rugby League content. There is interest in the game, evidenced by the thousands who will show up for a Socceroos World Cup qualifier, or to see Manchester City play Real Madrid in 2015, or the thousands who were turned away from seeing Kevin Keegan play for Blacktown because Marconi Stadium was fit to burst.

The challenge for National League football in Australia has long been turning those glimmers of interest into flames of passion for local clubs. Converting the couch Australian football fan—who has often found it easier to slide into love with teams from the homeland of their parents or grandparents—is the driving force behind clubs offering short-term contracts to 'name' players.

Be My Guest focuses on guest players on short-term contracts who were welcomed by Australian clubs as lightning rods for media and fan attention.

There have been a mix of world class, average-quality class and frayed stickers to slap on a billboard. Some guests worked out, and some didn't. Some pulled crowds but were abject on the field. Others were three classes above their opponents (and teammates) but didn't influence crowds.

But they have one thing in common. They all manifested someone's vision of a prosperous Australian National League, a league worthy of the football royalty.

These comets have burnt bright for a week or two during the domestic season and then left a void that struggles to be refilled.

There is little doubt that these guests tick the boxes in terms of increased local crowds and TV ratings. But the initial sugar hit doesn't encourage the theatre-goers to come back and watch the rest of the season or become lifelong fans of that particular club.

The football clinics, autographs and selfies allow for some nostalgia and great memories for the fans of the world game, but surely these have been existing football fans who follow the game either here or overseas.

They have, however, become a point of reference for the global football community. The Brazilians know of the A-League through Romario, the Japanese via Kazu and Shinji Ono, and the Italians thanks to Alessandro Del Piero.

Some of Australia's wacky recruitment methods, such as scouting players via ten-year-old YouTube highlights, Legends games or from other sports, have probably undone the hard work Australian football achieved.

What it does show us is that Australia has so many football stories worth telling.

We hope you enjoy the read as much as we enjoyed researching and writing it.

TIMELINE

Alex 'Sandy' Young
Tongala,
2 games, 1 goal

Peter Price
Gladesville-Ryde,
10 games, 9 goals

STATE LEAGUE ERA

Takis Loukanidis
Pan-Hellenic,
9 games, 1 goal

STATE LEAGUE ERA

1976

Francis Lee
St George,
2 games, 0 goals

Mimis Papaioannou
Heidelberg United
(Fitzroy Alexander),
2 games, 2 goals

STATE LEAGUE ERA

Charlie George
St George,
6 games, 1 goal

Malcolm Macdonald
South Melbourne,
3 games, 3 goals

Graeme Souness
West Adelaide,
6 games, 1 goal

Adrian Alston
Canberra City,
9 games, 3 goals

NSL ERA

Peter Marinello
Canberra City,
11 games, 1 goal

Ray Clemence
St George,
2 games, 0 goals

Ralph Coates
St George,
11 games, 3 goals

Bobby Charlton
Newcastle KB United,
1 game, 0 goals

Craig Johnston
Newcastle KB United,
9 games, 0 goals

NSL ERA

Ian Callaghan
Canberra City,
9 games, 0 goals

Martin Peters
Frankston City,
5 games, 3 goals

Eamonn Bannon
Frankston City,
4 games, 2 goals

Mimis Papaioannou
Western Suburbs (VIC),
9 games, 6 goals

NSL ERA

1980

Martin Chivers
Frankston City,
2 games, 0 goals

Justin Fashanu
Adelaide City,
5 games, 3 goals

Bobby Charlton
Perth Azzurri,
3 games, 0 goals
Blacktown City,
1 game, 1 goal

NSL ERA

1981

Bob Latchford
Brisbane Lions,
5 games, 4 goals

Bobby Moore
Inglewood Kiev,
2 games, 0 goals
Rockingham United,
1 game, 0 goals
Cracovia,
4 games, 0 goals

Mick Channon
Newcastle KB United,
3 games, 3 goals
Gosnells City,
1 game, 1 goal

Justin Fashanu
Adelaide City,
6 games, 2 goals

NSL ERA

1982

Alan Ball
Floreat Athena,
4 games, 0 goals

Ted MacDougall
St George,
9 games, 2 goals
Floreat Athena,
4 games, 1 goal

Craig Johnston
Newcastle KB United,
4 games, 4 goals

NSL ERA

1983

George Best
Brisbane Lions,
4 games, 0 goals
West Adelaide,
1 game, 1 goal
Osborne Park Galeb,
1 game, 1 goal
Dee Why,
1 game, 1 goal

Mick Channon
Newcastle KB United,
6 games, 0 goals
Salisbury United,
1 game, 2 goals

NSL ERA

1985

Ossie Ardiles
St George,
1 game, 0 goals

David Provan
Sydney Olympic,
5 games, 5 goals

Kevin Keegan
Blacktown City,
2 games, 1 goal

Trevor Brooking
Kelmscott SC,
8 games, 3 goals

NSL ERA

1986

Eli Ohana
Sydney City,
5 games, 1 goal

NSL ERA

1987

Danny McGrain
Rochedale Rovers,
3 games, 0 goals

NSL ERA

5

1988

Ioannis (John) Samaras
South Melbourne,
1 game, 1 goal

Ciccio Graziani
APIA-Leichardt,
2 games, 0 goals

Alan Brazil
Wollongong City,
12 games, 4 goals

Trevor Francis
Wollongong City,
3 games, 2 goals

Paul Mariner
Wollongong City,
2 games, 0 goals

NSL ERA

1989

Kosta Kouis
Heidelberg United,
4 games, 1 goal

George Best
Devonport City,
1 games, 0 goals

NSL ERA

1993

Jimmy Case
British Wanneroo,
3 games, 0 goals

Andrea Icardi
Marconi, 1993-94,
8 games, 0 goals

NSL ERA

1999

Ian Rush
Sydney Olympic,
2 games, 1 goal

NSL ERA

2000

Peter Beardsley
Melbourne Knights,
2 games, 0 goals

Aljosa Asanovic
Sydney United, 2000-01,
2 games, 1 goal

NSL ERA

2001

Nicola Berti
Northern Spirit, 2001-02,
8 games, 0 goals

Aljosa Asanovic
Sydney United, 2001-02,
2 games, 0 goals

NSL ERA

2005

Kazuyoshi Miura
Sydney FC, 2005-06,
6 games, 2 goals

A-LEAGUE ERA

2006

Benito Carbone
Sydney FC 2006-07,
3 games, 2 goals

Romario
Adelaide United, 2006-07,
4 games, 1 goal

Gianfranco Zola
Marconi,
0.5 games, 0 goals
APIA-Leichardt,
0.5 games, 0 goals

A-LEAGUE ERA

2007

Mario Jardel
Newcastle Jets, 2007-08,
11 games, 0 goals

A-LEAGUE ERA

2013

William Gallas
Perth Glory, 2013-14,
15 games, 1 goal

A-LEAGUE ERA

2014

David Villa
Melbourne City, 2014-15,
4 games, 2 goals

A-LEAGUE ERA

2015

Luis Garcia
Central Coast Mariners,
2015-16,
10 games, 2 goals

Kostas Katsouranis
Heidelberg United, 2015,
1 game, 1 goal

A-LEAGUE ERA

2018

Usain Bolt
Central Coast Mariners,
2018-19,
2 games, 2 goals

A-LEAGUE ERA

Part 1:

The Guest Players Who Left an Impression on Australian Football

The Tongala Sensation: Australia's First Guest Alex 'Sandy' Young

Tongala, 1914, 2 games, 1 goal

When Alexander Simpson 'Sandy' Young left England to migrate to country Victoria, he was arguably Everton's greatest player. His 125 goals in all competitions between 1901 and 1911 had him miles in front of Everton records, and he led the league in the 1906–07 season. His 314 appearances at inside right had him third in their all-time appearances alongside captain Jack Taylor and right-forward partner Jack Sharp.

Young farewelled his remarkable career, which included Everton, Spurs, Manchester City, St Mirren and Falkirk, in 1914 to set up adjoining farms with his older brother John in the Goulburn Valley, six miles west of the town of Tongala, wedged between Echuca and Shepparton, and around 140 miles north of Melbourne.

This was a time before mega-wages, and so Young wasn't moving to country Victoria to count his premium bonds or set up garages full of Model Ts. He was migrating to establish a new life and a new vocation after his football curtain was drawn.

At his peak between 1905 and 1907, Young represented Scotland twice in the British Home Championships. He was Everton's leading scorer for five consecutive years from 1903–04 to 1907–08, driving the Toffees into three second-place league finishes and a third-place finish in 1906–07 when he scored a mind-bending 28 league goals—the third highest since the establishment of the First Division in 1893.

In 1906, Young was instrumental in Everton's finest pre-war moment. Young scored the solitary goal against Newcastle United to claim Everton's first FA Cup.

It was a summit that would take decades for Everton to reach again (in 1933), with a sharp comedown the following season in 1907 when the Toffees lost the final 2–1 to Sheffield Wednesday.

It was a remarkable, memorable career for Young at Everton.

At an advanced age for the time (31 years), Young was sold to Tottenham for £500, a 300% profit on the £120 Everton paid both St Mirren and Falkirk for Young. Indeed, upon leaving the club in 1911, Everton Chairman Dr James Baxter reflected on Young at the club's AGM: "Everton have never treated their players like oranges. At the proper time, his service will not be forgotten."

Baxter made another, more portentous comment: "There were many things that came to the knowledge of the directors that were quite unknown to the shareholders."

These "things" were most likely a reference to Young's solitary and anti-social behaviour, probably an undiagnosed mental health condition, which was barely acknowledged, let alone discussed, in 1911.

Having scored only three more goals for Tottenham and Manchester City, Young was sensing the end of his career in 1911, and he forwarded his football life savings to his brother John to invest in a small farm in regional Victoria.

By 1914, with more disappointing seasons behind him, Young said goodbye to English football and joined his brother John in Tongala.

Once on the boat to Australia, James Baxter's promise to preserve Young's legacy started to fade. While his name and records stood, he was mostly forgotten.

When he arrived in Tongala, Young seemed to integrate well into the local community. So well, in fact, that within a month word of his exploits for Scotland and Everton spread among the region. It wasn't long before Young would officially kick off the tradition of long-retired home country and continental stars pulling on the boots in Australia to pull crowds and evangelise football.

Reports from newspapers in nearby Kyabram have Young playing at least twice for Tongala against Kyabram XIs. The first report, on August 14, 1914, was dripping with enthusiasm and could have been written about Alessandro Del Piero 100 years later— if he had also recently taken over an irrigation block.

Kyabram were at full strength, with one exception, when they journeyed to Tongala on Wednesday last to meet the local team. Tongala hardly had their best side out, but had the assistance at centre forward of 'Sandy' Young, the brilliant Scottish international, who arrived in the district a month ago, and has taken over an irrigation block. Although on the shady side of 30, he still maintains a lot of his old dash, and gave a fine display. The game was very evenly contested. Kyabram were the first to score; T. Steele taking a neat pass from G. Markham and putting the ball through at 6 yards range. This reverse roused the Tongala players, and Young getting the bill, eluded several opponents and gave to F. Oldfield, who scored with a fast shot. After some exciting play on both sides, T. Steele again scored by bundling the goalkeeper through the posts while holding the ball. When the whistle was blown for time Young was in possession of the ball and making a bee line for the Kyabram goal. The game ended Kyabram, 2 goals ; Tongala, 1 goal. Kyabram have now won 4 games, drawn 1, lost 1. It is proposed to play two games, one against Tongala, the other against Ky-valley, in the local recreation ground at an early date. Admission will be charged and the proceeds given to charity. This should prove of interest to those desirous of witnessing the English soccer game.

The second report from the *Kyabram Guardian* roughly three weeks later on September 4, 1914 has an E Young—but almost certainly Sandy—getting on the scoresheet after a delightful combination with 'this player', and giving away a penalty, in an away 4–1 loss:

It was unfortunate that this fixture, played at Kyabram on Wednesday, should have clashed with other popular local events which carried away supporters of sport, who would otherwise doubtless have patronised the match. This was the first chance that the locals had of witnessing the English soccer game. Kyabram played their best side, whereas Tongala arrived minus two of their players and put in substitutes, but they were greatly strengthened by having the services of E. Young, the Scottish International player, at centre forward. Young was, when in his zenith, one of the finest forwards in the British Isles. Kyabram, having lost the toss, kicked off before a fair number of spectators. The play was very even, and after the ball had gone from end to end repeatedly, E Young got possession and pass to left wing ; this player centred, and Young taking it on the run, scored a good goal. This first blood to Tongala put the locals on their mettle, and they were seen making tracks for their opponents goal. They were soon rewarded, as Young gave away a penalty to Kyabram by handling the ball within the 12 yards area. 'Snowy' Walker took the kick, and put the ball through the sticks, the goal keeper failing to hold, although he touched it. Kyabram added another goal before half-time, and the teams crossed over with the scores — Kyabram 2, Tongala 1. The local players lasted better than their opponents, and put on two more goals before the close, the final result being — Kyabram 4 goals, Tongala 1 goal, 'Snowy' Walker played a great game for the winners at centre half, and E Young gave a good exhibition at times, but lacked support of the men close to him.

Drawing crowds to the "English Soccer", scoring goals: colonial life seemed to be going so well for Young.

However, there was much more going on in Young's life besides country football.

In December 1915, Young would be featured again in the regional press under the headline 'TONGALA SENSATION'. This time, they weren't talking about association football.

Young, Scotland International, Everton's legendary top goalscorer and winner of the 1906 FA Cup, had shot his brother John while John was milking a cow before walking home to turn the gun on himself.

The events are told as follows in the *Riverine Herald*:

For some time there had, it is stated, been differences of opinion between the brothers, and frequent quarrels ensued. A disturbance of more than usual violence is said to have taken place between them on Tuesday. The brothers were the joint owners of a dairy herd. Yesterday morning John Young left his home shortly after 7 o'clock for the cow shed. He was joined there shortly afterwards by his brother, Alexander Young, who was carrying a gun. Whether the quarrel of the previous day was renewed by them is not known. It is alleged, however, that Alexander discharged the gun in the direction of his brother, who was at the time milking. The charge struck John on the left shoulder and prostrated him on the ground. He did not lose consciousness, however, and states that after Alexander had fired the shot he said: "I am sorry for what I have done, John," and walked away in the direction of his house, taking the gun with him.

John did not die immediately from the wound, and neighbours found him bleeding in the shed and took him to the local doctor who was joined by the local constabulary. John relayed what had transpired to the police before he died from loss of blood.

"Alexander came to him at the cow yard and said, 'I'm going to shoot you.' He replied, 'Don't do that Alec,' but the latter discharged the shot which has resulted in his death," the police report noted.

Young was later found in his home bleeding from the face from a self-inflicted gunshot wound. Prison photos would later show the vicious scar across his face from the wound. The *Riverine Herald* noted that: "He had evidently intended to blow his brains out by placing the muzzle of his gun under the jaw, but the shot had passed outside the bone, tearing away a portion of his cheek and shattering the cheek-bone."

The *Riverine Herald* could not reconcile Young's actions with his public profile. He had, since he came to Tongala, aroused interest in the game of British association football, and his dexterity in the game was remarked upon as being extraordinary. He was well liked by the residents.

As reports filtered back to Liverpool at the end of 1915, and reports of his trial in Melbourne in January 1916 reached the *Liverpool Echo*, media shifted their characterisation of Young as a "sad case" to being more circumspect. He was now a tormented man, prone to long phases of solitude where he was, supposedly, conducting inner dialogues with demons.

At the trial, Young added more context to his fratricide, explaining that he was coaxed into the move to Australia by his brother.

Reported by the Kyabram Free Press after sentencing, Young told his barrister during his examination, "I wanted to leave, but he induced me to stay, saying I could make more money here than by footballing in Scotland. Everything I did was wrong, so John said, and we were always quarrelling."

Alex Young spoke of being struck and threatened at times with a loaded gun by his brother. Alex wanted out of Tongala, and wanted the money back that he had loaned his brother for the move.

Young described the events of that day to the court.

Early [on the morning of the shooting] I heard a noise, caused by someone moving about in the house. I got up and loaded a gun. I went down to the cow shed and saw John there. I said, "Were you in my house?" He replied "No." I said "Are you coming to Tongala to-day" [to settle Alex's exit]. He said "No." I said, "Where's my gun?" He said "Go to hell" and picked up a shovel and rushed at me.

The Everton club establishment, not forgetting Dr Baxter's promise to remember Young, wrote a character reference—of sorts—for Young, proclaiming "his mental unsoundness". That helped bump Young's verdict from murder to manslaughter by way of his mental unsoundness. He spent three years in a combination of prisons and local institutions (then known as lunatic asylums).

In 1920 he returned to the UK and lived out a quiet, impecunious life, dying in 1959.

The circumstances of his life and crime in Australia did not follow him all the way to Merseyside, beyond a handful of news articles buried in papers dedicating reams to the First World War.

Young was a footnote in Everton—and Australian football—history, and a giant mystery with a dash of intrigue until the Everton Heritage Society (EHS) went digging. Thanks to the work of the EHS, journalists and historians such as James Corbett, Billy Smith, Paul Wharton and Simon Burnton, we have all the pieces to put together Young's life. And now we also have the proof that Young did indeed play football on Australian soil.

In 2014 the EHS funded and unveiled a headstone for Young in Edinburgh's Seafield Cemetery in a ceremony featuring members of John Young's direct line, and one of only three men who later bested Young's goal tally for Everton, Graeme Sharp.

If not for the EHS and its members, Young's true life story would not be known. In the same way his impact, albeit fleeting, on football in Australia would also be lost to time.

While Young's story is amazing and shocking in many ways, from a purely modern football perspective it is remarkable.

In 1914, in the Victorian rural community of Tongala, Young became our first guest star, appearing in his new community and inspiring spectators to travel from far and wide to see a real International and FA Cup star in the flesh.

While the ripples of those appearances for Tongala in 1914 didn't cause a tsunami somewhere across the country, they did for a fleeting moment form a bond between Everton and the game in Australia. It was a bond forged in darkness, but it stands as one of the most remarkable brushes with football fame—and infamy—Australian football has had.

Bobby Charlton, Ambassador for Football

Newcastle KB United, 1978, 1 game, 0 goals
Perth Azzurri, 1980, 3 games, 0 goals
Blacktown City, 1980, 1 game, 1 goal

Sir Bobby Charlton occupies a unique position within the pantheon of football. World Cup winner, Ballon d'Or winner, Manchester United and England legend.

In 1978 Sir Bobby Charlton was merely 'Bobby' (he was knighted in 1994), a soon-to-be 41-year-old football statesman who was on a two-year journey to appear in the NSL twice.

Charlton was no stranger to Australia. He'd toured three times previously to massive outpourings of idolatry and adoration. In 1967 First Division champions Manchester United arrived in Australia where Charlton, the banner man for English football, was mobbed. The season before he had ascended to the World Cup and the Ballon d'Or, and was the hottest property in football. Charlton's celebrity transcended the game, even in Australia where football news was hidden in a corner of the Rugby -or Australian Rules-laden back pages.

In the official tour program Andrew Dettre, writing under a Soccer World pseudonym Paul Dean, set the scene for anyone in attendance who had been living under a rock.

Seeing Bobby Charlton play is an unforgettable experience. He is one of the most dynamic yet graceful footballers in the world today. And a great shot. And a tireless worker. And a man without temper. Ah, what a player!

United played eight games in 24 days in front of nearly 200,000 Australian fans. Charlton scored eight of United's 33 goals and left Australia with his reputation as a global elite affirmed.

Australia was a happy and accommodating starting point for Charlton's 1967–68 odyssey that culminated in his greatest club achievement: the European Cup. From there a fondness for Australia never left him. He returned (at least) four times to Australia in the years after 1967 and either played or coached in clinics. There were also, notably, some near misses where Charlton was reported but never arrived. "Unfortunately it's so far to travel, otherwise I would be sure to be doing it more often," he said of visiting and working in Australia.

Charlton saw Australia as fertile ground loaded with potential. "Your weather is perfect, you've got the facilities and all the space you need, there are so many kids playing in school … and Australians have such a competitive attitude. To put it into soccer seems natural."

Charlton was in Australia next after the Mexico World Cup in 1970 to run training camps. He had just hung up his boots for England after their disappointing exit in the Quarter Finals. He was next seen in Australia in June of 1977, when his 'Bobby Charlton All-Star Team' stopped by on a global tour for a matchup against the Socceroos at Olympic Park in Melbourne.

In between the two visits Charlton had officially retired as a player, saying goodbye to Manchester United as their most capped player in 1973. His timing was immaculate as it spared him the indignity of the relegation season of 1974. He moved to Preston North End for a season as player-manager with minimal success, and then picked up a handful of games in the League of Ireland with Waterford, linking up with former teammate and friend Shay Brennan.

A complete break from football was never going to be possible for Charlton. He ran a travel business but it wasn't enough. So in 1977, aged 39, he placed a few calls and toured the world with his All-Star side. His All Stars were a mix of playing, retired and near-retired stars of the English top flight who went on to play league football for Australian clubs. Charlton, Ian Callaghan, Ralph Coates and Alan Ball all returned to play in Australia.

For Charlton, the 1977 Australian pitstop was fruitful on a number of fronts. First, he was approached by the Victorian State Federation with USD$45,000 in hand, eager to bring back his All-Stars in 1978. Second, and most compellingly, Charlton started fielding offers to appear in the NSL as a guest player for the 1978 season.

Western Suburbs was a foundation NSL club and on the eve of the 1978 season they announced a recruiting bonanza, having signed a series of big English names. They had convinced English Second Division striker Ian Moores from Stoke to arrive on a guest contract. They'd also signed two more Second Division players from Bristol Rovers—Josh Vernon and Brian O'Donnell. It was a fine bounty, but somewhat spoiled in the club's press release by the inclusion that they had baulked at the chance of signing Bobby Charlton for two matches for $12,000.

But there were other fish in the pond ready to nibble at Charlton's lure.

The VSF deal for the All Stars in 1978 ultimately fell through, but Charlton was signed by NSL new boys Newcastle KB United. Like so many guest signings, corporate interests played a key part. Charlton was first linked to Newcastle during the unveiling of the club's primary sponsor Tooths Brewery who contributed $100,000 into the new club in a three-year sponsorship deal.

It wasn't quite RB Leipzig, but there were a lot of brand assets offered up to Tooths in the deal. Namely, the 'KB' was a nod to Tooths main product, the 'KB Lager'. The sweetener was Bobby Charlton, who would join as a guest player to help the sponsorship pay off.

Unlike most NSL clubs, Newcastle KB United was assembled as a rep team from the football mad Hunter Valley as opposed to being a pre-existing club from the State Leagues. The league had considered the Canberra City experiment—a team established from nothing to represent a football-mad region—a success, and identified Newcastle as another green field. The region had produced Australia's most exciting football export, Craig Johnston, and it was seen as deserving a National League side for that alone.

Charlton linked up with Newcastle for his package of two games for Newcastle KB United, one of which was in the NSL, as well as four coaching clinics and seminars in regional Grafton, Lismore, Coffs Harbour and Newcastle. To cap it off, a 'celebrity sportsman's dinner' was held in Charlton's honour at the club rooms of local side Adamstown Rosebuds after his NSL appearance for Newcastle against Marconi, which was the final match of the 1978 NSL season.

The second game was an exhibition game three days before the NSL match, against a blended NSL Brisbane 'all star' side in Lismore, with players drawn from Brisbane Lions and Brisbane City which had also missed the NSL finals. No record of the friendly has to date been found, but round 26 of the NSL certainly did, and Charlton laced up his boots for his first dose of NSL.

Charlton's Newcastle teammates were a mix of experienced pros, kids and a familiar face. Local boy Col Curran was a well-known player for Newcastle and Australia after a long and distinguished career with the Socceroos including all three games in the 1974 World Cup. Officially Curran was the first Australian to find the back of the net in a World Cup; sadly it was an own goal for East Germany.

Curran had brushes with fame earlier in his career when he spent twelve months in 1965–66 with the Manchester United youth team, alongside fellow Novacastrian

Ray Baartz. Curran would never forget his experience at Manchester United and his exposure to star player Bobby Charlton—and Charlton never forgot Curran.

Curran recalls Charlton greeting him in Newcastle as an old friend. "After he arrived we were going somewhere on the bus and he came up and said 'How are you, Col?' He remembered me from back in Manchester. You can imagine how that made me feel! A man of that calibre. He was a lovely fella and when we trained with him back in England, you were always just one of the boys."

Playing alongside Curran was Ken Boden, Newcastle's star player who was awarded 'Yugoslav Airlines Soccer Action Player of the Year' for the 1978 season. Boden had bounced around the English pyramid before, at age 28, being recommended to Newcastle manager and fellow Englishman Alan Vest. Boden enchanted the Newcastle fans, drawing massive crowds which set the region abuzz. He wasn't quite in Charlton's class, but he was adored in Newcastle.

As round 26 approached, the excitement was palpable. Signing Charlton was marketing genius and ensured an otherwise meaningless game would draw a huge crowd, with Boden and Charlton in the Newcastle midfield facing Marconi's Roberto Vieri and Jim Rooney.

Newcastle's first season saw them finish 10th (of 14 teams) with only six wins from 26 games, but in a sign of a good side that didn't quite gel they earned a lot of draws.

The official program for the game was brimming with excitement: "It is hard to estimate the value of Bobby Charlton as a player and a soccer ambassador but his world-wide reputation and the tremendous regard for him by all soccer fans makes his appearance for United the greatest Philips League promotion of the season."

The 16,614 fans who turned up for Charlton's one NSL appearance in 1978 makes it hard to argue with the program editor. Newcastle's season average crowd had been 8,437.

The result was also a win. A single goal from 18-year-old striker Neil Endacott just after half-time, with another disallowed in the first half, was the difference in a 1–0 win to Newcastle.

The first half was fairly ordinary from both sides, but Newcastle came out breathing fire in the second. With one of the greatest of all time in their midst, one wonders what was said at half-time to dial them up to 11. Endacott's goal demonstrated this new level of inspiration. He had been anonymous in the first half but found a new gear in the second. From a corner he received a flick on, and with his back to goal took a touch and pivoted to volley home. Another youngster, Peter Tredinnick—who would go on to play for the Young Socceroos and also join the FFA Board—also dazzled alongside Charlton in the second half.

Both Charlton and Boden found the woodwork in the second half to keep the fans on the edges of their seats. Charlton brought "a roar from the crowd every time he touched the ball", and the keenness of his eye and anticipation hadn't diminished one bit. A Charlton second-half pile driver from 25 metres slammed into the upright with a ferocious rattle that had fans fit to burst.

Boden was man of the match, but it was Charlton they had come to see.

Curran recalls the game as a vintage Charlton display: "He played like he used to play in England, I mean he wasn't as fit but his touch and his skill and his knowledge of placing the ball really stood out."

Charlton's performance also left an indelible impression on Marconi's manager Rale Rasic, partly because the wind played havoc with Charlton's legendary comb-over, but also because of the battle of the titans between Bobby Charlton and Roberto Vieri.

"Vieri really brilliantly pushed the ball through Bobby's legs and Bobby swore and his hair went up in the air and Roberto Vieri pushed the ball second time through his legs. Bobby—I won't tell you what Bobby said—won the ball and played it 40 metres to the left [to a teammate who won the corner]. They then scored, and that was 1–0, so Bobby goes to Vieri and he said, 'One, two, you. Three, me—1–0.' Amazing! Amazing story about two champion people."

Rasic, a famously studious manager, didn't even bother opening a file on Charlton. "[Winning the game] was really dependent on the mood of Bobby Charlton. Players like Bobby Charlton … these people on their day, you could not plan, they were unstoppable."

He was right. Charlton was given licence to roam around midfield in a free role and basically could not be matched. Rasic recalls "Bobby Charlton was a free agent. Bobby Charlton played where Bobby Charlton wanted to play."

Charlton left shortly after the Marconi game, but stayed behind in spirit agreeing to be a patron of Newcastle KB United. He professed that he "fell in love" with the club and reports surfaced that he might return for more games. "I'm now proud to be a patron of the club. They have a very good go-ahead board, they have good ideas, good workers, good supporters, and they do a lot for the community."

A top crowd, a win against a top four side, and 90 minutes of Charlton magic, and oh so nearly a goal. Charlton's time at Newcastle was a resounding success.

*   *   *

Charlton returned to Australia two years later, this time on a goodwill marketing mission with Dunlop.

Dunlop were early innovators in Australian football in the NSL era, and had a hand in many appearances made by their 'ambassador' players.

Ian Callaghan had played with Canberra City in 1979 on the company's dime, but Charlton was their main man and was contracted to the footwear company worldwide. Charlton was still eager to play where he could, and made himself available in 1980 for appearances across Australia.

He agreed to appear in Blacktown City's debut NSL match, but before then signed a deal to represent Perth Azzurri in their 1980 pre-season 'Night Series'.

His expectations for Perth football had been set by the 1967 tour, when over 20,000 fans poured into the WACA to watch Charlton score twice in a 7–0 deconstruction of the WA state side. It was a battering—especially considering Denis Law was sent off after half an hour with the score at 3–0—but few locals would have heeded the result. With a soon-to-be European Champion side in town representing the elite of the English First Division, and reigning Ballon d'Or winner Charlton leading the line, few would have cared about the fortunes of the local side.

The Soccer Federation of WA's yearbook from that year noted that: "One of the highlights of the game was the elegant artistry of Bobby Charlton, who lived up to every inch of his great reputation."

By 1980 crowds for exhibition or WA rep matches had dwindled to four figures. The NSL had been operating for three seasons with no representative from Western Australia. There was a growing sense that WA football needed an injection of energy to revitalise the sport.

There was love for the game, plenty of British expats who idolised their stars, but a creeping malaise affecting crowds and the Federation's coffers.

Like so many guest signings, the "getting bums on seats and putting us on the map" logic seemed watertight and a 42-year-old Charlton was offered $13,000 for three exhibition matches over three weeks.

The 'Solahart Night Soccer Series' was the traditional opener to the Perth football calendar. As a pre-season competition in January, mercifully scheduled at night given Perth's heat, all ten top division clubs met in a round robin tournament for some match practice, bragging rights and some cash via sponsor Solahart—an early innovator in solar power solutions for the home. Solahart put in nearly half of Charlton's appearance fee, and the rest was met by the WA Federation ($6,000) with Perth Azzurri adding the remaining $1,500.

Mixed in with the matches were a series of coaching sessions in schools, and appearances. Charlton attended hospitals, shopping centres, social gatherings and spoke at pro-football seminars, including at Perth Concert Hall where he appeared on an eclectic bill with comedian Max Bygraves and actor and female impersonator Danny La Rue.

While he was in town, Charlton went out of his way to integrate into his temporary football home. There was a dinner held for the players after training one night at a committee member's home, and another on a Sunday afternoon. Charlton made a genuine effort to blend in.

Club vice-president and life member, Dom Stillitano, remembers Charlton's visit fondly and got to know the man behind the football legend. "In between his engagements myself and [player and life member] Frank Rossi showed him around some Perth sites and our beautiful beaches. We also enjoyed a few beers with him at the WA Italian Club adjoining Dorrien Gardens [the Azzurri ground]. He was a pure gentleman, very friendly with everyone and a big success."

In between basking in the wonders of a Perth summer, the congeniality of his teammates and the fabric of the club, Charlton had three matches to play, which even with his famous longevity and constitution would not be easy on 42-year-old legs. But Charlton managed to find form in spectacular style.

In three matches for Perth Azzurri Charlton scored twice. The first game against Tricolore was a loss. In the second, a 3–1 win over Gosnells City, he awed the huge crowd with a moment of vintage Charlton. A low cross from teammate Chris Proctor found Bobby Charlton in enough space to wheel around and volley the ball on the turn and into the far corner. It was a top finish with too much power for beleaguered keeper Owen Nuttridge to save.

Charlton scored again in his third and final game against Kingsway Olympic. It was a loss for his Azzurri side, but Charlton got on the scoresheet after a goal of sublime quality. According to a match report, Charlton collected possession "near the halfway line" and, in a goal that reads like a portent for Maradona in 1986, took on the entire Kingsway half on his own, "outpacing" them before "deftly [placing] the ball past Willie McNally [Kingsway Keeper]."

Eric Marocchi was a teammate in those three games. Marocchi recalls Charlton adopting a free role, sitting in midfield and occasionally—like he did with his goal—making runs into the box.

"He could still move. That experience when you play in the high grades you play more with your head than your legs. You know where to move and where to position yourself. You can read the game a little bit better and you don't have to cover as much ground. And he was still fit."

The venue, the small scuffed patch of grass inside a velodrome, also played to the advantage of Charlton's 42-year-old legs.

Azzurri with Charlton won one and lost two, but would ultimately finish fourth and earn a semi-final with Kingsway Olympic. In a 3–2 loss Azzurri were out, and Kingsway went on to lift the trophy.

But that didn't matter. According to the Federation's annual report Charlton's three appearances each pulled numbers "more than that attended any of the International matches for 1980".

The President's Message in the WA Federation's 1980 annual report lauded the success of the initiative. "Solahart, the Federation, and Perth Azzurri were all to be commended for their initiative in bringing the revered Bobby Charlton to Perth to play three games during the 1980 night series. His visit was a breath of fresh air that helped dispel a smog of tedium, and the ordinary."

*   *   *

Charlton's third and final experience with Australian club football was a few weeks later with Blacktown City in the NSL. 1980 was Blacktown's first season in the NSL and it had been a meteoric rise for the club on the outskirts of Sydney's west.

They had finished third in the 1979 NSW State League season, but were elected anyway into the NSL at the expense of the relegated Sydney Olympic, and Sydney Croatia which reportedly turned down the option to join.

Club president Howard Bradley said, "We were surprised when we were elected to the league because Wollongong was considered the favourite."

Blacktown was progressive by NSL standards. They owned their ground Gabbie Stadium, had three youth teams, had a fully licensed clubroom with 1,500 members and a steady turnover of $500,000 per year. They had a sponsorship with Bradmill Group—the makers of King Gee and Yakka clothing—and with Traveland. On the face of it they had a sustainable business model. Their first year football budget was only $250,000, and they had spent only a handful of that on signings as they picked up players from defunct NSL club (and neighbour) Western Suburbs, as well as keeping the bulk of their promotion squad together.

Headlining their inaugural squad was captain Cliff Pointer who had arrived in Australia from London as a non-League player, and quickly established himself at the heart of the Blacktown defence.

Joining Pointer for the 1980 NSL season was 34-year-old midfielder Dave Harding, who had over 20 caps for the Socceroos, and young striker Alan Fisher who impressed with Western Suburbs, scoring 9 goals in the 1978 NSL season. On the eve of the season they also picked up a couple of veterans in 1976 NSW Player of the Year, Bruce Stowell, and George Harris, a 28-time capped Socceroo. Both Harding and Harris had played for the Socceroos in 1977 against the Bobby Charlton All-Stars and Harding got on the scoresheet.

Blacktown were going to keep things tight financially, but were also very eager to avoid a one-and-done NSL season. They were going into the 1980 season relegation favourites, and needed a grand gesture to give their fans, players and the region a boost. They might not have the money to buy a marquee player, but they sure could get one in temporarily.

Enter Bobby Charlton.

Pointer had grown up a Manchester United supporter in the south of London and never dreamed he would soon be suiting up beside his idol Bobby Charlton. "I was fortunate enough to be captain in those days and it was a magnificent opportunity to run out with a childhood hero."

Pointer remembers where he was when he discovered he was about to become Bobby Charlton's teammate.

"The first I heard of it was two weeks before the start of the season. We were playing Melita [in a practice match] ... they announced it to the players obviously that Bobby would be coming to play a game. We were just stunned. The magnitude of the player!"

Local Dunlop marketing exec and part-time referee Terry Seacy is credited with making the Charlton deal happen for Blacktown. He connected the dots and got Charlton a final appearance for his Australian tour.

Charlton was asked at the time by the *Sydney Morning Herald's* Brian Curran why he was still making himself available for appearances at his venerable age. "They keep asking me ... I still like playing and [am] happy to help a newly formed club like Blacktown." Charlton had amazing longevity and just couldn't let football go. Blacktown had made the call and Charlton answered.

When Charlton arrived at training a week before kick off in round one of the 1980 season, his new teammates were still in shock. "He walked in with the guy who was looking after him, and everyone looked at the ground. I still remember that. No one looked at him. It was almost like you're in the presence of greatness. You couldn't believe you were in the same room as him."

Charlton's reaction to that first training session suggests they might have taken their nerves out onto the pitch. In the piece with Brian Curran, Charlton was quoted as asking Blacktown manager Mick Jones, "Have the boys been training or what?"

Charlton was a tough competitor and fitness freak who was able to push his body for years after his First Division retirement to keep playing the game he loved. If Charlton thought his teammates were unfit on the eve of a new season, it would have come to Mick Jones as a wake-up call.

Charlton's single game for Blacktown against St George was at hand. The official match programme sought to answer the question on every fan's lips; what was Charlton driving while he was in town? It was a 2.6 litre Sigma station sedan, graciously supplied by Chrysler Australia.

"Don't sell us short; we will go out to win and entertain," Mick Jones told the media on the eve of the match.

Mick Jones was right, with goals galore and cherished memories all on the menu. At the age of 42, after seven years out of the English top flight, Bobby Charlton scored Blacktown's opener in the sixth minute in a 4–2 rout. To have Bobby Charlton as your club's inaugural scorer (which was also his last goal in league football) in the top flight is an amazing footnote in Blacktown City's history, and everything they had hoped for.

However, fans weren't treated to a volley in the box, or a long, skilful run beating multiple defenders like at Perth Azzurri. Nor was it one of his thunderbolts from outside the box that went agonisingly close for Newcastle KB United.

It was a miss-hit that somehow wriggled over the line. St George switched off in defence and allowed Dave Harding to race into space and put in a cross for Fisher who knocked it down to Charlton lurking just outside the six yard box to poke home. He mistimed the shot but was so close and with no St George players near him it still found a way to trickle over the line. It wasn't vintage Charlton, but at least Blacktown could write his name into their record books.

While the goal didn't wow the crowds, the rest of his performance did. He sat deep in midfield, reprising his usual late-career Regista role, and sprayed passes all day into dangerous areas.

George Harris, Charlton's Blacktown teammate, witnessed the game on the sidelines having picked up an injury in the pre-season. With the added advantage of being able to survey the entire field, he remembers Charlton's performance vividly: "He was well and truly past his peak then, but [he] had a real influence on the game, even though he wasn't running all over the place."

Blacktown were playing through Charlton, who was getting the ball long and wide into space looking for his wingers to put in crosses. It was simple, but effective, and made St George sweat all afternoon.

Cliff Pointer remembers an excellent crowd—biggest of the season—and markedly higher than the other crowds they received that year, and more impressive than the rather disappointing official crowd of 3,478. No matter the actual attendance, driving rain in an uncovered grandstand was what thousands of fans braved for a glimpse of the English legend.

Unlike in Perth where he had three matches and a fair amount of socialising, Charlton was mostly absent to his teammates after the match. "We didn't see much of him after the game, which was a little bit of a disappointment. We had a function upstairs above the changing room," Pointer recalls, and there actually wasn't a lot of fraternisation with Charlton outside of training and playing. Charlton was there to do a job, and do a job he did.

And then, just like that, he was gone. Blacktown had been witness to one of the greatest players of all time who inspired them to glory in their first-ever game in the NSL.

So how did Blacktown go in round two with Charlton out of the side?

They were embarrassed 9–0 by Marconi. Merciless Eddie Krncevic—who had just won the Oceania Cup with the Socceroos—scored four times, Peter Sharne got three and Roberto Vieri also got on the scoresheet. George Harris, like all his teammates, remembers that round two turnaround wryly. "I was the only change in the team, replacing Bobby Charlton."

Blacktown ultimately finished fourth bottom in 1980 just surviving the drop as St George. But there were some bright spots. The home fixture against Marconi later in the year was a 5–1 win, and the Blacktown players were 'chaired off' after their 14 goal turnaround.

Horsing Around
with Mick Channon

Newcastle KB United, 1981, 3 games, 3 goals
Gosnells City, 1981, 1 game, 1 goal
Newcastle KB United, 1983, 6 games, 0 goals
Salisbury United, 1983, 1 game, 2 goals

In the United Kingdom in the 1970s, when Mick Channon scored for Southampton, Manchester City or England, he would celebrate with a one-handed windmill celebration. It was very much in the mode of The Who guitarist Pete Townsend, although Channon said it was to get his breath back after running so far.

"The old windmill, that was just something that happened over the years, once you start something like that you have to keep it going. People expect it."

After starting as an apprentice with Southampton in 1965, Channon would celebrate often. He scored 157 goals in 391 games in his first stint with the Saints. This included their upset 1976 FA Cup win when the Second Division Southampton knocked off their more fancied rivals, the Tommy Docherty-managed Manchester United, 1–0.

An avid gambler and horse lover, Channon's first stint at Southampton saw him play a guest stint in South Africa with Durban Celtic, in order to give himself a little pocket money.

In 1977 Channon was sold to Manchester City for £300,000 as the Blues were looking to consolidate a good run in the First Division. Scoring 11 and 12 goals in his two seasons at City, Channon managed to make it back to South Africa, this time for a guest stint with Cape Town City, presumably for another off-season stint to top up his funds.

Channon returned to Southampton at the end of 1979 and it was during this stint back at the Dell that he found himself out on loan for a guest stint in northern NSW with Newcastle KB United in 1981. Channon was coaxed into his Australian guest stint by former England teammate Paul Reaney, a Leeds United legend with over 500 appearances to his name, who was finishing his career in the sunshine with his last couple of seasons being played in Australia's NSL.

Channon's family joined him for his Australian adventure. His son Michael had spent a lot of time in Australia previously working for the Chris Waller stables in Sydney. He remembers the trip fondly.

"We came out for a holiday, the one and only time I came to Australia as a kid. I imagined Newcastle was going to be like Newcastle in England and you couldn't get any further apart.

"It was just a really friendly place and I remember we had an apartment, he got given a yellow Volvo and because he was part-time, we'd nick a few days break here and there.

"I remember seeing the Sydney Harbour Bridge and getting on the ferry and all that. I loved my fishing, Mick came with me and he was bored senseless, but he was trying to be a family man, he wasn't great at that.

"It was a holiday for us, but we could see what the Aussies were trying to do making a big stink about this English player Mick Channon."

Channon Junior's love of horse racing obviously came from his dad, with the avid punter Channon Senior once driving 11 hours from Sydney to Brisbane to attend a race during his time in Australia.

Channon's three games in the NSL resulted in three goals for the Englishman, value for money in any language. With all of his games played at home, he scored in two wins and a draw.

His debut game for Newcastle came in a whirl of publicity; Newcastle's coach Alan Vest was replaced as manager by 'mutual agreement'. His position was filled by local legend and former Socceroo Ray Baartz.

Adding some more star factor to Channon's debut, the Newcastle KB United Raiders were lining up against Channon's former English strike partner Bob Latchford, the Everton star out for a guest stint with Brisbane Lions .

The hype didn't live up to the contest when a hamstring injury, a recurring theme for Latchford, kept him out of the Brisbane team. The game ended in a 1–1 draw and Channon scored in the 62nd minute, unloading his trademark windmill celebration in front of over 6,000 spectators, a big crowd for the times.

The stark differences between the English First Division and Australia's fledgling NSL were obvious, but they are best summed up from a child's perspective, as son Mick Channon Junior remembers.

"There was a big fuss made of dad on his debut, the stand at the time was packed, it was very rustic, it's a proper stadium now. The ground had a very non-league feel to it, like a semi-professional soccer field from England.

"At Southampton, at the Dell, as a kid I was football mad and would be in the players' lounge with the likes of Alan Ball and Kevin Keegan getting autographs after matches.

"At Newcastle it was a friendlier atmosphere, at the end of the match we went down and had a barbecue. On the pitch!"

Channon's following two home games saw him score in a 4–2 win over West Adelaide, followed by another goal in a 4–1 win over APIA-Leichhardt, the opposition being managed by former Hearts, Celtic and Scotland player Willie Wallace, who would spend the last 30 years of his life residing in Australia.

After Channon's guest stint in Newcastle, having left the family to make their own way home, Channon flew home to the United Kingdom via Perth, Western Australia. It was here where he ended up playing a one-game cameo for local side Gosnells City. The recently deposed Newcastle KB United coach Alan Vest had previously worked in Western Australia and had it arranged as part of his Australian visit.

Gosnells City was coached by John Davies, whose brother Reg Davies was a Welsh international who had played for Newcastle United and Swansea before emigrating to Western Australia in 1971. Channon told Davies that he wanted to play in the midfield but he was reminded that people paid to see him play upfront.

Channon dutifully scored in a 1–1 draw against Greek club Kingsway Olympic, local Perth legend Len Dundo scoring the equaliser.

Four games in Australia for four goals. Not a bad return.

Following his game with Gosnells, Southhampton alumni John Sydnenham and his family accepted an offer for dinner with Channon at his hotel.

"Mick came to Southampton as a 15-year-old when I was an established player, so I'd known Mick and his family since he was a boy. We were pretty close so he took Jean, my daughter Tracey and I to have a meal with him at the Sheraton.

"We had a decadent meal and were drinking the best champagne and having a great time. We thought he was treating us, we thought it was on Mick."

Little did the Sydenhams know that Channon had spent most of his time in the hotel on the phone back to his horse trainers in the United Kingdom at a time when phone bills to the UK were extraordinarily expensive. Channon left the phone bill, the hotel bill and the dinner bill for Gosnells City to pick up.

Jean Sydenham recalls: "I remember John Davies sorting the bill out, the look on his face! I think it nearly finished Gosnells City!"

Mick Channon loved his time in Australia, and when asked about the Sheraton bill,

Channon laughed and said, "I've always said first class all the way in. Life's not a rehearsal is it!"

A little unsettled after his time in Australia, Channon snuck off to Hong Kong for some guest games before bouncing around England trying to earn some further money before he retired. Short stints in England at Newcastle United and then Bristol Rovers proceeded the final significant chapter of his career when he joined Norwich City at age 34.

In his three seasons at Norwich City, Channon managed to play plenty of guest roles again in his off seasons. He returned to South Africa, this time with Durban City, had another stint in Australia with Newcastle KB United, as well as being flown to Adelaide to play in a friendly for Second Division club Salisbury United, and finished with games for University in Auckland, New Zealand and in County Donegal, Ireland with Finn Harps.

If his first stint at Newcastle United was a success with three goals in four games, then the second was not as fruitful. Six games and zero goals, ageing legs not helping him on the harder and faster Australian pitches.

Unlike the big home crowds that came out the season before in 1982 to see local boy done good Craig Johnston, Channon's return was relatively low key in terms of supporter numbers.

A crowd of 4,950 saw his return in a 0–0 draw against the Tommy Docherty-led Sydney Olympic. This would be the biggest Australian crowd he would play in front of on this occasion.

A home loss to Marconi-Fairfield was followed by a 3–0 win over Footscray JUST. Channon only played the one away game in his six-game guest stint, a 3–2 loss to APIA- Leichhardt before a week off and then facing Brisbane City.

After playing at home against Brisbane City on the Saturday, Salisbury United's ambitious club benefactor, the car sales mogul Steve Jarvis, flew him to Adelaide to take part in a friendly the next day.

Channon made the 20-kilometre trip north from the city to suit up for Salisbury United that Sunday. This northern region of Adelaide is famous for being the childhood home of musician Jimmy Barnes, housing the Holden factory, as well as producing test cricketer Darren Lehmann.

The Second Division side with the fancy ring-in known as the 'Bears' duly defeated the First Division Elizabeth City 4–3.

Channon repaid his benefactors by scoring two of Salisbury United's goals in front of a large crowd for the region. It was standing room only as 2,000 people watched this game.

Keith Hughes is a life member of Elizabeth City having played more than 15 years with the club. Normally a striker, he played against Channon that day, lining up in the midfield, and remembers the class of his goals.

"He was very clever, he took players on, feigned to go one way then feigned to go the other then smacked them in."

His trademark windmill celebration came out and delighted the crowd. "The crowd went mental after that."

Hughes also ended up on the scoresheet with a brace himself.

"I scored two in the second half, but they were consolation goals. Salisbury changed their side around. They had a fantastic goalkeeper called Frank Ostendorf but they took him off at half-time and put a young lad on. I don't think I would have beaten Frank with the two shots I took!

"One thing I do remember, Channon was coming down from full back on me and he was going to do his turn, I had seen it on TV that many times, where he'd go to feign. I knew what he was going to do. He kept doing it and I wouldn't let him pass and the crowd was going each time 'Ole! Ole!' and I made him pass the ball backwards, I was so pleased.

"Later when I saw him in the club rooms he patted me on the head and said 'Well done lad!'"

Channon's reputation for a drink was upheld as he partied with his teammates and opponents, first in the clubrooms that evening and then at a disco in Glenelg.

The ambitious Salisbury United finished that 1983 season as Second Division champions, only losing the one game. A mere two seasons later in 1985 they were the First Division champions.

Channon's final NSL game in Australia was a 2–1 win over Preston; unfortunately his goalscoring exploits of two seasons previously couldn't be replicated.

A quick recap of Channon's Australian club career is impressive: 11 games for three clubs, in three different states, scoring seven goals.

Alan Ball: Making Dough
Floreat Athena, 1982, 4 games, 0 goals

In 1982 Alan Ball was brought to Perth to play for the Greek-backed Floreat Athena club by brothers John and Peter Pilkadaris, owners of the VIP bread manufacturing company, which was later bought out by Buttercup Bakery.

The Pilkadaris family have been involved with the Floreat Athena soccer club since it started in 1951. John Pilkadaris recalls his involvement with the club.

"I joined the club when I came to Australia when I was 18, in 1954. My father was already here in Australia, and I followed with my mother, brother and sister.

"My father was one of the first players to play for the club. He was their first goalkeeper. I joined the club at 18, they were then in the Third Division. After two years we got promoted to second division and then to the first division.

"I played for about 14 years for Athena, and made the Western Australian state team as well."

In the 1970s with their playing days behind them, the Pilkadaris brothers and their highly successful bakery located in Victoria Park became the backbone of the Floreat Athena club. Their sponsorship allowed for the club to bring quality football players to assist them on the park.

This was most successfully achieved in 1974 when they recruited a couple of former pros, who were now playing semi-professionally with Bath City, in John Sydenham and Steve Stacey.

Sydenham was a member of the England Youth team alongside the legendary Jimmy Greaves and played more than 400 times for Southampton, competing with and against all of the England squad who won the 1966 World Cup.

Stacey was the first player with an African-American background to play professionally in the United Kingdom with stints with Bristol City, Wrexham, Ipswich Town and Exeter City. He even released his own book in 2019 called *The Colour of Football*.

This was shrewd recruiting by Floreat Athena as both of these gentlemen are now members of Western Australia's Football Hall of Fame and still reside in Australia. Pilkadaris explains:

"The club brought about a dozen players from England over ten years, the most successful were John Sydenham and Steve Stacey, they were very good players for the club and made Athena a lot stronger.

"It was very hard to find jobs for the players in those days. We had to find decent jobs for the players in Perth. Conditions in our bakery weren't great for soccer players, when you're talking about coming to work at four or five in the morning, delivering bread to the supermarkets and that sort of thing. But they had to have a job.

"We gave John Sydenham a job. He'd come at five in the morning and finish about nine o'clock. The club paid him some money here and there."

John's son Stan Pilakadaris remembers how Floreat Athena and VIP Bakery worked together over that period.

"We employed quite a few people involved with Athena. They would be progressive and bring players over and then the club would ask if there was any chance of giving these players a job. We were more than happy to do that and helped each other."

Alan Ball was destined for a career in football. His father, also Alan, was a capable player with the likes of Southport, Oldham Athletic and Rochdale and then turned to management. Ball Senior managed Halifax Town, Preston North End and Southport, as well as clubs in Sweden.

Alan Ball started to really make his mark in football in the early 1960s with over 100 games at Blackpool, so much so that he was the youngest member of England's winning 1966 World Cup side at 22. He made quite the contribution in the final too.

Full of running, it was a corner that Ball took which led to a Martin Peters goal to put England 2–1, up as well as his chase and low cross that set up Geoff Hurst's second goal that saw them go ahead 3–2. Socks down in the final, Ball ran and ran and ran, one of the better players in their famous victory.

From Blackpool he went to Everton where they would be chanting for the perpetual motion machine, "Who's the greatest of them all? Little, curly, Alan Ball!"

Ball played over 200 games at Everton and that included going to the 1970 World Cup with England. A close friendship with Bobby Moore then saw him move to London, although not to Moore's West Ham; he joined Arsenal. His friendship with Bobby Moore saw him at nightclubs, casinos and mixing with many of London's 'colourful identities'. These after-football activities mixed with Ball's happy-go-lucky nature saw him lose money in a number of ventures such as pubs and garages. Ball's high lifestyle in London saw him living above his means. As he mentions in his 2004 autobiography *Playing Extra Time* about he and his wife Lesley's time in London:

"We were happy spenders. We spent on clothes; we ate out a lot and generally lived it up. We were regulars at the famous nightclub Tramp, entertaining people. We did not need an excuse to hit the town. We were just silly spendthrifts."

In the 1976 off season, Ball had committed to a guest stint in South Africa to play with Hellenic Football Club in Cape Town. Hellenic, known as 'The Greek Gods', were managed by former England international John 'Budgie' Byrne. A prodigious striker at Crystal Palace and West Ham, Byrne left for South Africa after one season at Fulham and would manage football clubs there through the 1970s and 1980s.

On returning to England, the appointment of Terry Neill at Arsenal saw Ball move on and leave for Southampton, then in England's second tier. With no money, no house and no car, Ball signed for £60,000 and headed south to join the Saints.

At Southampton, Alan Ball's stereotypical lifestyle of an English footballer with his love of gambling, horses and drinking was appreciated by many of his Saints teammates at the Dell who had the same vices, particularly other players in this book such as Ted MacDougall, Mick Channon, Charlie George and Kevin Keegan.

Ball helped Southampton earn promotion to the First Division in 1978 and was made club captain by manager Lawrie McMenemy as well.

During his first two seasons at Southampton, Ball spent his off season being loaned out to the North American Soccer League. Firstly he joined Saints teammate Peter Osgood at Philadelphia Fury, a new club that counted musician Peter Frampton as one of its chief powerbrokers. Ball even managed to become player/manager that year when the Fury manager Richard Dinnis, former manager of Newcastle United, resigned mid-season.

His guest stint at Philadelphia over, Ball was given a $US5,000 bonus cheque as he departed for England. Ball was picked up at Heathrow and taken by his mates straight to Salisbury races. After a few drinks at the track, they decided to buy a horse, and with that the cheque was gone.

The next season in 1979 Ball went to the Vancouver Whitecaps, winning the 'Soccer Bowl' and winning their MVP before returning to join Blackpool as player-manager for season 1980/81.

He took Ted MacDougall with him and when his time at Blackpool wasn't successful, Ball rejoined Southampton for season 1981/82.

In 1982 both MacDougall and Ball joined Floreat Athena. Amazingly McMenemy allowed Ball to travel down under without any insurance. He was on a handshake deal with club legend and ex-pat John Sydenham. Sydenham was playing coach of

Floreat Athena at the time.

"I knew Lawrie McMenemy fairly well, he was never my manager, but I knew him. He agreed to let him come for a month, no question of insurance or anything like that. Can you imagine that today?"

The money for Ball's visit was covered by the Pilkadaris brothers.

"We were very close with John Sydenham, and he was making a lot of contact with players who were coming to Western Australia from England.

"John told the committee that Alan Ball would love to come to Australia and spend five weeks here.

"So I said we'll bring him over and our company paid for all of his expenses during his five weeks."

Due to Ball's gambling problem and spendthrift nature, he had specific contract instructions for Sydenham to make his payment.

"It was £1,000 for the month and Alan said 'Listen I want the thousand pounds in cash, but I want it the day I leave, don't give it to me before.'

"He was a terrible gambler and was off to the races every week."

Assistant coach to Sydenham at Floreat Athena that year was Alf De Bono. Maltese-born De Bono was such a playing talent that he represented Western Australia as a 16-year-old. He would end up in the WA Football Hall of Fame through his decades-long involvement at club level.

De Bono remembers a player that clearly had been enjoying the Australian hospitality when he turned up to training, but a player who never shirked when it came to the contest.

"You could smell alcohol on him at almost every training session, yet he could outrun most of us. He was just a machine when it came to running, even at that late stage of his career."

On the pitch Ball was an outstanding success, Sydenham not restricting him with any coaching or tactics, but allowing him to do what he wanted.

"These Greeks guys will never forget what he put into the game, I think he played five games and what he contributed was great.

"I said to Alan, just go wherever you want to go on the field, he said 'Great that's what I want to hear.' So he would be picking the ball up from the 'keeper and starting the runs, and I was fortunate as I was able to play at that time and then Ted started scoring goals for me which he hadn't been doing before.

"It all worked out great and was a great experience for Floreat Athena."

The Pilkadaris family made sure he wasn't just available to Floreat Athena, but also to the entire Perth football community.

"We made sure that he didn't come just for the club. He went to every other club. In fact we put on a lunch for him at the club, we had about 300 people having lunch. And afterwards he invited everyone that wanted to talk to him that they could.

"He lived a good life, but I never saw a fitter person than him, an incredibly fit player. The way he trained and the way he was talking to young kids, promoting the game.

"For me he was the best person who ever came to Perth from England as far as playing and promoting the game."

Playing against fellow Greek side Olympic Kingsway, more than 3,000 people saw Ball, Sydenham and Ted MacDougall star; in fact, it was Sydenham's pass that saw MacDougall score the first goal in a 4–1 win.

Ball played a further two games against Perth Azzuri and Gosnells City and a Cup game against Forestfield which they won 5–2. He even managed to line up in the touring Bournemouth side when they played against the Western Australian state team.

Floreat Athena finished eighth of 12 teams in the State League, Ball playing in two of their seven wins for the season. Pilkadaris remembers what an amazing ambassador Ball was for football, but also for their bakery and business.

"He was a person who loved the game so much he wanted to pass it on to people. We spent a heck of a lot of time together when he was in Perth.

"He used to come at 9am to the bakery and spend an hour or two with me every morning, and we would have visitors like young kids and people interviewing him.

"Then we would have lunch together with him. Ted MacDougall, John Sydenham and a few others would join us too. Then they would take him to do promotions and some coaching clinics with young kids, he never really stopped.

"He did a TV commercial for us, which was the first time our bakery business had done it. At the time we had a new loaf of bread we had in the market and we wanted to promote that, he promoted that for us on TV and radio.

"It did boost our business up a heck of a lot!"

Since their father started VIP Bakery on his arrival in Australia, production had increased from 350 loaves of bread per day to 3,500 loaves per hour. The VIP Bakery was bought by Buttercup Bakery two years after Ball's stint with the club.

It is bit fanciful to say that the Alan Ball sponsorship led to the sale, but it certainly didn't harm them with all the publicity it generated.

He looks fondly back on Ball's contribution to both their football club and the family business.

"It's fair to say that what he gave back to us, was worth the money. Just his interaction on a daily basis, to come in every morning. What he did, not only for Athena, but for the rest of the community, you would have paid double or even triple!"

The success of Ball's stint for Floreat Athena is best summed up by Sydenham when he reflects on the return for the club's benefactors.

"Ball did some advertisements for VIP Bakery and they eventually sold out for millions to Buttercup Bakery, a huge bakery in the eastern states.

"I was told that the only way they even heard of VIP Bakery was that they followed the Alan Ball story. So that bakery actually got sold through Alan Ball being here.

"When they sold their business, I jokingly asked VIP for commission."

According to Sydenham when Ball arrived back at Heathrow from his Western Australian visit, he was picked up by his wife Lesley and was driven straight to Ascot for a week spent at the Royal Ascot horse racing carnival. With the Floreat Athena funds from VIP Bakery in his pocket, Ball had turned the £1,000 into £10,000 by the middle of the week.

By the end of the week it was all gone. An indication on how the Balls lived, Alan and Lesley regarded it as one of the best weeks of their life!

After Floreat Athena, Ball's playing career was seemingly at a dead end with Southampton. In 1982/83 McMenemy allowed for him to be loaned out for a guest stint with Eastern Athletic in Hong Kong. This was a club managed by good friend Bobby Moore, where Ball again cashed in on his name.

The Pilkadaris family and Ball remained in contact throughout his post Floreat Athena career, sending him congratulations when he was appointed manager of Southampton. John and Peter received a letter back.

"We never lost contact at all, when he was appointed coach of Southampton, we got a letter back from him and it read 'I still recall my time with you all with affection'."

A sentiment that still gives John Pilkadaris chills.

After Southampton, former England teammate and millionaire Francis Lee purchased Manchester City and he poached Ball to be his manager. Not the most popular signing amongst the City faithful, the 1995–96 season saw City relegated in controversial fashion on goal difference.

With relegation not decided until the last game of the season, Ball was told during the match that other results meant a draw would be enough for City to stay up. He instructed his team to play for a draw; his players were dribbling into corners in order to wind down the clock. When City player Niall Quinn was subbed off, he noticed the live scores on the television in the tunnel and saw that a draw would mean City would go down. Sprinting back up the field to tell Ball, City then had to change tact and play for the win, which they could not pinch in the dying minutes.

A calamitous end to their season.

Following Manchester City, Ball took a break from football before being asked to manage Portsmouth in 1998. Here his Australian connection would continue. The Terry Venables-led revolution at Portsmouth saw them have five Australians on their books following on from Venables' tenure as Socceroos coach. Fast running out of money when Ball arrived, he was forced into selling most of his squad in order for the club to stay afloat. The two most high profile of these Australians were John Aloisi and Craig Foster. Forced to leave for Portsmouth to cut its wage bill, in Alan Ball's 2004 biography *Playing Extra Time* he recalls a furious row with Foster as he let him go on a free transfer to get him off the books. Foster played only 19 times for Pompey and would then move to Crystal Palace.

With 26 goals in 60 games, Aloisi was Portsmouth's best player. Ball moved him to Coventry City for £1 million, a bargain price given that West Bromwich-Albion's striker Lee Hughes, who had scored three less goals than Aloisi, was being shopped around for £5.5 million. Ball finished his football career in management after that disastrous season at Portsmouth.

Ball died suddenly and tragically of a heart attack in 2007 when he was trying to put out a bonfire at his home. An England World Cup legend, Ball touched many people in Perth in his short time there in 1982.

Fed to the Lions:
George Best's Tours of Australia

Brisbane Lions, 1983, 4 games, 0 goals
West Adelaide, 1983, 1 game, 1 goal
Osborne Park Galeb, 1983, 1 game, 1 goal
Dee Why, 1983, 1 game, 1 goal
Devonport City, 1989, 1 games, 0 goals

Australia is a place of special significance in the George Best story. His first visit with Manchester United in 1967 was a springboard to what became Best, the legend. His second, in 1983, was remarkable for the opposite reasons.

By 1983 he was battling depression, the breakdown of his marriage to Angie, and another failed effort to redeem himself in England with Bournemouth. But Best was determined to keep going and so he agreed to play in four league matches with the Brisbane Lions in the 1983 NSL season.

There was another compelling lure for Best to accept the contract from Brisbane Lions. He had marvellous memories of Australia.

In 1967 on the preseason tour with United, Best wiped the floor with the national and state rep sides. Their only falter was a 1–1 draw against Victoria where United rested Denis Law, Paddy Crerand and Bill Foulkes, and only conceded an own goal. Best scored nine times in eight games, and had particular joy in Brisbane and Perth, scoring five goals in those games in identical 7–0 drubbings. The only solace for Australian football fans was the 8–1 and 11–0 hidings handed to teams in Auckland and Christchurch were worse. That 1967 Australian tour stuck in Best's mind as the starting point for his greatest triumph.

The years after were witness to Best's descent. He drank, stopped showing up to training and matches and spent more time in his Manchester nightclub than the training pitch. His drinking became a running joke in the press. His career with United was over in 1974, playing his last game on New Year's Day before being sacked by manager Tommy Docherty after another extended absence. United were relegated later that season after 36 years in the top flight.

Best played in hundreds of testimonial and exhibition games throughout the years, which began as soon as he left United with the occasional performance adding to his legend. Rumours would spread about the old magic being back, and he was approached constantly by clubs looking to lock him down to a contract. He nearly joined Middlesbrough, had a spell in Bournemouth, and in 1985 turned down an offer from Ron Atkinson to rejoin Manchester United. He knew his time at the top was over, and loved United too much to let her down.

Instead, he preferred the itinerant route. After 1981 he turned away from contracts in the US and bounced around other parts of the globe picking up games.

Best's girlfriend was former Miss World winner Mary Stavin, but he was nonetheless devastated when his wife Angie finally, officially left him with their young son Calum, in May 1983.

With his Bournemouth contract torn up, his club football career in the UK was effectively over as well. But rather than let the grief consume him via drink, Best realised that he needed to change.

So on the very cusp of joining Brisbane Lions, Best adopted sobriety. London-based writer Bill Mellor quoted Best as saying, "Now I stick to tea … at last, at 36, I feel I've grown up … This year I have learned more and changed more than any other year in my life." Mellor's response to this quote was, "Readers could be forgiven for treating these statements with some skepticism", and labelled the claim a media stunt.

Only it wasn't. Best was desperate to get his life back on track.

Just over a month before Best jetted off for Brisbane, Manchester United had made it to the FA Cup final, and Best appeared in the coverage with his old teammates Denis Law and Bobby Charlton in feeds from all over the world. Best looked bright, spritely, and in good humour, despite the debris of his life still in view.

Having played around 50 matches around the world in Northern Ireland, Iceland and Hong Kong, as well as for Bournemouth in the prior season, Best had a modicum of fitness to go along with his abstinence.

He also knew that for the Brisbane Lions he would have to face his bitter rival, Tommy Docherty, who was then coach of Sydney Olympic. For the shy and non-confrontational Best, dealing with Docherty would feel like being thrown to the lions. And, sure enough, Docherty was about to do everything he could to make Best's life in Brisbane miserable.

Perhaps the most amazing footnote to Best's 1983 trip to Australia is his description of it in *Blessed*.

"I flew off on a tour in the Far East with Bill McMurdo, playing for a couple of teams in Hong Kong and then for the Brisbane Lions in Australia. A guy named Ed Marconi owned them and we had some pretty good attendances in the three games I had agreed to play for them. So he asked me to play one final match, a special game he was trying to organise against their biggest rivals—I can't remember what they were called. It wasn't part of my deal, so he said 'Tell you what, George. It's bound to be a big gate, so I'll split the attendance money with you.'

"The Lions game turned out to be my last club appearance."

There is no Ed Marconi. Ed Marconi is obviously an amazing football manager NSL spawn name but he isn't real. The Lions Chairman in 1983 was a guy named John Morcus. In reality Best signed for three games with the Lions, and then opted for a fourth against Marconi where he got a share of the gate to appear.

*　　*　　*

On arrival at Brisbane Airport in 1983 he told local reporters, "I'm as fit as one can be at 37. Of course I don't compare for pace with the player I was ten years ago. But skill—that improves with age."

Skill, and giant helpings of it, was what the Lions were hoping Best would bring. That and of course a star billing. They were willing to pay through the nose for it. He was reportedly offered $50,000 for three games. It was a heck of a gamble for the Lions, especially considering one of the stars of the competition, John Kosmina, had attracted a mere $45,000 to transfer his entire contract to Sydney City in 1981. But the Lions had some fortune with imports before Best. Bob Latchford (1981) and Alan Sunderland (1982) had both scored goals and transformed fortunes on the pitch.

McMurdo explains how the deal went down, masterminded on the Lions side by former manager Joe Gilroy, and Dutch-born promoter and businessman and Lions booster, Hans Strik. Gilroy had been manager of the Lions in 1981 and 1982, but was replaced by Dutchman Simon Kistemeker for the 1983 season. It is likely then that the initial approach to Best occurred in 1982, but bore fruit in 1983.

"What happened was we were flying to LA from Glasgow, [Best] and I. We met a guy who used to play for Brisbane Lions, a Scotsman called Joe Gilroy, he was also a coach. We got talking on the plane. He said, 'would you come to Australia?' we said 'If the terms were right'. So I gave him my number. A guy called Hans Strik got in touch with us on behalf of Joe Gilroy.

"I said 'look, if you can put this whole thing together and it's worthwhile financially and all the rest of it then we would love the opportunity to do it but it has got to be a package, we need hotels and flights and cash and the whole bit.' After about two or three weeks of putting it all together we had Malaysian Airlines sponsor us first class all the way to Australia and back. On the way back in Kuala Lumpur we did a thing for the Malaysian FA where we did coaching schools."

It was a full package deal with speaking engagements, appearances and coaching clinics including the flights and accommodation. After agreeing to the deal, McMurdo went to work finding other opportunities for Best. He was hastily booked to appear on good friend Michael Parkinson's show. Parky was in Australia filming an Australian version of his successful British format with Channel 10. Other television and radio spots were booked, along with appearances in shops.

Before Best joined up with the Lions in 1983 the club had been trying to assemble a half decent side for new manager Simon Kistemaker, a boom recruit from the Netherlands. He had managed across the Eredivisie and was exactly the sort of coach the Dutch-leaning Lions needed after years of limited success and dour football.

They'd let other recent imports—Billy Williamson, Mark Atmore and Boudewijn de Geer—move on to make way for Best.

Their season had also not started well. In mid-May they were beaten resoundingly by cross-city rivals Brisbane City 4–0. Best's arrival represented an opportunity for the Lions to also turn a new page over on their faltering season.

Best, now a recovering alcoholic, arrived in Sydney's Mascot Airport on June 28 and was swamped by reporters. A press conference was set up, where Best sipped tea and told the Australian media throng that he was "on the wagon" and that he "hadn't touched the bottle in six months".

While that wasn't technically correct, he was no doubt exaggerating for the salivating press room, who filed reports with remarks about not detecting a "whiff of booze" on him. In front of cameras, microphones and baying reporters, some of whom were regular press who probably only knew two facts about him—he played soccer, and he was a drunk—Best was staring into the abyss once more.

"I don't have a drinking problem; I'm an alcoholic … there's a difference," he told the Sydney media who had their noses at the ready.

In truth most reporters were probably disappointed to meet the Best who alighted in Sydney. He looked lean and healthy. Almost serene, or sanguine. *The Age* was one of the rare places who picked up on this, reporting that "a sleek-looking athlete with black shiny hair, neatly clipped beard, lively face and dancing eyes bounced ahead of his manager and soccer officials into the VIP interview room at Mascot airport".

But the liveliness in his face, and his entire mood, must have dropped when he was led into the VIP room because waiting for him was Docherty.

Before they left London, McMurdo told AAP, "George and Tommy have crossed swords many times before. They have a special love-hate relationship which has lasted many years, but it's one tinged with mutual respect." But that wasn't quite true. Irrespective of what Docherty felt for his "enfante terrible" (to quote the *Sydney Morning Herald*), Best despised Docherty. He blamed him for his exit from United, and grew in time to resent Docherty for implying he had a part in United's relegation in 1974.

In 1972 Docherty took over at a faltering, ageing United. By this time the drink had gotten to Best, and his antics became more regular. Ultimately, United and Docherty said goodbye to Best for good, telling the press, "Bringing him back was a disaster. He was more trouble than he was worth."

It must have come as a shock to Best to find Docherty, as well as good friend Michael Parkinson, sitting on occupied seats alongside the Lions representative Hans Strik. When he entered the room, Docherty jumped up and hugged Best as if they were old friends. Docherty had been rubbishing Best's signing in the Australian Press since it was announced.

For Best on his road to salvation, his encounters with Docherty were tests. His mistakes were his, and he had to own them.

At the press conference Strik boldly predicted that Best would pull 4,000 extra fans for each of his matches. "We're paying him the highest ever fee offered by Australian soccer, but it's worth it."

After the media conference, Best was whisked away to a private interview with Channel 10 and established football journalist Tommy Anderson. This was the first of many interviews with Best in Australia preoccupied with his fall from grace. "Have you got any regrets, you know, if you'd had more discipline—for instance—that you could have really reached the top?" asked Anderson.

"Not really. I was at the top for 12 good years," replied the Ballon d'Or and European Cup winner.

Not everyone was impressed by this new, dry Best. SMH Rugby League writer Gary Lester seemed put out that Best hadn't smashed a glass on someone or vomited on the table. "On arrival Best even had the hide to sip tea ... reformed? Nothing has changed in soccer."

Best and McMurdo then jumped a flight to Brisbane to unite with his new teammates. When he arrived at training with his new side, there was another expat in the squad who recognised Best first-hand.

Mike Mulvey was a Manchester lad who went through United's academy before emigrating to Australia in late 1982 to join up with the Lions. Mulvey would go on to have a successful career in management, holding the reigns in the A-League with Gold Coast United (as caretaker), then Brisbane Roar before ultimately taking over the Central Coast Mariners and having the rare distinction of managing Usain Bolt.

Mulvey had grown up with Best as the cornerstone of the United sides he adored. Over a decade later they were teammates, and Best had just arrived at training. Best immediately integrated. He nutmegged his teammates at training to prove he still had it, while in the rooms he got the usual barrage of locker room interrogation. Goalkeeper Nigel Lowndes, an Englishman by birth, in particular used to grill Best about the film stars, models and Miss Worlds he may or may not have slept with.

Best was an elite trainer at his peak, and when he wasn't drinking he maintained a high standard. He had built up a base of fitness that he carried with him even in the 'exhibition' phase of his career. Clubs who bought cautiously based on his label were often surprised that he was, mostly, willing and able to do the work on the track.

Before his debut against Sydney Olympic, Best had to endure another appearance with Docherty in front of cameras. Seated between Docherty and Channel 7 presenter David Fordham, Best sat back while Docherty joked about Best's drinking and his penchant for not showing up to things. He also compared Best's knack for doing a runner to that of Hitler's right-hand man Martin Bormann.

All Best could do was wince. But inside Best was fuming. And—although it never made it to air—Best blasted back at Docherty while still on the set with cameras rolling.

In the lead-up to the first match against Sydney Olympic at Brisbane's Perry Park, Olympic star Peter Katholos, in his regular 'Kat's Corner' feature in *Soccer Action* (which had arranged for a photo of Best reading a copy surrounded by a group of women fans), seemed to have borrowed some of his manager Docherty's old jokes.

"Well Sydney Olympic and I are due to play against George Best on Sunday. I hope he turns up ... I reckon that signing him as a guest player doesn't say much for our soccer. To George Best I say welcome to Australia. I look forward to playing against you and having a drink with you after the game."

It was a tone-deaf piece to say the least, about a player on the wagon and who had won the European Cup and the Ballon d'Or, but one can only wonder what anecdotes Docherty had shared with his players.

On the morning of the game the mood was electric. TV, radio, journalists and autograph hunters descended on Perry Park with its official 5,000 capacity, but ample standing room on the hills. Programme sellers wore shirts saying "GEORGE DOES IT BEST", and before kick-off Best expressed a degree of nerves when he told TV reporters, "You know I'm not superman. Everybody plays badly once in a while. But I just hope that my bad games are little less than normal."

Before kick-off Simon Kistemaker approached Mike Mulvey with some words of inspiration.

"I remember him saying to me, look this is your boyhood hero, go and play and enjoy it this is something you will remember forever. He was right about that, but I didn't have a good game and I think I got pulled off just after half-time. I remember from the kick-off they kicked the ball to me and what do you do in a big game and your idol is on the field, you just give him the ball straight away. So I gave him the ball and about four players converged on him, and he danced in and around them and passed the ball off to someone else and then said to me 'anytime you like son'."

The first half started poorly for Best and the Lions, and got worse when Best dislocated his finger and had to push it back into place to play on. *The Courier-Mail* described his early impact as "[keeping] well clear of some robust midfield skirmishing, preferring to find space for himself in a deep-lying role on the left wing".

His lack of midfield skirmishing was abundantly evident after half an hour, when his right back opponent, Mike Coady, drove forward with the ball while Best jogged beside him, and put a ball into the channel for Katholos to run onto the pass and score.

Fans were starting to wonder what the Lions had signed up for with Best, who so far was only standing out for having a Malaysian Airlines logo on his jersey (his teammates had KLM logos, the Dutch club's major sponsor, on theirs). He only touched the ball 16 times and sprinted four times. But then, just before halftime, Best had a hand in the equaliser.

With five minutes left in the half Best took a ball on his chest, turned his opponent at the top of the box, feinted one way and moved the other to put his opponent off balance. Best's flick-on then caught the hand of the defender, whose arms were flailing as though calling for a lifeboat. It was a golden opportunity at the top of the box, but while everyone was watching Best line up to take the free-kick full-back Alan Niven snuck in like John Wilkes Booth to ruin the theatre for everyone. Niven slammed the quick routine into the comatosed wall, got his own rebound and then poked it home.

The Lions scored, and despite Niven taking the opportunity from Best, the whole thing seemed to enliven the crowd and the boy from Belfast. In a wonderful piece of pun-work from *Soccer Action's* Margaret McDonald—who must have personally counted Best's touch and run stats herself—"overheard on the terraces in the first half was 'I thought he was the world's best', and 'He's not George Best. He's more like

George 'just adequate'." McDonald continued: "but in the second half the Northern Irish soccer legend assumed a different identity, moving from just George Best to George 'absolutely marvellous'." "Every time he touched the ball he beat the tackler and flicked a superbly timed pass to one of his teammates, using an array of dazzling skills," reported *The Courier-Mail* laced with more than a little hyperbole.

A match report on Channel 10 seemed to agree. "Every time Best came onto the ball the crowd roared with anticipation. He played the position to perfection. Always the opportunist, often unmarked when receiving and passing with amazing accuracy. The years have not dulled the Best magic."

Best took all the corners, all inch perfect, and while taking his sixth corner a fan raced down the hill with his can of beer as an offering. Best waved him away and floated another perfect corner in the mixer.

It took Brisbane nearly the full 90 to find the winner, but it came in the 88th minute to Calvin Daunt. In Best's debut Brisbane were victorious and Best had worked his way into the game, eventually winning over the crowd. Officially the crowd was 5,000, but estimates of those present have the crowd much higher, potentially beyond 10,000. Taking into account the hill and the generally haphazard nature of official NSL crowds, it isn't clear precisely how many came out for Best.

After the game Docherty appeared on Channel 10 to discuss the outcome with Tommy Anderson. He called the crowd "one of the biggest seen at Perry Park in a long while". He repeated his stand-up routine about Best's unreliability, as well as his claim that Best had been a genius in 1973, but wouldn't stoop to real praise for Best's game against his side. "I thought he did quite well. I wouldn't sum him up any better than that. He's a good ambassador for the game. I thought he did well."

Docherty then reverted to form, calling for "overseas players to be banned" for depriving young Australian players of opportunities in the NSL. Presumably his ban wouldn't apply to managers.

Best was pleased with his performance, and had two games due in the following week, at home against St George and an away game against Marconi.

Originally, the Lions intended not to include the away game in Best's itinerary as they wouldn't receive any of the gate, but when Marconi got wind of this they approached Best and McMurdo to sign and play for them in the home fixture, offering to pay a $7,500 finder's fee to the Lions.

The Lions were reportedly open to Marconi's offer, but it didn't sit right with Best or McMurdo. After further negotiations Marconi offered to pay 75% of their gate receipts over $5,500 to Brisbane Lions.

There were other moves afoot. In that same piece in the *Sydney Morning Herald*, a Lions spokesperson denied rumours that Best had signed to play for one of the Adelaide NSL teams, which was mostly true. Best wasn't keen to appear in the league for a rival side. But he was willing to appear in an exhibition game for West Adelaide Hellas after his Lions obligations were complete.

It was also announced that he had signed to play two State League matches in Western Australia with Yugoslav side Osborne Park Galeb. The price tag was $8,500 per game, which was enough to send Soccer Action editors over the top.

"So while every NSL club struggles for financial survival the former Manchester United and Northern Ireland star flits in and out of the local scene with a hefty fee to take back to the UK."

It was a common criticism of Best while he was in town, and one hinted at by Docherty; that money could have been invested anywhere, and there were many embittered football people resentful that it went to Best.

The deal with Galeb had actually been agreed before Best arrived in Brisbane, but the Best camp wasn't keen to release it just yet to take the air out of the room for Brisbane. But with the debut and the barrage of PR out of the way, Best and McMurdo could turn their attention to extracting maximum value out of the tour, including the end of it. To aid in the marketing for Best and in advance of his arrival, Galeb sent a photographer from a Serbian language magazine to follow Best and McMurdo around for eight to ten hours to capture a day in the life of Best. The only problem was: the photographer they sent was a Serb who spoke no English.

"This guy comes through the hotel with all these fucking cases and cameras and shakes hands, doesn't speak a word of English right, and he is sat now at fucking breakfast. We go over to the lift; the lift is coming down. I turned around the guy is fucking clicking me, and the camera is on me, George is looking at me laughing. I said 'you're thinking what I'm thinking aren't you? He thinks I'm you' So we get in the lift and he's fucking clicking away at me, I said 'George we've got to fucking tell him, if he goes back to the magazine after paying all of that money'. George said 'I'm fucking loving this right'. So we kept it going for about an hour, but we tried to explain to him who was who and we thought we got it eventually sorted out. But then we went to different suites, and he follows me. I open the door and he's clicking away; George is rolling about laughing. It was very funny."

In between photo shoots, media appearances, training with the Lions, and announcing his intentions for the latter portion of his Australian tour, Best tried to connect with his teammates. There was the usual bawdy locker room talk, and Best hosted a lunch with his teammates at the Crest Hotel where he was staying. Mike Mulvey was young at the time and wasn't exposed to what Best got up to in the evenings, but he respected Best the professional.

"He was still a very charismatic quiet character, and he was one of the lads. He got in, he mucked in. I had Usain Bolt at Central Coast Mariners and I would say it was very similar, Usain came in and he was very unassuming, he turned up and did his work."

Best would be in bed at 9 p.m., with a cup of tea to read or do the crossword, which he could reportedly finish in a couple of minutes. Other players who, like Peter Katholos, were looking forward to a beer with the legendary drinker would be disappointed. Best didn't touch the stuff while he was in the country.

Best, the famous pants man, had also left that part of his life in England. He was a mixture of settled with Mary Stavin, and grieving the end of his marriage to Angie. Indeed while he was in Australia, Stavin was in South America promoting the Bond movie *Octopussy* where she was cast as one of 17 'Octopussy Girls'. McMurdo confirms that Best "never looked at a woman in Australia at all, which was unlike him".

The closest thing Best had to a night out in Brisbane was a couple of dinners out with actor Kenneth Branagh, who was in town. On his days off, McMurdo and Best explored the Gold Coast beaches and checked out the Great Barrier Reef. If Best was in Brisbane to party, then he was partying like an eight-year-old on holiday with his parents.

McMurdo still laughs today about this side of Best: the hidden saint inside the sinner. "When George wasn't drinking, he was the most boring fucking man in life."

Five days after his debut Best was set to face a rampaging St George side at Perry Park. St George was a top side, and ultimately won the NSL premiership that season. They easily defeated Brisbane Lions, 0–3. Although winners are grinners, Best's game made an impact on St George. In an interview in recent years, Robbie Slater confessed, "I was awestruck and you could see how good he'd been." St George Manager, Frank Arok, labelled Best a "brilliant artist" despite his team running rings around Best's Lions.

Two days later, Brisbane Lions and Best were at Marconi where officially 3,000 fans attended Bossley Park. Many claim the actual figure was closer to 10,000 or even 15,000 on par with the Kevin Keegan match numbers. The match ended 1–1.

The big crowd would have pleased all parties, especially Best who reportedly earned $3,000 from his take. But the biggest winner of the day was shareholders of the Gyprock Company, manufacturers of fine plasterboards. The Lions kit went missing on the trip from Brisbane so the Lions were forced to wear Marconi's away kit for the game. Gyprock, who was Marconi's shirt sponsor, got a massive freebie on one of Marconi's biggest nights.

Best had one game to go on his deal with the Lions, a week later at Richlands against Adelaide City. Before that game, and the completion of his deal with the Lions, Best had his appearance on the hugely popular *Parkinson* show scheduled for the Thursday night. Best and Parkinson had been friends for decades, first meeting when Best was a 17-year-old upstart with United and Parkinson was doing news shows on Manchester-based Granada Television.

Parkinson penned a biography of Best in the mid-1970s that threatened the friendship but they stayed close. While in Sydney for the show, Best and McMurdo stayed at Parkinson's place.

When Parkinson welcomed his great friend they played the footage of Best scoring six times for United in an FA Cup tie against Northampton in 1970. It might have been the only footage of Best that Channel 10 had, as they'd played it a few weeks earlier in a Tommy Anderson segment when it was announced Best had signed with Brisbane. When Best sat down, he remarked with a smirk, "He was a good player that lad, wasn't he?" to the titter of the audience.

That was the light point of the interview. Parkinson didn't leave any questions on the table, probing Best about where it had all gone wrong, and even if he had ever considered suicide. Parkinson was warm, and had probably worded Best up on the topics, but he didn't go easy on his friend. In fact, the interview was a platform for Best to be brutally honest while the audience squirmed and didn't know how to process his light entertainment.

PARKINSON: "I never ever thought that you were an alcoholic. I thought of you as a heavy drinker at times, a social drinker, but I never thought of you as an alcoholic but you say you are."

BEST: "You always hide it around friends. I think the longest time I went was 22 days. Drinking solidly without food. That's when I figured there was a problem."

Members of the audience didn't know whether to be shocked, horrified, cry for him or laugh: so they did them all.

BEST: "I went through a spell where I couldn't remember anything. There was maybe a week in between where I had a total blackout."

Best talked about checking into rehab and realising with the help of therapists that his drinking sessions were usually sparked by events in his life going well, and not the usual rock bottom narrative. The Australian trip was Best at rock bottom, and yet he remained sober and committed to performing for the Lions and fans. Most importantly, he just wanted to play football.

> BEST: "To this day it's still a big love to me. I enjoy it tremendously. I still get a big thrill and, you know, I still feel that buzz when I run onto that field. I know I can do things a little bit special and different to other people, and that excites me. It frightens me that one day it's going to be gone."

Best's final game was against the visiting Adelaide City, a mid-table team. But at Richlands in front of 3,600, Adelaide City played like United in 1967. The Lions were battered 4–0 and Best received withering reviews.

With that, Best left Brisbane. He was off to Adelaide for an exhibition game for West Adelaide against the Adelaide City side which had just humiliated him. With the Lions Best had played four games, scored no goals and provided no assists.

He had, however, caused a groundswell of press to descend on the Lions and—although these are debated—crowds burst while he was in town. He pushed the capacity of both Richlands and Perry Park, and many people, including Mike Mulvey, remember full houses for the Best matches. TV reports included long shots of capacity grandstands. The fact that the TV cameras were there was because of the lure of Best. To illustrate the point, in the final match of the 1983 season, the Lions hosted Canberra City at Richlands in front of 300 fans.

*　　*　　*

Best's next stop was Adelaide, where he had accepted a gig to appear in the 'Plaza Ceramic Challenge Cup' at Hindmarsh for West Adelaide Hellas. It was an annual exhibition game with their cross-town rival.

West Adelaide did the deal while Best was in town, agreeing the fee with McMurdo and picking up the bill for his flights and expenses. West Adelaide won the game 5–3 in front of 5,000 fans and a packed grandstand at Hindmarsh. Best seemed to extract some low-level revenge on Adelaide City, breaking his 1983 Australian duck, scoring one of the five from the spot and generally tormented his opponents with his devastating passing range all night. Photographs abound of Best with his West Adelaide teammates, and he was given a West Adelaide Hellas scarf that Bill McMurdo keeps to this day.

After Adelaide, Best travelled to Perth to meet his obligations with Osborne Park Galeb. But shortly after he arrived in Perth on a dawn flight from Adelaide, McMurdo took a call from the Dee Why Football Club, of the NSW State Second Division, wanting Best to return to Sydney for an exhibition game against local top-flight rivals. "Are you kidding, we've just flown 4,000 miles?" was McMurdo's response. "Just come, I'll make it worth your while," was the short response.

Best and McMurdo agreed on a return leg back in Sydney, after first earning their $8,500 appearance fee with Osborne Park Galeb. Best's deal with Galeb was sometimes written up as being for two games. But that seems to have been optimistic. Best was only ever out for one, and Galeb arranged a full marketing package for Best, including a dinner they arranged for him to speak at that attracted 2,000 fans. McMurdo remembers being "mobbed" at that event. Best and United were big deals in Perth. Best had knocked in a hat-trick on the 1967 tour in front of 20,000 fans in another 7–0 win.

While Western Australians were delighted to see Best, he was probably nearing the end of his rope when he arrived. His bags from Adelaide hadn't arrived, and at his first news conference he was swamped with questions of his off-field exploits.

John O'Connell, retired player and the voice of WA football for decades, was at that press conference, and famously interrupted the tabloid proceedings to say, "George I'm going to ask you a football question", to which Best replied, "Thank Christ for that."

To pay off O'Connell's kindness, or recognising a kindred football spirit, Best offered O'Connell a one-on-one. He told O'Connell he'd given the last ten years of his life to his fans, playing around the world, and his repayment—other than money of course—was to be treated as tabloid fodder. Few journalists stopped to consider that underneath the scandal was a human being trying to turn his life around.

Best's game for Galeb was against Melville Alemania. Galeb had been promoted this season, and were in the bottom half needing an injection of something to keep their heads above relegation. The Best deal had been announced weeks before, and with only a capacity of a few thousand, they didn't need to do much more to ensure a sell-out. O'Connell told the ABC that Galeb "had probably 20 or 30 people [normally] watching them on matchday, all of a sudden the ground was packed".

While the crowds figures are not in dispute—it was over 2,000 and massive for Galeb—the events on the pitch have grown into the stuff of legend over the years. What we do know is that Galeb won the game 2–1 and that their huge gamble on Best would have made the Lions swoon. Best scored the opener and set up the winner.

After Perth, Best and McMurdo jumped on another plane and returned to Sydney to stay at the Manly Pacific International and pick up an exhibition game on the beaches of North Sydney.

His fee was reportedly $5,000 to play at Manly-Warringah's Cromer Park. The game was scheduled for the same day that Best was originally supposed to reappear in court for his bankruptcy proceedings in London, but he had arranged a reschedule.

Officially 3,500, but unofficially closer to 4,000 or 5,000 people packed the hills to watch Best, and this time Bill McMurdo suited up at fullback for Manly-Warringah. Best, in his shiny white Dee Why shirt with the number 11, might have seemed like an apparition to the local supporters. In a way he was. The old, hobbled Brisbane Lions Best was left in Brisbane, and the ghost of European Cups past ran out for Dee Why.

Best scored, running onto a through ball and flicking it over the keeper and tapping it home. He also rattled the upright from a 40 yard lob as dessert. The crowd lifted as the Manly-Warringah keeper scrambled back, realising he had been done by the legendary George Best before the upright saved him. It was a lick of paint away from a folkloric Best goal.

When the game was over Best retired to the rooms to share a soft drink with his teammates and opponents, declining offers of a harder option from rabble-rousers. He'd delivered on the pitch, given the fans what they wanted and smashed attendance expectations for a midweek friendly.

*   *   *

After Best left the country, the tide of media opinion turned against him. There were dissenting voices from the start, namely from Andrew Dettre, mainly due to the fee, but other than poor performances in match reports, the press had mostly focused on Best the legendary player or strayed down the tabloid path.

Rale Rasic wrote of the Best tour: "Was George Best the right type of 'super star' to bring over for a guest stint? Let's face it, his football days were over, and with the Lions he turned out to be nothing more than 'Mr Ordinary'."

Johnny Warren in one of his pieces invoked Best as a stick to beat the Lions up with when they finished bottom.

Best himself was sick of it. While in Australia he and McMurdo teed up a three-match deal with Christchurch Mogal United in New Zealand for the end of August, but then mysteriously dropped in a 'no media contact' clause before he arrived. That left the Christchurch brass scrambling and scratching their heads. What was the point of Best if they couldn't get him to front the media? Understandably that deal didn't go through.

Best was sick of the grillings and recriminations. On his Australian trip he was given scant opportunity to be presented as just George Best the player. He constantly faced questions directed at George Best the womaniser, and George Best the man who had pissed his talent away. He had willingly walked into the colosseum, sober, to face his lions and serve his penance. But even though crowds flocked to him and there were moments of magic, he didn't have them swooning like in 1967. In fact he was mostly written off as over the hill.

As a nice footnote to his relationship with Australia, officially his final league match was with Galeb.

George Best returned to Australia in 1989 and in 1990, a very different man than in 1983, returning for The Best Australian Tour. The monastic life hadn't stuck and he was drinking again, but had stumbled upon a routine that worked for him: touring the world with McMurdo and playing in the odd exhibition or testimonial game. He was loving football again and had made peace with the end of his league career.

Best was approached by Billy Millen to tour Australia and pick up speaking gigs, coaching sessions and maybe the odd match. Millen had known Best as a boy in Belfast—Best had scored seven goals in a youth game against Millen's side—but their careers branched apart early before circling back around in 1989. Millen broke through at Linfield, where, according to the *Belfast Telegraph* he "terrorised defences and scored goals for fun". Millen was responsible for one of Linfield and Northern Ireland's greatest football nights when he scored both goals in a 2–1 home win against Manchester City in the 1970 Cup Winners Cup.

By 1974, when the Troubles were peaking, Millen left for Australia after first giving the South African league a shot. When he landed in Sydney he joined Marconi where he was given a job in the clubrooms to help supplement his match day income. "Everything was written in Italian. I said, oh what have I come to?" reflects Millen.

Marconi was one of Australia's biggest clubs but their facilities in the early 1970s were not exactly pristine. "I said, lads, there's an awful sound in the ceiling. So I popped the ceiling. I thought it was possums. It was not, it was rats. You should have seen the size of them. Oh my goodness, they were like cats."

That experience proved symbolic for Millen, who kept on bumping into rats in Australian football clubs, in ceilings and in management. Those experiences steeled Millen to ensure he was paid upfront for Best's appearance fees in 1989. "It was $3,000 a night [for clubs to book Best], so once it got to 10, I was like, George, here's $30,000." He had 18 appearances in total, Millen earned his cut from the other eight, and Best was booked to play in two games.

George and his girlfriend Mary Shatila flew to Australia probably not sure what to expect. The tour was sponsored by Nordmende TV because Millen worked there and talked the bosses into it.

Best's first stop on his 1989 tour was King Village, a hotel/spa deal in Wantirna, east of Melbourne. In the official programme for the tour, an ad for King Village is on the inside cover, featuring a model in a swimsuit lounging by a pool with the tagline: "King Village, the Best way to mix business and pleasure … at the end of the day George needs to relax and that is why he chose to stay at King Village."

King Village Club was also Best's first speaking gig. The next day he crossed town for the Geelong Soccer club, where a fresh-faced football writer newly arrived in Australia from London, Michael Lynch, was in the crowd. In an article in *The Age* years later, Lynch reflected on the night and his brush with football fame. Best was half an hour late after a detour via a local pub.

The following day Best was booked to play in a charity match at the home of the Doncaster Rovers Soccer Club in the north-eastern suburbs of Melbourne. The match was put together by the Celtic Supporters Club in Melbourne to raise money for the Biala School for disabled children.

It was a 'Celebrity XI' v 'Australian XI' match for charity, where some huge names were involved. Willie Wallace and Terry Hennessey took part, both of whom were in the country coaching, as well as five or six different former internationals. Millen also remembers David Hill, then Chairman of the Australian Broadcasting Corporation, who would become Chairman of the Australian Soccer Federation in 1995, was also part of the team.

The crowd of 300 plus was treated to a vintage second-half performance from Best. Driving at defenders, Best scored after a long run and then made it two from the penalty spot in the final moments. The match raised $10,000 for the charity.

There was also another living legend scheduled to be on the pitch that night. Ferenc Puskás, in town coaching South Melbourne Hellas, was booked to play but, according to Millen, in a somewhat apocryphal version of events, Puskás was turned away by an overly officious Doncaster official. "The guy told him, 'what's your name?' He said, 'Puskás', and he said, 'aye, and I'm John Wayne, fuck off'. But he was the real Puskás!"

That didn't prevent Best from spending time with one of his boyhood idols. Best long considered the Real Madrid of Di Stefano and Puskás to be his all-time favourite (outside of United of course), and his opportunity to lunch in Melbourne with Puskás turned out to be memorable on a couple of levels. "I've never seen anybody eat as many meatballs in all my life," remembers Millen of Puskás. "I would have done that for about two weeks. He had 40 meatballs."

After Melbourne Millen, Best and Shatila drove north to Canberra, where Best had a couple of speaking gigs at the Belconnen Soccer Club. On the drive Best had to beg Millen to stop at a pub so he could get a drink. After Canberra, they travelled south again to Tasmania to speak and play in a charity game with Devonport City Soccer club.

In Tasmania, Best was reunited with another former United graduate who had made Australia his home. Ken Morton is well known in Australian football, having coached in the NSL with Newcastle and Wollongong, before establishing himself in Tasmania and is to this day manager of one of Tasmania's biggest clubs, South Hobart. He also coached around the world in Malaysia, Vietnam and Ethiopia before returning to his adopted country. As a kid in the 1960s he come through at United just after Best, before finding opportunities greater elsewhere, namely at York City. But he will never forget his time at United with Best.

"I played with him in the A team, the B team and the youth team. We scored bags of goals together. When we played together we were a good partnership, we complemented each other."

Morton was in charge of Devonport City which faced a Tasmanian state rep side. In front of 1,800 supporters, Best again rolled back the clock to put on a show for the Apple Islanders.

As soon as the whistle blew Best was at home, although he hadn't figured on a Geordie named David Crosson invading that home in the opening minutes to send him flying. As Best lay in the dirt in agony, Morton screamed at Crosson, "If he goes, there's no game!"

But Best got up, unharmed, and played on. Crosson was told to cool it, and evidently he did after his one shot at glory.

Despite his right knee being in a state of continuous swelling, and a paunch under his shirt that wasn't there six years earlier, Best hadn't lost any of his touch. He created the first goal after his thunderous shot was parried out into the path of Devonport striker Anthony Rimmer. Then Best set up the second goal for Devonport just before half-time, when his majestic through-ball played in Rimmer to score.

Best had the ball on a string. He hit teammates 30 yards away with ease, and even got out his old tricks, like playing the ball off his opponent's shins as he once had for United. When football journalist Walter Pless asked Best after the game who was the greatest player of all time, he answered, "I was. Pelé said so, and he should know."

The game ended 2–2 with Best delighting fans. Afterward, thousands of miles away from any paparazzi or Fleet Street, Best cleaned the mud off his own boots and then downed a can of beer before hitting the showers. He also did something he didn't allow himself the luxury of doing in 1983: he drank with his teammates.

Morton had asked Mary Shatila what Best liked to drink. Her answer was Moet-

Chandon so Morton arranged for a couple of dozen bottles to be ordered for the local pub where they would retreat to after the game. After a few cans in the clubrooms the Devonport boys headed to the pub to keep the night going.

Around midnight Morton was approached by some locals, including the publican, to see if Best would be willing to join them for a game of snooker in the other room. Morton cleared it with Best, who was keen. That was the last time Morton saw Best that night. The next day Morton discovered that they'd played snooker all night, and that there was only one of the 24 bottles left. To his credit the publican, who had experienced an all-time epic evening, has never charged Morton for the Moet.

Best thoroughly enjoyed Tasmania. Millen and Best both recognised a little of Belfast in Tasmania, and Tasmania recognised Best. "I remember one day going to a small island nature reserve not far away and betting George $20 that no-one would know him there. We got off at Green Island and walked up like 100 yards, and there was the president of the Rangers supporters club from Melbourne. He said, 'Hello, George, how are you?' George said, 'Where's my 20 bucks?' He couldn't go anywhere."

After Tasmania, Best headed to Adelaide before finishing his tour in Sydney, which included a speaking gig at Marconi, where he was very likely warned not to check the ceiling. With the tour wrapped up Best famously won $10,000 in a casino one night, and then lost $18,000 the next night. The media caught the story and Millen had to hide him away for a couple of days. It was a sour end to the 1989 tour which contained a lot of great memories for Best.

In fact, he enjoyed his time so much that Millen had him return again in June the following year, this time bringing former teammate, Denis Law, with him.

Best's four tours of Australia represent the four faces of Best's battle with alcoholism. In 1967 he had not yet taken to drinking. In 1983 he was completely sober, having found some clarity and taken a handle of his problem. In 1989 he drank and embarrassed himself at times, but more often than not pulled it together and delivered for his fans. In 1990 he was often steaming.

In Sydney, Best was a no-show at a sportsman's night in Waverley, and also didn't appear at a 'Best XI vs Law XI' charity game at St George Stadium. In Melbourne, Lynch recalls an early engagement in Melbourne.

"[Best] was drunk at his speaking function and his language would make them blush on the Stretford End. Law, as he did many times for United, saved the day. Smart, sociable and a top speaker, he looked after his teammate that night, but could not help the Irishman giving Australia a first-hand look at his wild temper.

"One of the punters, who looked like he had as much to drink as Best, tried to convince the legend to dance with his wife. Best was having none of it, but the drunk persisted and then took offence and gave Best a piece of his mind. The Ulsterman responded by giving the drunk a piece of his fist. At that point Denis Law came in to save the day, and wheeled Best out of the venue."

This time, the trip wasn't going so well for Millen either. Best's rate was still $3,000 a speaking gig, but this time it had to be shared with Law. And Millen had forgotten his golden rule. One of his venues bounced their $9,000 cheque for three gigs, and Best's appearances fees were forfeited (and offered as charity to the Lidcombe hospital in the case of his Waverley event) for non-appearances.

Despite Law's debonair appearances and talk-show charm while on stage, Millen regretted inviting him.

"Denis Law wouldn't go anywhere. He wouldn't do anything. All he'd done was moan. I was trying to get Pat Crerand out. But for some reason, I couldn't bring Pat. So somebody said, bring Law out. It was the worst thing I could have done. Shocking. Just wouldn't mix with anybody. He shouldn't have come, you know. He just moaned the whole time."

Best was busy with coaching commitments while he was in Melbourne in 1990, but he may have been laying the groundwork for something more permanent. Before he left England, Fleet Street was reporting that he was considering relocating to Australia.

He told Melbourne's *The Sun* that he might be interested in coaching in the NSL, and that he was opening a business called 'George Best Sports Design' on Punt Road. He had always enjoyed coaching kids, had an affinity for the country, and was clearly contemplating something more permanent. If it was good enough for his hero Ferenc Puskás, it was good enough for him.

"We have formed a company in Melbourne so the incentive is there to be based here, and as long as the job appeals, I certainly would be interested in looking at it."

Nothing came of Best's 'offer' to take over an NSL team in Melbourne, and like so many of Best's endeavours, George Best Sports Design was another idea too good to be true.

While they were in Melbourne Ken Morton crossed Bass Strait to meet up with Best and book him for another exhibition game. This time Best would represent the 'Wrest Point Hotel Casino XI' against a 'British Airways World XI' at Morton's new home at Olympia in Hobart. Best and Law did a couple of speaking nights in Tassie beforehand, which were most memorable for only six people attending the second night. "They forgot to advertise it," claims Millen.

The game in Hobart featured a mixture of talents, including Morton who suited up at left back so he could feed Best the ball. David Crosson was selected, and was no doubt on his best behaviour. Law refused to play, but was made notional manager of the British Airways side.

It was a massive success. Between 2,000 and 5,000 fans flocked to see Best for one last time, including Walter Pless who again captured the game for the local media.

Accounts of Best's performance in the game have since fallen into legend. Pless was less than impressed describing his output as "showing little of the brilliance he exhibited last year". Some fans remember Best scoring a headed goal from a corner while sitting on the shoulders of a teammate. According to Pless, Best did find the back of the net, but under more charitable circumstances. When British Airways were given a corner at the death, they let Best—who was playing for the other team—take it for them. His goal made it 8–7.

Morton is grateful today for both of Best's visits, and Best himself would have just been thankful to be on the pitch before a gracious audience.

After the 1990 tour of Australia Best continued to tour and play in exhibition games right up until the late 1990s, playing 15 or 20 games a season. He died in London in 2005.

Billy Millen, a Linfield legend who took on and conquered Manchester City at Windsor Park, and rodent infestations at Marconi, sadly passed away in 2020 after a long illness.

Today Best's visits to Australia are warmly regarded in some circles, but are often wrapped up in heady debate about the value and cost of imports. In 1983, he was a poster child for clubs who thought buying a crowd was simpler than building a culture. Best did pull crowds, and he provided invaluable football memories for fans on the hills and grandstands; and in those matches, maybe he did stand on his teammates shoulders to head-in a goal, or steal the ball from his own teammates to go on a 40 yard run to score. Whether that happened or not is almost immaterial.

He was a legend, and in the years since fantastical tales were bound to merge with fact. Whether he weaved his magic on the pitch or a flop, or whether he was drunk, cavorting or completely sober, people saw what they wanted to see. The football god, the drunk, the magician, the man of the people.

Of all the football legends to ever play in Australia, he was the best.

Peak NSL:
When Kevin Keegan
Came to Blacktown

Blacktown City, 1985, 2 games, 1 goal

While Blacktown had the pulling power and money to attract Bobby Charlton, they didn't have the squad or facilities ready to sustain a NSL presence. They were relegated in 1981, but fought their way back into the Australian top flight in 1984.

They also retained their experienced heads, like Cliff Pointer, who stuck with Blacktown throughout the early 1980s.

The 1985 NSL season rightfully brought with it considerable hope for Blacktown. But they had a problem: they couldn't pull a crowd. In the early part of 1985, home attendances were good when one of the bigger Sydney clubs were in town—like the 4,550 who turned up with Sydney Olympic in round four—but they were averaging three figure crowds on other weeks.

Andrew Dettre penned a damning indictment on Blacktown in the early part of 1985. In an excursion to the west to see football in Blacktown (and Penrith) he wrote of Blacktown lacking an atmosphere, and reminding him of "a village ground somewhere in Europe where amateurs muck around for the love of the game, watched by their families". Dettre was one of Australia's most influential football writers and he was berating Blacktown for their lack of 'proper football'. Blacktown were a team of "honest hard-working, tradesman like" players. "Piano removalists rather than piano players".

Discontented with being considered piano removalists, Blacktown sought out football's Liberace. While it wasn't sustainable, as the Bobby Charlton experiment had proven, signing a big name could be good while it lasted. The club opened an old copy of France Football, skipped to the Ballon d'Or catalogue and picked out Kevin Keegan.

Outside of Charlton and Bobby Moore, there was no bigger name in English football than Kevin Keegan. He was a perennial winner, and only Fort Knox could compete with his collection of silverware. Two Ballon d'Ors in 1978 and 1979, four league titles (three with Liverpool and one with Hamburg), one European cup, two UEFA cups and multiple team-of-the-season appearances.

He remains the only Englishman to be awarded the Ballon d'Or twice. Michael Owen is the only English player to win it since.

Keegan's record as a player puts him on the adult table in the pantheon of football gods. But there was a lot more sense behind his signing by Blacktown than just his reputation. First, he was Liverpool. Like Charlton, Keegan's name and stature brought with it a tiny red magnet for fans of one of the biggest clubs in England.

Second, and most remarkably, Keegan was still only 34; in fact, he had just turned 34 on the cusp of the 1985 season, even though he had retired at the end of Newcastle's 1983/84 season after delivering on his promise to win them promotion. While he was a fair while out of professional football, he was playing in exhibition games and was nearly a decade younger than Bobby Charlton when he appeared for Blacktown.

Blacktown were getting a bona fide legend, without airs and graces, and with legs young enough for a fight.

On a much smaller scale, signing for Blacktown put Cliff Pointer into an extremely unique category. He is the only player to appear in club football with both Keegan and Bobby Charlton.

A snapshot of the media excitement over Keegan's arrival is offered by *Soccer Action*, who ran with the front page header 'Millionaire superstar Keegan!', and saw fit to include an exclamation mark just to underline their editorial opinion. *Australian Soccer Weekly's* 'Keegan will shake this city' reads as something of a threat, but one that hungry football fans will have been happy to accede to.

Keegan arrived in Sydney in April 1985, a little more than a week before his first game. He was booked to play in two matches, at home against Canberra City at Gabbie Stadium, and another home game against Sydney Croatia. Two training sessions were also advertised in the lead-up to his first match for fans eager to get in as much Keegan as possible.

Keegan was in the midst of an antipodean tour, having just come from New Zealand where he took on the All Whites with a 'select team'. The All Whites won 5–2, but Keegan scored both of his side's goals.

He was reported to be on $6,000 a game. At $5 a ticket, the club barely needed to sell any tickets to break even and with a big drawer fixture against Sydney Croatia on the schedule the club was bound to make a profit. Indeed, within days of Keegan landing in Sydney, Blacktown couldn't accommodate all the interest in tickets so the club moved the Croatia game to Marconi Stadium, about 30 minutes' drive away. Gabbie Stadium could only take 7,000 fans. Even before Keegan arrived the club knew they were on a massive earner.

"It's been disappointing switching our home game against Sydney Croatia to Marconi Stadium but where else could we play? I don't think 13,000 supporters would be able to fit in the Gabbie Stadium," long-time club man Peter Thorne told Andy Paschalidis.

Keegan, his family and his entourage were all staying at the Camperdown Travelodge for the duration of the contract, and the hotel was happy to let everyone know, stopping just short of actually advertising his room number. They ran ads after his debut featuring Keegan in a Blacktown jersey. "Kevin Keegan and his family should not be surprised if they meet sporting personalities like Imran Khan, Alex Hurricane Higgins, Jeff Fenech or Lisa Curry, all of whom are Camperdown customers," was the hotel's promise in an unsubtle advertorial piece.

Was $6,000 a game a lot? It seems a steal using revisionist maths on the payback expected from crowds. Conveniently, playing in the NSL in the same season was Celtic's Davie Provan who was on $600 per game with Sydney Olympic. And yet, even at ten times this rate Keegan seems tremendous value.

The only real debate about the fee from the enraptured media was the opportunity cost. $12,000 was a pretty healthy transfer fee by mid-1980s NSL standards. So Blacktown were banking on a return from crowds, more so than a lasting boost to the squad. Rather than buy a new player, they were ostensibly investing the money in marketing.

"Our main concern is to attract new people, and perhaps keep maybe 200 or 300 of them on a permanent basis. That's why we are eager to secure Keegan—for he's known to all sports lovers not just soccer fans." Peter Thorne told journalists.

On his arrival Keegan immediately bedded in with his new teammates. By now Cliff Pointer was an elder statesman at Blacktown, and onto his second Ballon d'Or winner. He had broken the ice with Charlton and, compared with a slightly standoffish Charlton, Keegan was a breeze. "He mixed with the boys in a different manner to Bobby. He saw it as having a bit of fun as well as playing two serious games of football."

Keegan made the effort, including spending the day with his new teammates at the races where, through connections, he gave them access to the inside track … or so they thought. Pointer remembers the day fondly. "As part of breaking the ice, we had a day at the races. I think as part of his agreement he was to present one of the winners with the winners rosette after the race. So all the boys organised a box, and we said to him 'you must be able to get some tips for us … get us a good tip'. So he came back to us and said 'get your money on Lounge Lizard'.

"So we all put our money on Lounge Lizard. The start happens, and Lounge Lizard's out of the box first and we're thinking 'we're onto a good one here'. But at the end of the race Lounge Lizard finished stone motherless last, three metres behind the next best horse. And I have this picture of him pinning the rosette to the winner in the enclosure and looking up at us and just shrugging his shoulders. We gave him heaps about that."

As well as appearances at the races, Keegan was booked for an assortment of speaking engagements and coaching clinics. The night before his debut against Canberra, fans were given the opportunity for $8 to experience 'An evening with Kevin Keegan', a speaking engagement scheduled at the social club of rival St George. It was a panel discussion, with iconic football journalists Les Murray, Tommy Anderson and George Donikian sharing the platform.

On the day of Keegan's debut there was a buzz around Blacktown. In the opening pages of the matchday programme, Keegan was welcomed to Australia, the NSL and Blacktown by both ASF President Arthur George and the Mayor of Blacktown, Leo Kelly. Praise was being heaped on the club from on high but, alas, congratulations were not the only thing pouring down. In the days leading up to the game Sydney experienced torrential, Noah-levels of rain. The rain was so heavy that the game was on a knife's edge and it looked like part of Blacktown's investment in Keegan would be washed away. Four NSL matches had to be cancelled that weekend in Sydney because of the rain. But there was no way that rain was going to ruin one of Blacktown's biggest days.

Pointer recalls it well. "His first game was against Canberra at home and it was a sell-out. I think [it was] the biggest crowd they had had at Blacktown."

Fans covered the perimeter of the ground despite the deluge. The rain mercifully stopped before kick-off, but to get the game going desperate measures had to be taken.

"There was so much surface water on the pitch that they thought they'd have to cancel it. On the morning of the game it stopped, so at the crack of dawn they got a helicopter to fly down to the ground to disperse the water. It was there for quite a while. The water was all over the pitch instead of certain heavy areas. And although the pitch was heavy it was ok to play on," says Pointer.

It may not be uncommon for clubs to commission a helicopter to get star players to games, but to enable one to play?

An official crowd of 3,567 assembled, slightly more than the Charlton game, but unofficially it was higher, and they got exactly what they hoped for.

Keegan, wearing the number 8 shirt, put in a blinder. Like Charlton he opened the scoring for Blacktown, and bossed the game like only a player of his class could.

The game itself was a loss (3–2 to Canberra), and Cliff Pointer scored an own goal, but few fans would have been bothered with the result.

Australian Soccer Weekly ran with the front page headline 'Keegan's Still England Class' for Tommy Anderson's article, who was still enchanted by Keegan from the event the night before. "Kevin Keegan is still one of the world's finest players and an entertainer second to none."

Blacktown had lost, but "with a little bit of support from his adopted teammates Canberra wouldn't have been in the race."

Pointer was also in awe of Keegan after the game. "He played that game as though it was an FA cup final. He was very, very good. He was a livewire. He put players under pressure. When they thought they had time, that time reduced when he was around, so they had to make decisions quicker. The thing that really, outside of being an altogether good bloke, surprised me and surprised me for how good it was, was his ability in the air for a not-very-tall guy."

Keegan's goal underlines Pointer's assessment, and was vintage Keegan. Unlike Charlton's scuffed dribbler, Keegan leapt above Canberra's defenders and powered home a header from Johnny McKie's cross.

Alex Vesic from Soccer Action was also quick to label the Keegan experiment a success. "I doubt that Blacktown would have had more than 500 spectators for this fixture with Canberra without Keegan."

After his fantastic debut, Blacktown got to know their new signing a little better. "That was the difference with Bobby," Pointer recalls. "We actually had a dining club area at the club when Kevin played, but we didn't have that with Bobby. He came in and mixed with all the players. He was very much about the rest of the players as well.

"While he was there everyone got better. Just the fact of having someone like him. The pressure was on. You didn't want to make a mistake because Kevin was there. When you get someone like Kevin into a training situation then no one wants to make a mistake, and everyone's concentrating so hard to make sure they're not the one who stuffs up. I can guarantee everyone got better!"

One of Keegan's other great virtues was his selflessness with fans. Keegan was always available to sign jerseys, cards, books or footballs for young fans. While Keegan was in town, clinics were set-up with Rale Rasic to run across Sydney with Keegan as the guest star.

Rasic recalls those sessions, and Keegan's devotion to his fans, fondly. "We had two and a half thousand applicants for one clinic. Then they announced two hundred winners for a clinic. When we arrived at Arlington [in inner suburban Sydney], Keegan saw the few thousand people around. I had eighteen coaches there to coach different groups, and Kevin would stay on the other end of the field so every player could kick the ball to Kevin Keegan and get a return.

"We had started at nine in the morning, and had an interview with ABC booked for 1pm. We were not even halfway through at that time. Kevin calls to me and says, 'go and tell them that we will do interview either late tonight or tomorrow morning. I will not leave this field until the last kid kicks the ball with me.' What a commitment and what an honour. Keegan to me is an amazing, amazing human being."

Pointer was at one of those sessions, and remembers Keegan passing on the advice—make sure the kids bring a camera.

"He made sure at the end of the session that every kid had the opportunity to have a photograph taken with him. And he wouldn't leave until all those kids had that experience. He was a real gentleman."

In the week before his final game against Sydney Croatia, Keegan provided his perspectives on football, and Australian football in particular, to *Australian Soccer Weekly*. In the piece titled 'Play to Your Strengths', Keegan offers an answer to a question nobody was asking. "I'm not nervous about playing for Blacktown. I know I can play football and I know I'm still very fit and I know I can add something … I've always said that with footballers like myself people expect miracles. And it's our job to try and provide them."

It was the perfect strapline for Keegan's final game for Blacktown against Sydney Croatia at Marconi Stadium. May 5, 1985 must be one of the most storied and unparalleled days in Australian football history. To accommodate the shifted fixture, Marconi staged a double header, with Keegan's Blacktown to appear second on the bill after Marconi first faced Canberra's Inter Monaro. Marconi wiped the floor with their Italian brothers 4–1 in the lunch-time kick-off as crowds grew for Keegan. The chat "Cro-atia, Cro-atia" filled the air. When Keegan ran out onto Marconi Stadium, 14,220 'officially counted' fans went into a frenzy.

Truthfully, no one has any idea what the actual attendance was. But whether there were 14,000, 15,000 or 20,000, it was a turnout nobody present will forget.

"I remember the crowd was packed at Marconi stadium, and apparently there were three or four thousand outside who couldn't get in," recalls Pointer, who sadly missed Keegan's final game with an injury.

Sydney Croatia, like Marconi, was a big Sydney club with a big supporter base who would have added to the enormous occasion. But despite the star-studded Croatia line-up, it was Keegan they had all come to see, as well as thousands outside the ground who couldn't get in. Police had to close the gates for safety reasons, which still didn't deter some fans who snuck in over fences.

But even with Keegan in the side, a result for Blacktown against Croatia seemed unlikely. Sydney Croatia were brimming with internationals. Socceroo Jim Patikas, in his only season with the club, was on the brink of joining AEK Athens where he would go on to play for eight seasons. Twenty-two-year-old Graham Arnold, who was appointed manager of the national team in 2019, led the line for Croatia while a playmaker Žarko Odžakov slotted in just behind him.

Odžakov had toured in the 1970s with Macedonian side Vardar, fell in love with Australia and moved to Melbourne to play for Preston Makedonia. After three seasons, aged 29, he moved to Sydney Croatia and immediately caught alight. He would go on to be hastily naturalised at the behest of then Socceroo manager Frank Arok, and parachuted into the national side as they sought to qualify for the 1986 World Cup.

Here, he was playing in one of the biggest games of his career facing up against Kevin Keegan, in front of a crowd more fitting of a Yugoslav First Division match than an NSL Northern Conference mid-season bout.

The game ended 1–1 but despite the result, not a single fan that day left with an empty feeling. The game was an epic display of skill, from two world-class footballers, that is still discussed with affection decades later.

'Glimpses of genius from Keegan, but Odžakov steals the show', was Andrew Dettre's headline in Soccer Action.

Blacktown started stronger. Keegan nearly opened the scoring early on, but his shot was parried by Croatia keeper Greg Woodhouse, for strike-partner Johnny McKie to pounce and fluff his chance from the rebound. Keegan was photographed with his head in his hands after McKie's miss, but then Keegan started the ball rolling with a trademark glimpse of genius.

Keegan created Blacktown's opener by laying the ball on a plate for McKie, after some fantastic combination play between Keegan, McKie and former Socceroo Phil O'Connor. With his back to goal, Kcegan collected a ball on the half-turn and played McKie into space at the edge of the box. This time McKie belted his shot into the top corner with so much power that it could have been felt at the Kop. 1–0 to Blacktown with Keegan in vintage form.

But after the early Blacktown flurry Odžakov took over. But when a Jim Patikas goal was disallowed for reasons no-one could discern, Odžakov seemed to get mad. With only minutes to spare and facing a loss, Odžakov was rolled an indirect free-kick which he belted so hard the net nearly tore. It was a thunder-bastard from 25 metres which stunned the crowd and made it 1–1. A rich reward for Croatia who had largely bossed the game through their Macedonian general.

On the pitch after the game in a TV interview Keegan was full of praise for both sides, and the energy the game was played in. He lauded his strike partner McKie and picked out Croatia's 22-year-old Socceroo Jim Patikas for specific praise. Later that year Patikas became a key player in Australia's World Cup qualifying campaign, before being signed by AEK Athens (where he won a league title).

It was Keegan's final hit out for Blacktown. He had scored, set up another, dazzled enormous crowds, but only helped Blacktown to a single point in two matches. Whatever happened on the pitch barely mattered to Blacktown, who reportedly pocketed a tidy $20,000 profit on the investment.

Andrew Dettre moralised on Keegan's guest appearances after the Croatia match. Dettre was generally sceptical of marquee signings, but in Keegan he had seen a player still somewhere near his prime, who had both boosted attendances and rewarded those who came with his performances. "Keegan richly repaid those who had the courage to plunge into this expensive promotion with him—let's hope those entrepreneurs and clubs will repeat the exercise."

Keegan's parting gesture to Australian football was an interview with Les Shorrock and *National Soccer Monthly*. He was "pleasantly surprised" by the standard of the football: "tremendously entertaining" with "a high level of skill". He then summarised decades of Socceroo supporter neuroses by saying, "I can't for the life of me understand why you don't do better at international level."

After Keegan departed, Blacktown meandered through the rest of the season and finished mid-table in the Northern Conference. Like Charlton in 1980 his time on the pitch hadn't triggered any long-term success, and Blacktown receded to the mean. They did, however, avoid a repeat of the 9–0 embarrassment in the week after Charlton departed—this time managing an extremely healthy 3–0 away win at APIA Leichhardt.

The following season they finished a mid-table ninth, but were relegated anyway along with 10 other clubs as the NSL farewelled its Conference structure.

Blacktown City were back in 1989 after winning the NSW First Division title, and had two more seasons in the NSL but couldn't break the trends of the early 1980s, winning only nine games in two seasons. They were relegated after the first 'summer soccer' season in 1989–90, never to return to the National League.

Blacktown City, ultimately, just couldn't bridge that gap between State League and National League, but were more than willing to give it a go. While their seasons in the NSL were unremarkable, fielding Ballon d'Ors winners Bobby Charlton and Kevin Keegan left a permanent impression on Australian football that will never be forgotten.

Memories of Keegan's guest stint in Australia still live large in Australian football folklore. By football people he is described equally as a two-time Ballon d'Or winner and as the man who stood in the rain for 90 minutes after Blacktown training signing autographs so no kid would miss out. And while he only appeared in two games, the fact that he appeared in Australia at all has set in concrete his legendary status in Australia.

Ground Breakers:
Early Guests Who Set The Trend

The late 1950s and 1960s were a golden era of football in Australia. Geared around State Leagues, clubs emerged from post-war migrant booms and became powerful institutions. As they grew, and crowds swelled—some drawing regular five-figure crowds—so did the money in the game.

With boosted coffers came approaches to international players. AEK Athens legend Kostas Nestoridis migrated to South Melbourne for a couple of seasons in the mid-1960s as player coach. Young English starlet Alick Jeffrey chose to recover from a broken leg with Sydney Prague in 1961. And, infamously, Leo Baumgartner joined Prague on a 'no transfer' in 1958, setting in motion Australia's FIFA ban from 1960–63.

Clubs around the country also started to try the 'budget' transfer option: signing guest players. If that player had also played at the highest level in the 'mother' country of the signing club (as with Takis Loukanidis at Pan-Hellenic), then it was a match made in heaven.

Peter Price: Gladesville-Ryde, 1963,
10 games, 9 goals

Ayr United in Scotland is probably most famous as the last senior playing club of Sir Alex Ferguson (24 games and nine goals) before he launched his managerial career.

However, in the 1950s and 1960s Ayr United had a prolific goalscorer in Peter Price, who remains the club's all-time leading goalscorer, having put 213 into the net from 251 games.

Price moved to Australia in 1963 reportedly to immigrate and it would be difficult to find a better debut performance from an international star.

The centre-forward scored with his first touch and went on to register a hat-trick by the 25th minute, giving Gladesville-Ryde a 3–1 lead at half-time in front of 2,000 people at Somerset Park in the NSW First Division. Their opponents Hakoah bounced back in the second half and the game ended in a 3–3 draw.

Soccer World reported that Price's wife and two children were set to join him in Australia in four weeks. He was given a job as a process worker at Tennyson's Textiles before they arrived.

Then in the July 19 edition of *Soccer World*, it was reported that Price had left to return to Scotland, without notifying his club.

"Peter Price left for Scotland last Wednesday week without notifying Gladesville. The club is considering what action to take to recoup some of the money paid to Price for services not rendered."

Given Australia were in the middle of a FIFA ban because they were not paying transfer fees to overseas clubs, citing immigration instead of football contracts, Gladesville-Ryde had little legal room to move.

When Price passed away in 2015, the newspaper mentioned that he had not settled during his brief time in Australia. When he returned to Scotland he saw out his career with local side Whittlets Victoria.

Price was an incredible talent who Sydney only saw fleetingly. He ended with 10 games for nine goals, including a run of five games in a row where he scored against Yugal, South Coast United, Auburn, Croatia and Canterbury. A truly remarkable goalscorer.

*   *   *

Takis Loukanidis: Pan-Hellenic, 1968, 9 games, 1 goal

Sydney Olympic have always been a club willing to consider big name guests, and their success in signing Takis Loukanidis in 1968 lay the groundwork for a trend that would lead to Davie Provan and Ian Rush in subsequent years.

Olympic has its roots in Sydney's Greek community, and was established in the 1950s as Pan-Hellenic.

Sydney Olympic's transition from local to State powerhouse—and later foundation club of the NSL—was on the back of giants, and none was more giant than Takis Loukanidis, Pan-Hellenic's first major guest player in 1968.

A four-time Greek champion in the 1960s, Loukanidis scored 59 goals in 142 appearances for Panathinaikos. He represented his country with aplomb on 23 occasions, and represented his countrymen just as well when he visited Sydney in 1968.

Journalist Andrew Dettre wrote in *Soccer World* that 2,000 Greeks were on hand for Loukanidis's arrival at Sydney Airport to greet "the greatest Greek footballer in the world".

Crowds never dipped below 10,000 for any of his matches whilst the clubhouse got a nightly (instead of weekly) bonanza as people flocked to speak with the international footballer.

Sydneysider David Jack has a great football pedigree. He was an accomplished player, and he is also from the line of Jacks that include father David, who was a respected football journalist in the UK and Australia, and grandfather David who was a champion footballer with Arsenal. Sydney's David Jack played against Loukanidis for Manly during his visit.

"In Loukanidis's first stint in Sydney with Pan-Hellenic, the best supported, but perennial under-achievers in the NSW Federation, Hellenic came second, their highest position during the Pan-Hellenic years. Loukanidis was an inspiration to the team and he was still sharp. Loukanidis's magnetism swelled the Hellenic crowds and the regular chant of 'Takis Takis' reverberated around their Wentworth Park home ground."

Pan-Hellenic's recruitment of Loukanidis paid off in spades in crowds and clubhouse activity, but despite fleeting glimpses of brilliance his performances on the pitch left a little to be desired.

Soccer World noted that: "Nobody denies his skill, finesse and experience-but his fitness was questionable and his understanding with other key players was often pathetic."

Loukanidis reportedly tried to force his style on the other 10 and became disheartened when that failed.

Despite the less-than-flattering summary of his season he helped Pan-Hellenic to second in the Championship, falling short in the final, losing 4–2 to Hakoah in front of 22,111 spectators at the Sydney Sportsground. The first of Pan-Hellenic's goal was an equaliser by Loukanidis, described by *Soccer World*:

"Counting on the benevolent assistance of a strong wind, Loukanidis let go a sudden snapshot from 35 yards in the 26th minute; Fuzes (the Hakoah goalkeeper) dived too late and could only push it into the corner of the net for the equaliser."

On his return to Greece, the 33-year-old Loukanidis intimated that he would be retiring from playing, only for Pan-Hellenic to get him back again in 1969, this time as their player-coach.

His influence somewhat diminished according to David Jack. "Loukanidis returned to Sydney the following year as player coach, but a year older his impact was less profound and Hellenic struggled for much of the season."

As a marketing exercise, Loukanidis was a success. More than 150,000 spectators attended his matches, eclipsing the next best, 103,753, who attended APIA's matches.

On the field he was less successful, but still capable of moments of magic, his skill undiminished with the years.

*   *   *

Mimis Papaioannou:
Heidelberg United (Fitzroy Alexander), 1976, 2 games, 2 goals; Western Suburbs (VIC), 1979, 9 games, 6 goals

There are few more revered names in Greek football than Mimis Papaioannou. At AEK Athens he is an icon, playing a record 480 games and scoring 234 goals. He played in five Greek championships, including in 1978 and 1979, and won three Greek Cups, including the double in 1978. Papaioannou was also capped 61 times for his country, and scored 21 goals for Greece.

Papaioannou is his country's Bobby Charlton. A one-club man who broke countless records with AEK, a paragon of his national team side breaking countless records in the process, and with seemingly limitless physical resources allowing him to play at a high level across the globe well into his 40s. He was said to have once been a target for Real Madrid, but knocked them back to stay at AEK.

It was a massive coup for the Melbourne club then known as Fitzroy-Alexander (later Heidelberg United) to sign Papaioannou. Greek rivals South Melbourne set the trend when they brought out AEK's Kostas Nestoridis in 1966 and 1967 as player coach, and Fitzroy- Alexander followed by splashing $3,000 on his former AEK strike partner Papaioannou for two exhibition games against interstate rivals.

Around 7,000 fans descended on Olympic Park for the two matches. Those in the terraces were treated to some outstanding football (and a sneak preview of a young star in 20-year- old future Socceroo Gary Cole). A 3–2 win over West Adelaide was followed by 4–4 against Marconi where Papaioannou scored twice from his preferred position of outside left.

Melbourne must have made a serious impression on Papaioannou. He had toured with the Greek national team in 1969, but 1976 left him with a taste for suburban Melbourne and a real opportunity to extend his career in front of adoring fans.

In 1977 Fitzroy-Alexander, on the cusp of their NSL debut as a club, announced that they had signed the AEK legend for "six to eight weeks" of the upcoming season.

Fitzroy was thrilled. Since his exhibition appearances the year before, the club had worked desperately to make a league deal possible. What better stage than the inaugural NSL to make such a statement signing? They reportedly beat Sydney Olympic to his signature to boot. But what put Fitzroy's offer over the top? Papaioannou's cousin, George Tsakiridis, was on the Fitzroy committee.

"Tell the fans not to worry," Papaioannou told reporters at *Soccer Action*. "I'll definitely be in Melbourne when the Greek season is over."

But he never arrived, and it's not clear why.

Players definitely coming and never arriving was not unusual for early NSL fans, or football historians. But fans who wanted a fix of Papaioannou wouldn't have to wait too long. A couple of years later he turned up in Melbourne again, to play in the most improbable of places.

In 1979, aged 36, he returned to Melbourne to play for the Western Suburbs Soccer Club (not to be mistaken for the Western Suburbs Soccer Club of NSW which competed in the inaugural NSL season). This Western Suburbs Soccer Club were playing in the Victorian State second tier, and represented a wave of young Greek migrants who had settled in Melbourne's inner west.

Western Suburbs today are in the fifth tier of Victorian football, but in 1979 they were at their peak. According to current day club President Stratos Tzanoudakis— who was a "young kid on the fringes of the first team" in 1979—that late 1970s period was the finest in the club's history.

"That was the glory days of the club. There was money around, a lot of the members and officials of the club ran businesses, and there was a lot of sponsorship. And there was a big Greek community aged in their 30s to 40s. A lot of people on-hand to help."

Papaioannou's signing was the brainchild of the club President Dimitris 'Jim' Tsambasidis, who was a radio DJ with Radio Hellas 3XY. Tsambasidis would sign off his program with "I love youse all", and spun tunes for Greeks and Anglos alike. Radio

3XY was a staple of the Greek community, and was active in fundraising for Greek community services. This included promoting Greek clubs like Heidelberg, South Melbourne—and Western Suburbs SC.

"We've got the best Greek support in Australia. I wish I were a millionaire so I could bring more Greek stars to make our fans happy. They deserve it," was Tsambasidis's patriotic boast when he announced Papaiounnou's end-of-season deal worth $30,000.

Tzanoudakis was young at the time, but still recalls the circumstances around Papaiounnou's signing. "He (was brought) out to build our crowds and they went through the roof. Greeks who remembered him in Greece came to see him play. There was no official connection to Mimis that I know of. I thought they may have been related or there was a friendship there but I think it went through somebody else who knew him. He came out with his wife. The President owned a shop at the time, and while Mimis was here he lived above it. It wasn't the lap of luxury just an ordinary 2-3 bedroom above the shops."

Western Suburbs started 1979 with serious ambition. Within their ranks was star centre-back Mike Glykokalamos who had captained Greek First Division club Panetolikos and butted heads with Papaioannou before immigrating to Melbourne.

The club had also just hosted 30-year-old journeyman playboy Ulysses Kokkinos for two matches. The South Melbourne icon had just been released from HM Pentridge Prison on a 19-month blackmail conviction that was reduced to six months. After Kokkinos, Western Suburbs signed Cypriot midfielder Andros Miamiliotis, who played for APOEL and represented his country nine times. He was roped into playing in a 1–0 win for Western Suburbs against local rivals Maribyrnong Polonia. It was an easy sell: Miamiliotis was in town already visiting relatives.

The Polonia game was also expected to be Papaioannou's debut, and he made it to the ground by the skin of his teeth. Tzanoudakis recalls him landing in Melbourne on game-day itself after a delay to his flight. He was ferried straight to the game with seconds left.

"A couple of the players went to get him at the airport. He was due to arrive on the day … but they were a little bit late and the coach Ray Pocock made contingency plans to play somebody else. But he did arrive and there was a bit of a kerfuffle around whether he'd start on the bench because the coach had already organised the line-up. To Papanioannou's credit he said 'Hold on boys, I've just arrived here. Mr President, I don't want to create any problems.' He wasn't too big to worry about stuff like that. So he started on the bench and came on in the second half."

On the Sunday night after the Polonia match, Papaioannou was unveiled (with

Miamiliotis) to fans at a "gala reception", where the legend told his adoring fans he would "play in goal" if he was asked to by player-coach Ray Pocock. Pocock, the pragmatist, responded by saying he would probably play him upfront.

Papaioannou made his starting debut the following week against Keilor City and showed no signs of cobwebs, rust or any other impediment. He scored twice in a 3–0 win. The crowd got everything they bargained for in that win. Papaioannou's goals both came against the grain, poking home with his vastly less preferred right foot after skipping past a couple of defenders, and then nodding home a header despite being just 170 cm tall.

The game was moved to the Schintler Reserve—home of nearby NSL Club Footscray JUST to accommodate the expected crowds. 2,500 people attended, which would have been enormous for the small club, whose regular home ground Ralph Reserve was described by Tzanoudakis as a "tin shed for a social club and change rooms".

"He must have arrived and thought 'what have I got myself in for?' Our facilities were terrible. They were really poor. It had a roller door if you can imagine what that would look like," says Tzanoudakis.

Going from regular crowds of over 25,000 at the Nikos Goumas Stadium with AEK, to a tin shed with a roller door must have been a comedown of sorts for Papaioannou. But if it was, Papaioannou didn't let it betray him with his performances on or off the pitch.

The following week he scored again in a 2–1 win over Doveton, this time in front of the roller door at Ralph Reserve. Papaioannou went on to play out that season with Western Suburbs, scoring at least six times to power Western Suburbs to the Second Division title and promotion into the top flight.

He left an indelible impression on the small club, its mostly young squad and fanbase of young first- or second-generation Greek immigrants. "In that short period of time even at training and during the games you could just tell, even at that age, his class was unbelievable," says Tzanoudakis.

Tzanoudakis also recalls at least a couple of his goals for Western Suburbs coming directly from corners, curlers with his powerful left boot which his amateur or, at best, part-time opposition never saw coming.

As an interesting footnote, AEK toured Australia in 1979, prompting suggestions that Papaioannou should be selected to play for the Victorian representative state side against his old teammates.

In the week before his final game for Western Suburbs, an exhibition match was hastily arranged at Olympic Park between Western Suburbs and South Melbourne

Hellas to serve up some more Papaioannou for Melbourne's Greek football fans. South Melbourne would finish last in the NSL that year but avoided relegation because they were too big to relegate. It may also have helped that their president Sam Papasavas was Chairman of the NSL. South Melbourne were considering signing Papaioannou for the 1980 season and wanted him to play the first half for Western Suburbs, and the second with South Melbourne to see how well he would fit into their set-up. There are doubts as to whether the half-time switch happened, and Tzanoudakis recalls Papaioannou playing the full 90 minutes for Western Suburbs, in front of one of the biggest crowds he ever played before.

"We got to the ground and there were lots of people arriving and the turnstiles were ticking over, but when we ran out onto the ground the grandstand was full. There must have been five to eight thousand people out on a midweek night for an exhibition game to see this guy play. He scored a goal, and the crowd went wild every time he touched the ball."

The deal with South Melbourne Hellas never eventuated because according to Papasavas he was too expensive at between $30,000 and $40,000 a year.

Papaioannou eventually joined the New York Pancyprian team in the USA's Cosmopolitan Soccer League as player/coach for three seasons. He played until he was 41 and helped the side to two championships.

One wonders what his appearance may have achieved for Western Suburbs, who were relegated from the Victorian top flight in 1980 on goal difference. To date the club has only appeared in the Victorian top division once since 1980. Considering his reported contract request from South Melbourne in 1980, one wonders how a club two divisions below South Melbourne were able to afford him. It is likely that his 1980 price tag was swollen by demand, especially as the US club was also sniffing around. While Western Suburbs weren't a big club, Tzanoudakis believes there were enough benefactors willing to put their hands in their pockets to walk alongside a legend.

A player of Papaioannou's stature appearing in the Victorian Second Division, in the same season that Martin Peters appeared in the Victorian top tier is unfathomable today. Indeed, it was rather unbelievable to Greeks back then as well, as Tzanoudakis discovered on a family trip to Greece.

"I remember going back to Greece in 1983 with my father and my sister and I told them [locals] I played with Mimis Papaioannou in the League and they wouldn't believe me. I had to show them evidence that it was true."

Absolute Bangers

The Goldilocks Zone for guest stars requires the player to pull crowds while also scoring goals for fun. Some guest stars can bring the eyeballs but—given the age of many of these recruits—can't put it together on Australian pitches anymore. Then there are others who might not bring marquee reputations, but take the Australian League by storm. Absolute Bangers are players who found the going too easy in Australia, scored goals for fun but didn't quite have the transformative effect on the balance sheet that they did on the pitch.

Bob Latchford: Brisbane Lions, 1981, 5 games, 4 goals

Bob Latchford's stellar guest stint with the Brisbane Lions in 1981 was a burst of raw football power that was under-appreciated and unparalleled in the NSL era until Davie Provan arrived at Sydney Olympic with a similar Midas-like aura in 1985.

Latchford was a massive star in England. Starting his career at Birmingham City, he blasted goals for fun in the Second Division before leading them to promotion to the top flight in 1971–72, and 10th in Division 1 the following season. In 1974 his transfer to Everton broke a British transfer record (£350,000 value in a mix of funds and player exchanges), a fee he would repay to Everton several times over. He was the club's top goalscorer for four consecutive years from 1975 to 1978, and in seven seasons to 1981 scored more than 130 goals in all competitions to jump to second on Everton's all-time goalscoring tally behind arch-deity Dixie Dean.

At Goodison Park they chanted "Bobby Latchford walks on water" as he blasted home 30 goals in 1977–78, and claimed a bonus £10,000 prize put up by the *Daily Express* which didn't think a 30-goal season would be achievable. He was, quite literally, a god at Everton.

Today he still sits third on Everton's top goalscoring charts (he was eclipsed by the striker who replaced him at Everton, Graeme Sharp), and is also ninth on Birmingham

City's. He won 12 caps for England, battling for selection and minutes with other 75 world-class strikers England had at the time: Trevor Francis, Kevin Keegan, Mick Channon and Tony Woodcock.

By the end of the 1980–81 Everton season, Latchford knew his time at Goodison had come. He had turned 30, and at the start of the season manager Gordon Lee purchased the young Scottish tyro Graeme Sharp who was eagerly waiting in the wings. In May 1980, with Everton's season in peril, Howard Kendall was appointed manager and Latchford could see the warning signs. Kendall—who coincidentally was one of the players Everton traded for Latchford in 1974—leaned toward Sharp and a general squad rejuvenation.

Despite that, Latchford and Kendall got on well. The manager wanted Latchford to stay and work with Sharp. But Latchford needed a fresh challenge and by the end of 1981 Latchford faced a bigger threat to his longevity in the game than a new regime at Goodison. The second half of his 1980–81 season had been decimated by a hamstring injury that recurred as often as it healed. He only managed 18 games and had the spectre of a degenerative hamstring hanging over him.

"It was a time to ponder the future. I was thirty and my contract had expired. It had been a testing two years. I felt I'd stagnated. I'd lost my place in the England team. I wanted to play and I wanted to play at the same standards I had set earlier in my career," reflects Latchford.

Brisbane Lions were a foundation club in the NSL, joining alongside Brisbane City as Queensland's two NSL entrants. The Lions trace their roots to the Dutch community, and were originally formed in 1957 as Hollandia-Inala Soccer Club but dropped the Dutch convention in the 1970s. They kept the Oranje colour scheme, however, and still maintain a cultural dotted line into Brisbane Roar in the A-League. They also enjoyed a significant financial windfall from the Brisbane Lions AFL side to take the name, then becoming Queensland Lions in the National Premier League.

The Lions signed many players including George Best (in 1983) and Arsenal's 1979 FA Cup final scorer Alan Sunderland (in 1982), but Bob Latchford stands out as a real coup, a signing who would delight and amaze the small but loyal Lions supporter base.

"The name's not just enough. Bob Latchford, in England he was well known but he was also a real professional. He was a good player. He really showed what a striker should be like. He was the most successful one we signed."

That endorsement comes from Henk Mollee, a living legend at the Lions who has been involved with the club for over 50 years as a Board member and player. Mollee summarises Latchford's signing as a mixture of luck and good timing. Latchford had missed the second half of the season and was just fit again for the final week.

He had missed an opportunity to showcase his return to fitness to potential employers who, like Latchford himself, were wary of the health of his hamstrings.

Today, Latchford reflects on how precarious his hamstrings were.

"Basically in early November of the 1980–81 season I pulled a hamstring at Goodison Park and I did not play again until the very last game of the season, which ... turned out to be my last game for Everton football club. I kept getting back to full fitness but sprinting was the thing that was yay or nay as to whether you were ok, and I kept pulling it. And I kept having to go back to the beginning and start all over again. This dragged on for four or five months."

The Brisbane Lions offer came as something of a godsend. It was the chance to work on his fitness away from the bubble and scrutiny of the English football media, and the off-field perks were too good to refuse.

"So this offer came in," he recalls, "it must have been toward the middle to the end of April, and I was quite surprised. The club [Everton] said it might be a way to regain a bit of fitness, you know, and obviously it's a fantastic opportunity to go to Australia with the family for nine weeks, and everything's paid for. So it wasn't really a hard decision to make. And that's basically how it all came to be."

Unknown to either Everton or Latchford, Brisbane was the perfect place for Latchford to be heading. Few realised it at the time, but Brisbane in 1981 was an early incubator of the practice of sports science.

So in May 1981, while Everton's first squad travelled to Japan for their end-of-season camp, Latchford landed in Brisbane.

It was a nine-week, six-League and one-Cup match deal. Convenient scheduling meant that four games would be at home. For good measure a number of speaking gigs and coaching clinics were included and some extra time at the end to spend with the family and enjoy the sun.

Latchford arrived, settled in at the Gold Coast, but then had to get to work. The fingers of every Lions fan, director and Latchford himself were crossed, hoping for goals and dependable hamstrings.

Goals were exactly what they got in Latchford's first game for Brisbane. Footscray JUST was the fodder. In front of 3,000 fans the Lions routed the boys from Melbourne's west 4–0. Latchford opened the scoring and fired home a brace while strike partner Ron Millman—father of tennis pro John—also got on the scoresheet before breaking his leg in the first half after a clash with Footscray keeper Dennis Boland when they were one-on-one. 'Too easy for Bob Latchford' headlined the match review in *Soccer Action*.

Game two was another big win. A week later, also at home at Richlands Stadium, the Lions carved up West Adelaide 3–1. The Lions were cruising at 2–0 before Vic Bozanic, father of 2014 World Cup Socceroo Oliver, pulled it back to 2–1. Latchford powered home the winner seven minutes later to make it two wins and three goals. He got on the end of a short cross—exactly the kind of finish the Lions had paid for.

But then tragedy struck. Latchford's hamstring went.

Latchford was forced off in Brisbane's next fixture, a NSL Cup quarter-final against St Kilda Hakoah that the NSL side won 1–0 in front of only 900 fans.

It is no understatement to say that Latchford's career was on the line until he was treated by pioneering sports scientist, Dr Kevin Hobbs.

Hobbs was at the time president of the Australian Sports Medicine Federation and, for many years, the Chief Medical Officer of Queensland Rugby League. He helped establish the practice of sports science in Australia, and was awarded a Member of the Order of Australia for his service to the field.

It was pure luck that Latchford happened to be based in the same city. Hobbs was about to make a lot of English First Division fans happy by turning around Latchford's poor luck with his hamstrings.

Hobbs spent an intensive week with Latchford which led to a full recovery in record time (two weeks), allowing Latchford to complete the final games of his contract and the remainder of his career.

Sadly for Latchford and the 6,060 spectators at the Newcastle International Sports Centre, one of the missed games was a 1–1 draw away to a Newcastle KB United side featuring Latchford's former England teammate and strike partner Mick Channon, and Leeds United hardman Paul Reaney. Channon was on his own guest contract, while Reaney had joined in 1980 to top up his pension. Jim Hermiston saved a point for Brisbane with a late penalty after Channon had opened the scoring with his only goal for Newcastle.

The chance to see two First Division and England goalscoring legends at either end would be a remarkable slice of Australian football history. Channon kept up his end by scoring. Latchford wasn't quite fit enough to complete the billing.

Latchford missed the following week as well, this time a 0–0 home draw in front of around 2,000 fans against APIA Leichhardt. Latchford was close to a return but ruled himself out at the last minute.

In an away game against Wollongong, Latchford was brought on in the 75th minute but couldn't make the difference on the scoreboard, despite causing "immediate confusion in the Wolves defence". He set up three golden chances for teammates in 15 minutes but all three were either saved or struck the woodwork resulting in a 1–1 draw.

But it was another point gained and with Latchford approaching full fitness, the air was electric for Latchford's final hit-out in Round 19 at Richlands, against NSL powerhouse South Melbourne Hellas. South Melbourne were top of the table, and brought with them the former Wolves and Liverpool striker Alun Evans, who had been a derby rival of Latchford's at Aston Villa. In front of 3,000 fans, South Melbourne were brushed aside 2–0.

While South Melbourne looked the better side in the first half they could not beat the Lions' block and conceded against the run of play. The Lions woke up in the second half and Latchford set up three gettable chances for teammates before scoring himself to get his fourth for Brisbane. Paul Ontong's long hoof forward caught Hellas defender Arthur Xanthopolous "mesmerised" (according to the *Soccer Action* report) and allowed Latchford to control it, dribble into the box, and then slot it past the keeper and two defenders with "ice-cool professionalism".

Latchford played in three and a bit league games for Brisbane, a fraction of a Cup game, scored four times and ensured a 100% record in the games he started. It was an exceptional output on the field and by far exceeded the expectations of the club.

Off the field his impact was also exemplary. Henk Mollee recalls the consummate professional whose attitude and generosity spread throughout the entire club.

"He coached kids, he was involved in everything the club wanted him to do. He was a really good example of the sort of person you want to promote your club and to improve the mentality of your players."

Latchford did the rounds on the after-dinner circuit for the Lions, and also teamed-up with Brisbane manager Joe Gilroy on the '4BC Bob Latchford Soccer Clinic', a four-day extravaganza of coaching sponsored by the 4BC radio station for local kids offering four half-day sessions both morning and afternoon. Admission was $20 per child for the four half days—a bargain for access to one of England's finest strikers.

Latchford was able to slip into Brisbane unchecked by the English media, and then returned and continued his career as though the whole thing had never happened.

"It was something done under the radar, if you like. I don't think the press in the UK knew much about it, and I don't think the players at Everton knew much about it. It was really done very quietly. If it happened today it would be all over social media. But back then it was just a personal thing between me, Everton and the Brisbane Lions."

Ultimately, Latchford reflects on his time in Brisbane as a paid working holiday for he and his young family.

The rejuvenating Queensland sun gave Latchford a new lease on his career. While he had been somewhat on the fence before, he was now determined to seek a new experience away from Everton.

The Lions were so enamoured with Latchford that they tried a 'hail mary' to intervene on any English transfer as he was due to depart. Brisbane called on favours to some wealthy benefactors and creditors to put together a $700,000 transfer offer to Everton for Latchford. Given that star NSL players were being transferred for five-figure fees (the record at the time was $45,000 for John Kosmina), that fee would have smashed multiple NSL records. Alas, they couldn't put the funds together and it was unlikely to have tempted Latchford anyway.

"Being in Australia really cemented the thought that I needed to change. So I got back and had a meeting with Howard [Kendall], then Chairman of Everton. Howard wanted me to stay and I said 'no', I'd made up my mind—partly while I was away—that I needed a fresh start. Partly because being over in Australia was fresh and new. I think that really put it in my mind. It was fresh, new, exciting. And I thought 'I need some of this. But I need it at a high level'."

Latchford was snapped up by Swansea City for £150,000 who had just been promoted into the English First Division under the stewardship of player-manager John Toshack. It had been a meteoric rise from the depths of the English pyramid and Latchford, who had experience playing with a promoted side in Birmingham City, was the perfect fit.

"The level of football was just the level I needed. I wasn't fully fit, but it was at a level where I could cope with it that didn't make any great demands on me. In terms of pushing my body too much. I was pushing myself enough to gain that little bit more fitness.

"It was a wonderful, wonderful experience."

*   *   *

David Provan: Sydney Olympic 1985, 5 games, 5 goals

In 1985, David Provan was enjoying a renaissance in his Glasgow Celtic career. He was 29 and had just scored a decisive equaliser in the 1985 Scottish Cup Final against Dundee United—direct from a free kick—to turn the tide and lead Celtic to a 2-1 win.

Provan had been terrorising defenders in Scotland for years. He joined Celtic as a record Scottish transfer fee in 1978 from Kilmarnock for £120,000. He was voted SPFA Player of the Season in 1980. He won four titles in his time (1978–79, 1980–81, 1981–82 and later 1985–86), won two Scottish Cups (1980 and 1985), and the Scottish

League Cup in 1982–83. These were the days of Celtic treble-trebling for fun. Success was earned on the back of players like Provan, who was of an international class.

On the pitch Provan was an artisan on the right. As Celtic's number 7 he had the pace and control to mesmerise defenders with the ball at his feet, and the ability to cut in or continue outside to put in lethal crosses. His flowing perm danced as he beat opponents on the ball, but he had a razor edge that saw him capable of doing jobs all across the park when his team needed him.

He had represented Scotland 10 times in a period of strong Scotland squads, including being a squad member for Spain 1982 without seeing any action. In late 1985 he was being tipped for a recall to the Scottish national team for qualifiers for Mexico 1986, in what would become showdowns with the Socceroos in November and December of 1985. His health intervened but, in May 1985 at the peak of his game, Provan did something impossible in the modern game. He left Glasgow for a five-match contract with Sydney Olympic.

Pound for pound, end-product for end-product, David Provan can lay claim to be Australian football's most impactful guest player of all time.

He was brilliant on the field, inspired younger players like Chris Kalantzis and Robbie Slater, and single-handedly turned around Sydney Olympic's 1985 season.

At the time, Olympic were down their starting sweeper, Tony Dakos, with a busted left knee. Peter Katholos had also damaged a knee and was on the sidelines for two months. Captain Peter Raskopolous, Kalantzis and striker Marshall Soper were all suffering with knocks.

"The club needed a quick fix, someone who could come in and replace the high calibre of Jim Patikas so they stumbled across a number of players one of whom was Davie Provan," explains agent Tony Rallis, who was a boy at the time.

Olympic's offer to Provan, brokered by Club President (and father-in-law of Rallis), Jim Petinellis and Thomson, was for a five-game guest contract.

Provan came to work. His first act when he landed after the 24-hour flight was to join training.

Olympic had been floundering that season so far. From 11 games they'd managed four wins, six losses and a draw and hadn't tasted success since Round 6. In Round 10 they were humiliated away to rivals Sydney Croatia, where Olympic exile Patikas and Graham Arnold both scored twice in a 5–0 rout.

Provan's first game for Olympic was a home clash against Newcastle Rosebud United on May 26th—eight days after his triumph at Hampden against Dundee United, and the day after arriving in Australia.

His teammates in that game were not star-studded on every line, but there was enough gold to complement Provan's magic. Marshall Soper, one of Olympic's greatest strikers and a regular Socceroo, played upfront, while international teammate Graham Jennings and Chris Kalantzis held down the left.

When asked why he had agreed to play on only a couple of hours of sleep in 48 hours Provan said, "I didn't want to let anyone down."

He needn't have worried. On debut, Provan opened the scoring in the 36th minute, cutting in onto his left before dancing around the 'beleaguered' Newcastle defence to slide a shot past the keeper.

"I was told before the match that I would get a lot of kicking but, to be fair, the Newcastle lads gave me a chance to play," said Provan following the match.

Newcastle manager Willie Gallagher labelled Provan the difference in a boys-against-men assessment.

The 18-year-old tasked with marking Provan that day was Mark Jones in his first season of a nine-season NSL career with Newcastle, Sydney United and Marconi.

"He seemed to have a lot of time on the ball, but then he would turn and be passed before I knew what happened," Jones said after the match.

The win was in front of 2,985 at Pratten Park. It was a lower turnout than Olympic hoped for but President Jim Pantellidis wasn't too disappointed.

"We didn't really know whether Davie would play until he got off the plane. With time to promote the matches I'm sure the crowds will come."

Provan's second appearance was away in Canberra, and a 3–1 win where Soper and Kalantzis both got on the scoresheet in front of a measly 1,620 fans. A week later Olympic were home again to Blacktown and found themselves two goals down in the 22nd minute. Provan got Olympic back into the game in the 35th minute, and then book-ended a Kalantzis goal in the 62nd minute to haunt the Blacktown defence.

That particular game left a big impact on young Tony Rallis, and Provan's winner is still lionised by Olympic fans. Of his second goal, Rallis recalls "he rounded the keeper and rounded him again. That sent the fan base delirious. He walked past the goalkeeper. He was very much a true British footballer in the ilk of Hoddle, Waddle, Barnes, Souness. He could keep the ball on a string".

Kalantzis's goal was a header from a Provan free kick, and the two goals he scored himself "single-handedly lifted the game from impending mediocrity", according to a match report.

Provan was philosophical in his assessment of his match-thrilling performance. "People judge you by the goals you score and it was great to get one like that."

After his final match against APIA, Provan spoke to fans about his experiences in the NSL. At a time when few Australians players had ventured overseas, Provan said that the standard was high. He singled out certain teammates for high praise. He labelled Peter Raskopolous and Marshall Soper as English First Division quality, but worried about them adjusting to English football as older pros.

He reserved special praise for Chris Kalantzis. "Chris Kalantzis is better than anything we've got back in Scotland of the same age," he said. Provan was so impressed with Kalantzis that he organised a trial for the 17-year-old with Liverpool, soon to be managed by Scotland teammate, Kenny Dalglish.

But the young, bullet-proof and "naive" (according to some) Kalantzis didn't get that trial. On the back of that gruelling match schedule and preparations for the Australian Under 20s World Cup in August, Kalantzis was exhausted. He asked Provan to delay the trial, and it never happened.

The impression Provan made with his skill and professionalism reached deeper than just his teammates and Olympic fans. In the St George match he lined up against then 20-year- old Robbie Slater.

"He was brilliant," Slater recalls. "His skill and the things he did he were on another level. I remember being in awe of him. I was a kid and that was the level that I wanted to get to. I can remember thinking wow I'm going to have to train a lot harder if I'm going to get to that level."

Provan played five times for Olympic in just under a month. He scored five goals and was the catalyst for five Olympic wins. With Provan pulling the strings, both Soper and Kalantzis also scored twice. Provan's performances quite literally elevated Olympic out of mediocrity into genuine title contention.

His impact gave Olympic sufficient momentum for them to win three of the final six games, draw two others, and take a finals place. One of those three wins was a 3-1 win against Sydney Croatia, with goals from Raskopoulos, Soper and Kalantzis, reversing the 5–0 beating they suffered a fortnight before Provan arrived.

Davie Provan took a flatlining season, blasted five shots of adrenaline into it, with five individual goals and five wins, and inspired the side to a finals run and a domestic Cup.

Provan was mindful of the next stage of his career and was open to Olympic playing a part in it. Olympic president Jim Petinellis offered Provan another contract for the 1986 season, but this time as player-coach. Provan was considering the offer.

However, something intervened in Provan's life that changed his life—not just his career—forever.

Late in 1985 Provan was diagnosed with Myalgic Encephalomyelitis. According to Provan, a virus caused him to lose a lot of weight but he kept training. Training hard defined Provan, but in this case his immune system was so depleted that the ME took over. The disease devastated Provan's career, and forced him into retirement in 1987 after being unable to fully rehabilitate.

In the bigger picture, Provan's early retirement was a great loss to Celtic, to football and to Provan the man. He has since found ways to manage his ME and is now a successful pundit with *Sky Sports* and the *Scottish Sun*.

But on a smaller scale, his diagnosis curtailed any chance Sydney Olympic had of a second coming of Provan, this time as player-coach.

Provan was arguably the most successful guest contract to appear in an Australian First Division, and it might have been much more than that. The success of Provan's 1985 visit is etched into the fabric of Sydney Olympic, and certainly helped fuel the back room enthusiasm for the Ian Rush signing 14 years later.

In football, where passion is the highest currency, mythology is history. And today Davie Provan would be welcomed back in the Greek coffee shops of Sydney as one of their gods..

*   *   *

Benito Carbone: Sydney FC 2006-07, 3 games, 2 goals

After winning the first A-League grand final in 2005–06 with Sydney FC, marquee striker Dwight Yorke answered the call from former Manchester United teammate Roy Keane to return to the English Premier League with Sunderland.

Yorke had brought the crowds and scored the goals for 'Bling FC' who were now on the hunt for a new talisman. Enter Italian Benito Carbone.

Carbone was a bit of a football journeyman, playing for seven Italian clubs which included Torino, Napoli and Inter Milan before moving to England in 1996 to join Sheffield Wednesday. From there stints at Aston Villa, Bradford City, Derby County and Middlesbrough followed before winding his career down in Italy in a mix of Serie A and Serie B clubs.

Carbone was brought to Sydney FC on a four-game guest contract, almost an in-season trial, to see if he was worth being offered a season long deal with the Sky Blues.

Debuting in Round 6 at Hindmarsh Stadium away to Adelaide United, Carbone got off to a great start, scoring once and providing two assists in a 4–1 win to the visitors. A bumper crowd of 15,119 was at that game with many believing that Carbone would have a bigger on-field impact than Yorke did.

A draw at home against Queensland Roar was followed with another goal at Central Coast Stadium, Carbone giving Sydney FC a 1–0 lead in the 12th minute, before succumbing to a hamstring injury. He was subbed off in the 57th minute and had contributed Sydney FC's only goal in a 3–1 loss to the Central Coast. Legendary Australian striker Damian Mori scored twice for the Mariners.

Carbone's hamstring injury would keep him out for seven weeks and spell the end for his guest stint at the club.

With two goals and two assists in his three games, he delivered. His A-League form warranted a longer-term contract and Sydney FC went to the table offering him a marquee contract for when he recovered from injury.

According to a *Sydney Morning Herald* report, their offer to Carbone was way off his expectations with Carbone apparently requesting a wage comparable to Dwight Yorke's estimated $800,00 per season.

Sydney chief executive of the time Tim Parker remembers recruiting Carbone, but they didn't try to utilise him for any marketing, believing they already captured the Italian community.

In a Sydney FC fan interview Carbone remembered his brief time in Australia. He was coming to play under a former English captain in Terry Butcher and had an amazing lifestyle to look forward to, hopefully to finish his professional career.

Training on the beach and having coffees at Bondi beach with Steve Corica, Carbone hoped his four-game guest stint would lead to a longer-term contract but injury curtailed his hopes.

Six years later when Alessandro Del Piero was considering his move to Sydney FC, his brother called Carbone to ask about Australia, Sydney, and the standard of football.

Carbone allegedly said, "Tell Alex to go straight away!" paving the way for Sydney FC to have Del Piero grace their pitches for two years.

Sydney FC was Carbone's 17th professional club. He finished his playing career in Italy with Serie C club Pavia before becoming their manager in 2010.

Off Season Preparation

In the 1970s and 1980s, Australia benefited from pre-season tours when club teams from the United Kingdom and Europe would tour Australia and play club teams, state sides and sometimes the Socceroos. Over time Australian fans have seen the likes of Manchester United, Liverpool, Arsenal, Juventus, AS Roma and Real Madrid. They have also seen Middlesbrough and Norwich City.

The early winter seasons of the NSL didn't clash with the northern hemisphere, which meant players from the UK and Europe could pop down for a couple of games in their off season before returning to their clubs. For a competitive off season, increasing fitness levels or recuperating from injury, some quality younger players also answered the call and came to the NSL.

Graeme Souness: West Adelaide, 1977, 6 games, 1 goal

In 1977 Middlesbrough toured Australia with a young Scottish player, Graeme Souness, a part of the team that played against South Australia. This was prior to his career-defining move to Liverpool.

Neil McGachey played for South Australia that day, and a chance conversation post game led to Souness lining up for West Adelaide Hellas for six games in their first NSL season.

McGachey was born in Scotland, but grew up in Adelaide, playing juniors with West Adelaide before becoming their inaugural NSL captain. A midfielder like Souness, McGachey directly opposed him in the Middlesbrough vs South Australia game which led to their conversation post game.

"After the game, Graeme and I had a bit of a chinwag, and he said he had been approached by Liverpool and it looked very much like he would be heading there.

"They were targeting the transfer for January so he decided that he would be better finishing off with Middlesbrough and then thought he would spend the time visiting Australia. He was thinking about the Gold Coast and the Whitsundays and having a nice holiday.

"I said to him that if he wanted to spend a few games with us he could fly around Australia, keep himself fit before the Liverpool transfer, and the National League would benefit from his presence. He didn't reject it out of hand, his words were 'Well that's interesting' and as soon as he didn't shut the door I got a hold of the president and said 'What can we do?'"

McGachey's swift action in alerting the West Adelaide committee to Souness's availability led to results.

In Souness's 2017 book *Football: My Life, My Passion* he mentions that the club covered his accommodation and he received $750 a game. If he scored or played well, the supporters would put extra cash in his pockets. He claims that he had never earned so much money in his life.

"There were a couple of places that we would go back to like the Grecian Barbecue in Hindley Street. These places were owned by the supporters, businessmen. We used to enjoy our time there and we also had a place in Hindmarsh Square that was owned by a couple of the players, which was called the 'After Dark Club'," McGlachey recalls.

He was hardly homesick either, with West Adelaide Hellas having a large Scottish contingent. As well as McGlachey, there was also Gordon McCulloch, Graeme Honeyman, Ian McGregor and Peter Boyle. According to McGlachey, his teammates appreciated the type of player Souness was and he made them better.

"Our whole midfield was Scottish, so we all appreciated the physical side of the game. But he took it to another level."

McGlachey says Souness did not treat it as a working holiday, but genuinely used it as a springboard for his move to Liverpool.

"That kindled a similar ethic, everybody lifted that little bit. That was the major influence I remember.

"He was a class above. He also worked harder than what we were used to. In those days it was part time and we were all held down by jobs; Graeme came from the professional background of Middlesbrough. The way he applied himself in training was a great wake-up call to me and the other boys too.

"Graeme is a very personable guy off the field, but in training and in games it was very much professional, he was a winner. He was very much an aggressive player in the true sense. In those days it was a much more physical game than it is today.

"But the biggest standout was Graeme's work ethic and his will to win. The effort he put into training was quite stark in comparison to what we were used to."

McGlachey also says that Souness was a 'player's player'.

"He won the ball and he always wanted the ball, but when he released the ball to you, you were in space. He never put you in a position whereby he released the ball to you and you were pressured. He took the pressure and had the ability to hold the ball at will so he always released you in space. The game is all about time and space and when you have a player who makes that space, it makes everything so much easier.

"In the middle of the park he was a dominant figure."

Souness's first game for West Adelaide was in a derby against Adelaide City, where a familiar face greeted him in the tunnel. Compatriot Dixie Deans was walking out for Adelaide City, the two of them having debuted in the same game for Scotland in 1974.

Gary Marocchi is a Western Australian football legend and a former Socceroo who played in the NSL with Adelaide City in 1977 and remembers Souness's debut.

"We played at Hindmarsh and it was a full house. The Adelaide derby always used to fill out. In those days you had the grandstand on one side and standing room on the other three sides. The atmosphere in those games was electric."

Adelaide City won the derby 4–1 but Souness made an impression on the opposition with his play in midfield.

"A very hard man. He was a fantastic player. He was very strong in a tackle, he was one you could tell had been playing at a high level for a long time. The muscle definition in his legs, you could see why he was renowned for being a strong tackler in midfield."

Souness's work ethic and preparation, as well as his obvious skill, proved to be the catapult West Adelaide needed. In 1978, the season following Souness's six games for Hellas, West Adelaide finished the season on top of the NSL.

Graeme Souness played more than 200 times for Liverpool, and later for Sampdoria in Serie A before becoming player-manager of Glasgow Rangers. His managerial career would see him in charge of Liverpool, Southampton, Blackburn Rovers and Newcastle United in England, Galatasary in Turkey, Torino in Italy and Benfica in Portugal. He is now a regular expert commentator on television.

Australia was lucky to see him for six games prior to these wonderful football achievements.

*   *   *

Craig Johnston: Newcastle KB United, 1978, 9 games, 0 goals 1982, 4 games, 4 goals

Newcastle has a rich football history, one that helped to produce local sensation Craig Johnston. While Johnston famously never represented the Socceroos, he did have some club cameos in his hometown of Newcastle, playing nine games in the NSL for Newcastle KB United in 1978 as a 17-year-old on loan from Middlesbrough and then a further four games in 1982, just before his title-laden career with Liverpool took off.

In 1978 Johnston was coming back to Australia in form on the back of a goal for Middlesbrough against West Ham, saying to Australia's weekly football publication *Soccer Action* that people should lower their expectations.

"I hope the Newcastle fans don't expect miracles from me because of how I am playing at Middlesbrough.

"The game here is far different to the one being played in Australia. Here it's more of a team game with teammates running on to your passes; over there that won't be on as much."

Alongside Johnston in that Newcastle team was Socceroos legend Col Curran. A 1974 World Cup veteran, Curran was such a great player in his day that he was offered a contract from Sir Matt Busby at Manchester United. Curran remembers playing with Johnston who was 14 years his junior and knew he would go on to greater things.

"He told me one day that when he was a kid he had my pictures on his bedroom wall, and I said well later in life I'll have your pictures on my wall!"

Curran appreciated the talent that Johnston had and recognised his value as a teammate.

"He played nine games with us in a loan type situation as it was the English off season. You could see how much he had progressed when he played back here. He had the team fired up and playing well, he was just one of those never say die players. He had everything to go with it.

"He was a good player to play with, he didn't care who you were, if you needed the ball he'd give it to you. He wasn't greedy in any way, he was a team player. I can remember when we played Dundee here, he could have scored himself but he passed me the ball and I scored the winner. I think it was 2–1. He was very unselfish, he could do it all."

Johnston's 1978 nine-game NSL cameo saw only three wins and two draws. Newcastle did not have the best of seasons finishing 11th out of 14 sides.

In 1982, Johnston returned, this time a more accomplished footballer and as a Liverpool player. In the shadow of the World Cup, Johnston was trying to get a few games in for pre-season. His celebrity had risen to the extent that he even had a column in the Newcastle programs.

Newcastle KB United were in the middle of a mediocre campaign when Johnston arrived and the crowds weren't coming either. Averaging less than 3,500 people for the eight home games previously, Round 18 saw a massive crowd of 10,351 as the prodigal son returned.

Johnston dutifully scored a penalty in the 74th minute as Newcastle KB United ran over Adelaide City 2–0.

Johnston played in a 3–0 loss away to St George-Budapest and then his finest moment on Australian soil came in Round 20.

At the International Sports Centre against the Brisbane Lions a crowd of 6,524 witnessed Craig Johnston score a hat-trick. With goals in the 7th, 52nd and 85th minute the home side ended up winning 3–1.

Johnston's final game in front of another good crowd of 7,489 in Newcastle saw them go down to the Ken Morton-coached Wollongong City.

In the space of four seasons Johnston had turned into a superstar, and the Newcastle crowd came out to see him. Once Johnston returned to England the Newcastle home crowds reverted to an average of less than 3,500.

Craig Johnston's career at Liverpool went on an upward trajectory after his second NSL stint. He played 190 games for the Reds including scoring the second goal (Ian Rush scored the other two) in the 1986 FA Cup final 3–1 win over Everton, as well as winning five First Division titles, two league cups, a charity shield and a European Cup.

He is by far and away one of Australia's most accomplished footballers.

*   *   *

Justin Fashanu: Adelaide City, 1980, 5 games, 3 goals; and Adelaide City, 1981, 6 games, 2 goals

A troubled soul with a back story and a tragic ending, Justinus Soni 'Justin' Fashanu's star was on the rise in 1980.

Fashanu and his brother John were fostered out as children when their parents split. His father, a barrister, returned to Nigeria while two of Justin and John's siblings remained with their mother who remarried and had another child.

Justin and John were adopted by their foster parents. He became an apprentice at Norwich City, he scored the BBC goal of the season in the English First Division in 1979–80, was the first black player in Britain to attract a £1 million transfer when signed by the legendary Brian Clough, was the first openly gay footballer, was subsequently ostracised by his brother John, and took his own life in 1998 at 37 years old.

Ahead of the 1980 NSL Fashanu joined Adelaide City on loan for a five-game guest stint. Fashanu was hot property at the time, having just won goal of the season.

Rale Rasic brought Fashanu to Adelaide City on a guest stint after seeing him play for Norwich City on their pre-season tour to Australia and New Zealand the year before.

"I was approached by his manager for him to play and I jumped at the chance.

"We already had Dixie Deans, he was our idol in Adelaide. I thought to get Fashanu for a period of time and with Dixie playing also, it would be great.

"They were sought by the media and by the public and appreciated so much.

Because they were both giving so much back."

Fashanu worked hard in Adelaide, running clinics, promoting the game with the local media and even making a film for the education department.

"If you asked every player at Adelaide City, they will tell you he was an absolute gentleman. He was the symbol of a real professional as a sportsman."

Gary Marocchi recalls his teammate Fashanu.

"He was such an athletic guy. Not muscly, just tall, lean and very athletic.

"He was strong on the ball, good in the air and for his size you'd expect that. Typical English centre-forward for that time. The role has evolved over time. You don't have the big target men anymore."

Tony Dorrigo was a youngster at Adelaide City at the time, and he remembers being in awe of Fashanu and pestering him all the time, asking all about professional football in England. It paved the way for Dorrigo to approach clubs and end up in the youth set-up of Aston Villa.

According to Marocchi that is the primary benefit of having guest players behave as the consummate professionals.

"They can have a lot of influence over the young kids in this country and if they see someone with ability, then hopefully that gives them the contacts overseas."

In the first season at Adelaide City, Fashanu scored three goals from his five games helping them to four wins as well.

He was slow to get started after a 2–1 away loss to Sydney City, helped them to a 3–2 win at home to Blacktown City before scoring consecutively in his last three hit outs in Australia. These included the winner in Brisbane in a 2–1 victory over Brisbane

City, the second in a 2–0 win over the Willie Wallace coached APIA-Leichhardt and finally an 80th minute strike against Footscray JUST, the final goal in a 3–1 win. Rasic remembers his impact.

"He was only 19 and he became a superstar. Well-deserved."

But most of all, it was his humility that impressed Rasic. He focused on promoting his time as an apprentice at Norwich City in his weekly column in *Soccer Action* talking about how he had to clean boots and fix the pitch, keeping him humble.

"He was so well spoken, so well groomed, so hospitable, so polite. Justin would come to my office and ask, he said, 'Mr Rasic, would you mind if I ring mum? I haven't spoken to her for two days.' He was referring to his adopted mum in Norwich.

"He would come to my office and call his mum and speak to her every second day and would always finish by asking "How is the dog?"

On his return to the Canaries for the 1980/81 season, Fashanu lit up the English First Division with 19 league goals in the season, the third highest scorer. He ended up with 22 goals across all competitions, incredible for a player who only turned 20 during that season.

Fashanu's off season was busy. Norwich City toured the USA for three games straight after the season, and he was then selected for the England Under 21 team, before returning for another stint in Australia.

Fashanu's second season in the NSL was not as successful. With Rale Rasic now coaching Blacktown City in Sydney, there were murmurings that he would unite with the former Socceroos coach, but he returned to Adelaide City featuring in six games for two goals. He also courted some controversy when red carded against Heidelberg at Olympic Park for a headbutt, which he claimed he didn't do.

His second season at Adelaide City may have been interrupted with Fashanu's signature being pursued by three clubs in England: Crystal Palace, Newcastle United and Nottingham Forest. He went to Forest under Brian Clough and became the first black footballer to attract a seven-figure transfer fee.

Fashanu's time at Nottingham Forest was the beginning of the end of a promising career.

After 35 goals in 90 games for Norwich City, a culture of bullying, coming directly from Clough, would have a lasting impact on Fashanu as a player and person.

He only managed three goals in 35 appearances for Forest. Clough wrote of a confrontation in his biography, which no doubt summed up the homophobic culture of early 1980s football in the United Kingdom.

Including Adelaide City, he ended up playing for 19 different football clubs with stints in Scotland, New Zealand, Canada and the USA. After Norwich City the most games he played with any one club was 64 with Notts County.

Rale Rasic says Fashanu's troubles started at Nottingham Forest.

"I read Brian Clough's memoirs and he said that he failed in his coaching. He did not pay attention to Justin Fashanu to try and understand the problems he had off the pitch."

Fashanu tragically took his own life in 1998 following sexual assault allegations in the USA. Clough wrote about him in an updated biography after Fashanu's death.

When you hear of a lad taking his life in such squalid circumstances like that, a lad you once worked with and were responsible for, you have to look back and wonder if you could have done things differently. I know I should have dealt with Fashanu differently, certainly with a little more compassion and understanding.

According to Rasic: "Tragedies do come against all expectations. We never ever know what causes those problems. But Justin Fashanu, in my memory, will always be a gentleman and a beautiful human being. I dealt with a lot of wonderful ambassadors for football and Justin was amongst them."

*   *   *

Eli Ohana: Sydney City, 1986, 5 games, 1 goal

In 1985 when the Frank Arok-led Socceroos were competing for a spot in the 1986 World Cup in Mexico, they came up against a spirited Israel in the qualifying phase. After defeating them 2–1 in Tel Aviv, they hosted them in Melbourne in front of 27,000 people at Olympic Park. In what must have been a major embarrassment, the West German national anthem was played instead of the Israeli one at the commencement of the match. The game ended in a 1–1 draw, but there was a young Israeli star named Eli Ohana who was a standout in that clash.

The Jewish community of Sydney formed the Hakoah club in 1939, which was known as Eastern Suburbs Hakoah at the start of the NSL, followed by Sydney City Hakoah and finally, the Sydney City Slickers. Today it is known as Maccabi Hakoah Sydney City East FC.

Eli Ohana was young, talented and available to pick up a few games, and lure in a few new fans from the local Jewish community. For Ohana, the chance to stay fit proved to be the catalyst for a stint in Australia.

The 1986 Sydney City side was a star-studded side that included Socceroos Alex Robertson, John Kosmina, Steve O'Connor, Joe Watson, David Mitchell and Frank Farina.

Farina remembers Ohana well.

"I played against Eli in the Under 20 World Cup and later the World Cup Qualifiers with the Socceroos. He killed us in Frank Arok's last World Cup campaign when we drew 1–1.

"I told the other guys that he was a class act. He fitted in well and we had no problem accepting him. We were one of the top sides then, so not any player could just walk in, but he came with great pedigree."

Twenty-two-year-old Ohana managed to score one goal in the NSL, contributing to his team's total in a 7–0 thrashing of St George, but his influence was limited with three draws and a loss in his other four games.

His arrival hardly changed anything at the gate for Sydney City; the only time he played in front of more than 2,000 people was when they played Sydney United.

"We were the best team in the league, but in terms of following we didn't have a lot," says Farina.

Following Sydney City, Ohana would later play in Belgium and Portugal reacquainting himself with Farina again as they shared a manager in Belgium. On returning to Israel, Ohana would rejoin Beitar Jerusalem, the club he joined as an 11-year-old. After his playing career, Ohana managed Beitar Jerusalem as well as the national team, and later became chairman of his boyhood club.

Although successful on the pitch, Sydney City, under then chairman Frank Lowy, withdrew from the NSL a few games into the 1987 season because the governing body would not agree to allow the NSL to operate independently from the soccer federation. Almost three decades later, Lowy and his son Steven took the opposite position, strongly resisting separation of the A-League from the federation which they chaired consecutively from 2003 to 2018.

Football's Biggest Perthonalities

Outside of small Pacific Islands, the Western Australian capital, Perth, is the most isolated city in the world.

Perth also comes close to being the most British city outside of the United Kingdom with more than 8% of the Western Australian population born in England.

As a consequence, despite not joining the NSL until the 1990s, Perth's Knockout Cup competition dates back to 1899 and there is a strong football culture, only enhanced by the significant expat British community.

In the 1980s Perth saw guest stints by Bobby Charlton, Bobby Moore, Mick Channon, Alan Ball, Ted Macdougall, George Best and Trevor Brooking.

Bobby Moore: Inglewood Kiev, 1981, 2 games, 0 goals; Rockingham United, 1981, 1 game, 0 goals; Cracovia, 1981, 4 games, 0 goals

Bobby Moore is the man at the centre of England's greatest triumph, defeating West Germany for the 1966 World Cup at Wembley Stadium. After more than 500 games with West Ham United and a further 100 plus at Fulham, Moore had short stints playing in the USA and Denmark.

Following the World Cup win, Moore and his wife Tina reportedly lived the high life in London, but Moore also made a number of poor investments and by the early 1980s needed money.

Consequently, in 1981 at the age of 40, with the lure of some quick dollars to move around his ageing legs for a few games and some speaking gigs, Moore travelled to Perth to line up for Inglewood Kiev.

Inglewood Kiev was established in 1951 by Ukranian migrants and have been known as Inglewood United since 2000. In 1981 they were coached by former Socceroo Jimmy Pearson. The Scottish-born Pearson scored 13 goals in 66 Scottish League appearances before immigrating to Australia at the age of 24 to join Melbourne Hungaria. He was then recruited to Pan-Hellenic and represented the Socceroos in 1965 in Australia's first World Cup qualifying campaign. From Pan-Hellenic, Pearson coached in South Africa, Zimbabwe, Finland, Singapore, Malaysia and Zambia before returning to Perth and, eventually, Inglewood Kiev.

Pearson knew it would be great for the club to have Moore play, but at training he soon discovered that Moore wasn't quite the player he once was, even for club level football in Perth.

"When Bobby came out, he trained a couple of times with us, and I thought I'm much fitter than Bobby. We're the exact same age so I played against him at training and I went past him like he wasn't there a few times. I said 'Bobby you're finished man,' and he said 'Yeah I know'.

"So now I've got a problem, I have two young centre halves who I had brought through from 16, 17 years of age to Inglewood. What happened was I had to put one out to fit Bobby in and it meant reconstructing the team.

"I had to move a centre half to full back and that kind of thing, and why we got beaten and I knew we'd get beaten, I told the committee we'd get beaten. It's a good publicity thing and we got massive crowds. That was the idea of it, it was to further the game, it was not to further me."

Captain of Inglewood Kiev at the time was John Davidson. Davidson was a Scottish youth international who moved to Australia as an 18-year-old in 1970. He had playing stints in Sydney, Melbourne and Hong Kong, and also represented Australia at Under 23 level. In 1981 the team found out they were going to have a World Cup winning skipper line-up in their team.

"The next thing we know he was turning up to training.

"The night before the game Jim said, 'Bobby, you can captain the side'. He said, No, John's the captain, he can be the captain. I'll just come to the centre for the toss up and the photos,' which he did, he didn't take the captaincy for the day."

Inglewood played host to Perth Azzurri with both clubs near the top of the table. In front of a crowd of 4,000, Kiev lost 1–0. Davidson remembers the game fondly.

"We were going well but Azzurri were the top side at the time. It was pretty electrifying but pretty daunting for us guys playing with Bobby Moore, but once we settled in it was alright."

Moore's defensive tactics infuriated Pearson.

"You know the 18-yard line, that's where he stayed! We couldn't push up the pitch because he had no pace. The other team attacked us non-stop. It wasn't his fault, he was finished.

"His ability was good but when you're done you're done. That's what happened, they attacked us non-stop and we had a reasonably good side. It killed us."

The next game was against Gosnells City, a team which would have Mick Channon cameo for them later that season. Gosnells City defeated Inglewood Kiev 2–0.

Despite the results, Inglewood recouped much of their $5,000 payment to Moore via the gate, canteen and bar takings.

"The publicity side of it did the game the world of good, and that was the point of it in the first place. Bob brought the big crowds to Inglewood."

After the two games for Inglewood Kiev, Moore was hastily cleared to Rockingham United, to play with them in Division 2 for a one-off appearance against Perth City.

Rockingham United were formed in 1970 and played in Perth's Second Division. Located around 50 kilometres south of Perth, Rockingham was rebranded Rockingham City in 1988 when officially granted City status. But in 1981, it was almost like a country town.

Sponsored by the local real estate agents Summit Realty, a crowd of 1,500 paid entry fees of $2 for adults, and 50 cents for pensioners and children. The Scottish-backed Perth City drew 2–2 with Rockingham, Moore missing an easy shot in front of goal.

Moore played this game sporting a huge bruise on his upper hamstring; the crowd quipped that this was due to his heavy wallet smacking against him due to the level of income he earned from his Western Australian cameos.

Moore was rumoured to have been paid $1,500 for his one-off appearance at Rockingham. The clubrooms were packed afterwards as everyone wanted to meet the World-Cup-winning skipper.

Later the same year, Moore joined Perth club Cracovia for a four-game guest stint in their tour of Malaysia.

Formed in 1950 by members of Perth's Polish community, Cracovia established itself on the back of their recruitment in the mid-1960s of Pawel Sobek, a 36-year-old former five-time Polish international, along with Polish club footballers Władysław Musiał of Lechia Gdansk and Zygmunt Pieda, a former Legiua Warsaw captain who made the Western Australia Football Hall of Fame. Pieda stayed in Western Australia coaching the likes of Inglewood Kiev, Morley Windmills, Osborne Park,

Cracovia and the state team. In the mid-1990s the club dropped from semi-professional to amateur status.

The trip to Malaysia was Cracovia's first overseas tour. They played four games in just over a week. Moore played in all of their games as they drew 1–1 with Sandakan Select, defeated a Tawau Invitational XI 3–1, drew 2–2 with the Sabah State Team and were beaten 4–0 against a Sabah Select XI.

Cracovia now play in the Perth equivalent of a sixth Division with each captain of their junior sides, the White Eagles, wearing the number 6 in a nod to their special past player in Moore.

Moore's Australian club career reads seven games for only one win.

*   *   *

Trevor Brooking: Kelmscott SC, 1985, 8 games, 3 goals

In 1985 Perth's English connections saw Kelmscott Soccer Club play host to Trevor Brooking.

Established in 1969, the Kelmscott Soccer Club, known as the 'Roos, is located 23 kilometres south east of the city—at the time, the end of suburbia—and was in the Second Division.

Only three years earlier, Brooking had been playing for England at the 1982 World Cup in Spain, and two years before that, heading home the winning goal in the 1980 FA Cup for West Ham. How did it eventuate that a player who had played 647 games for West Ham and 47 games for England was not playing for an Australian State League Second Division side?

First, it was his old mate Bobby Moore who told him what it would be like to head down under. The second was through his family book binding business, which had connections in Perth through members of Kelmscott Soccer Club.

Brooking decided to make his trip to Perth a proper football holiday.

Through fundraising and sponsors, Kelmscott were able to generate enough funds to allow for Brooking not to earn crazy money, but to have an all expenses trip to Western Australia covered.

Jim Butterfill was the Kelmscott club president at the time and recalls their efforts. "There was nobody more surprised than us when he agreed to come. He came at a price of about $12,000 for six weeks. We got local sponsors to raise the money to get him out here.

"Toyota supplied him with a car—he just had to do an advert jumping up and down doing the 'Oh what a feeling'. Our shirt sponsor 'Film Show Video' also got him to do an advert.

"The local hotel supplied him with accommodation. He did promotions for Kmart and coaching clinics with the kids. Everything seemed to fall into place."

Such was Brooking's status in the UK, his stint in Australia even made the newspapers with the headline 'Brooking Down Under'. Outside of his games against suburban Perth clubs such as Rockingham, Wanneroo and Balcatta, Brooking had a full calendar, with dinners, promotional work and clinics.

Brian Wheatley was club trainer for the 'Roos in 1985 and he remembers how Brooking adapted to the drop in playing standard and made the team better, even from just observing.

"He wasn't taking training sessions, he was just making finer points and adjustments to training sessions. He would collect the ball and pass it and everyone would go, 'Oh now I see why you passed it there!'

"His thinking was two or three chess moves ahead of his teammates, and they were pretty smart footballers. They came to an understanding where he would take his football thinking down a notch and they would lift their thinking up a notch.

"Little things like it's the player who's passing the ball who does the work on the ball, not the player who's receiving the ball."

That year, with Brooking in the team, Kelmscott hosted premier local club Floreat Athena in the knockout D'Orsogna Cup, where 1,500 people turned up to the game—a far cry from the usual 100 or so made up of family and friends. The Cup now serves as the qualifier for Australia's FFA Cup.

Brooking ended up playing six league games, the D'Orsogna Cup tie and an exhibition game against a Western Australia select XI, scoring and setting up a few goals in the process. Former Southampton winger and Western Australian Football Hall of Fame member John Sydenham remembers Brooking's visit well.

"After we played in that exhibition game, we took Trevor to Yanchep Sun City for the day to play golf. A couple of us laid it all on for him. After golf we came back for a meal and when I was about to organise to pay for him, he wouldn't hear of it. He absolutely insisted, got out his wallet and paid for the golf and the food.

"He is just an absolute gentleman. Just delightful."

Brooking being a gentleman is a common theme from all of those who have crossed his path. He didn't drink, he didn't smoke, he liked reading and he liked playing golf.

In his player profile published in the Kelmscott match day program, when asked what occupation he would be if he wasn't a footballer he said 'accountant'.

His impeccable skills and values for the game helped Kelmscott have a great season. The senior side finished second in 1985, four points adrift of leaders Gosnells City, whilst their reserve team finished on top losing only twice for the year. They were rewarded with promotion to play in Perth's semi-professional Premier League the next season.

They were relegated after one season in 1986 but they did manage to win their only D'Orsogna Cup against Kingsway Olympic in a great final winning 2–1 after trailing 1–0.

"We went back down the next year," says Butterfill, "but as Trevor said you don't want to stray too much from being a local club. Once you go up you need more dollars."

Following Brooking's Kelmscott appearances, he managed West Ham in 2003, became the FA's Director of Football Development from 2004 to 2014, was knighted in 2004, and in 2009 Upton Park named a grandstand after him.

Such is his status in the UK that Sir Trevor Brooking was even a guest at the wedding of Prince William and Kate Middleton. Hopefully the catering at the royal wedding compared favourably with the fish and chips and mushy peas supper served at Kelmscott Soccer Club for their West Ham Reunion night.

It is an incredible piece of Australian football history that these gentlemen of English football graced the pitches of Perth in the 1980s.

Getting Bums on Seats

While all guest stars who arrive are expected to boost attendance, few have managed to truly turn the dial and cut through to non-regular football fans. Sometimes the player isn't high profile enough, or didn't play for the right clubs to really get casual football fans off their couches. But sometimes Australian clubs strike gold and reach into the community with a football proposition too good to refuse.

Malcolm Macdonald: South Melbourne
1977, 3 games, 3 goals

With the worldwide popularity of the English Premier League can you imagine what it would be like if Mohamed Salah came to Australia in his pre-season for a couple of games for Brisbane Roar? Imagine Perth Glory if they had Harry Kane up front for a little bit of pocket money before the season started.

The equivalent to this happened in 1977 when it was announced that Malcolm Macdonald, Arsenal's 1976–77 winner of the English First Divisions golden boot, would be joining South Melbourne Hellas for four games.

It wouldn't be Macdonald's first brush with Australia; that occurred in 1970 when the Rale Rasic-led touring Socceroos took on his Luton Town team in front of 6,140 people at Kenilworth Road. Then in the English Second Division, Macdonald headed home the first goal of the match before Socceroos Mike Denton and Adrian Alston scored to win the game 2–1.

Not long after that brush with Australia, Macdonald's career took off in England when he joined Newcastle United in 1971. Playing in his first home game for Newcastle United against Liverpool, the burly centre forward scored a hat-trick, and the Geordie fans went wild and his nickname of 'SuperMac' began.

To the tune of Jesus Christ Superstar, the chant began in the terraces.

"SuperMac, Superstar, how many goals have you scored so far?"

He would be a goalscoring sensation for Newcastle United, becoming the fifth highest goalscorer of all time, not bad company when you consider Alan Shearer, Jackie Milburn, Len White and Hughie Gallacher are ahead of him, with former Melbourne Knight guest Peter Beardsley just below him!

He won the golden boot with Newcastle United in 1974–75 and a season afterwards was sold to Arsenal for a record transfer fee at the time £333,333. The rock star striker was moving to London.

Macdonald picked up where he left off with the Gunners scoring 19 goals in his first season, before scoring 25 goals in the 1976–77 season and sharing the golden boot with Aston Villa's Andy Gray. In the process Arsenal were lifted from 17th to 8th.

At the peak of his powers aged 27, Macdonald's four-game stint included an away game in a Greek derby against West Adelaide Hellas, before two home games to be played on a long weekend against Brisbane Lions and St George-Budapest who would be bringing their own superstar guest in Charlie George. His final game was an away game against Canberra City.

South Melbourne Hellas paid a $2,000 insurance premium to ensure Macdonald's health and safety, insuring him for $500,000. He was paid $2,000 per game, with his time in Melbourne including writing a column for *The Age* newspaper and running a soccer clinic for kids at Middle Park.

In what was a sign of things to come in the future of Melbourne media, Macdonald was also involved in a cross-code promotion for Australian Rules football. He posed for photographs with Richmond footballers Kevin Bartlett and Royce Hart, wearing the sleeveless jumper worn in AFL.

Ted Smith was assistant coach to Manny Poulakakis in 1977 at South Melbourne Hellas. Smith, who represented Australia at the 1956 Olympics, also acted as Macdonald's driver for a lot of his Australian stay.

"It was great momentum for the NSL. I'm not sure how they afforded a player like that, but one thing about Hellas at that time, if they needed money, they could raise it very quickly," Smith recalls.

"Having seen him on TV with his goalscoring, I thought he would be an arrogant bloke, but he was most friendly. He did some clinics down at La Trobe, I offered to take him. But he got a car and took himself so he got a bit of an understanding of what Australia was like."

A heaving crowd of 7,500 at Hindmarsh stadium in Adelaide were on hand for Macdonald's Australian club debut. Neil McGachey was playing for West Adelaide in that game and remembers the hype.

"There were about 10,000 people for the Greek derby, I remember that! The league was enriched by SuperMac and these other stars."

West Adelaide went ahead 1–0 before Macdonald scored a penalty 10 minutes to draw the game. Quoted in *Soccer Action*, Macdonald was humble about his goal.

> I wanted one of the other lads to take it because the goal could have been crucial to the players when it comes to the top goalscorers at the end of the season.

Macdonald's second game against Brisbane Lions at home attracted only 4,800 people at Middle Park to see South Melbourne win 1–0, a tiny crowd when you consider the calibre of star that Macdonald was.

Australian football writer Patrick Mangan is an Arsenal tragic. Born in London he moved to Australia as a child and found it hard to stay in touch with the game and his beloved Gunners. His 2010 book *Offsider* would detail the level of excitement he had for this clash as a 12-year-old to watch SuperMac. He claimed in his book that Macdonald was here for a couple of reasons.

> He was set to indoctrinate Victorians in the dual fine arts of lethal finishing and the proper cultivation of sideburns.

Such was Mangan's appreciation of Arsenal and Macdonald, the fact that Charlie George was also an Arsenal favourite really didn't resonate. At the time of their guest stints, George was at Derby County.

"I was just a bit too young to have followed Arsenal when they won the FA Cup/league championship double in 1971, and that was Charlie George's finest moment, scoring the winning goal in the FA Cup final.

"I really got into supporting Arsenal around 1973–74, which makes me one of a very small group of Arsenal fans that place Malcolm MacDonald on a higher pedestal than Charlie George. You had to have been an Arsenal fan when Malcolm Macdonald joined Arsenal to get a sense of how absurd it was that he would choose an Arsenal team that was bound for relegation, or so it looked like.

"For a couple of years we were 16th or 17th in consecutive seasons. So when SuperMac joined it was a revelation to me, suddenly Arsenal had been transformed into a glamourous club.

"The focus for me was on SuperMac rather than Charlie. Which is an embarrassing thing for an Arsenal fan to admit.

"Charlie George grew up supporting the club and watching from the north bank.

He was proper Arsenal."

George and Macdonald had played against each other twice that English season. Both were scoreless draws.

The crowd for the second home match for Macdonald facing Charlie George with St George-Budapest was huge. So much so that they announced that children were allowed inside the stadium to sit on the grass, right near the sidelines.

George Harris was the St George-Budapest captain playing in that game and was nervous with the crowd situation.

"I don't know exactly what the crowd was but they were letting people in to sit inside the fence and they were three or four deep!

"It wasn't that long before that I had been attacked in a match against West Adelaide in the same season. They were also a Greek supported team. A spectator attacked a linesman and I came in and was clocked from behind.

"I had ten stitches and had it been half an inch lower I could have lost my eye. That was the only time I made the front page of the newspapers! So that was still very much in my mind."

The estimated crowd was 15,000—an amazing figure considering Melbourne also hosted three Australian Rules games on the same day.

Football historian George Cotsanis remembers the hype around this game vividly because as a kid he went with his dad to football games and then alternately he went with his stepdad to Australian Rules football games. He knew that this clash was special because it was his stepdad that took him to Middle Park to see SuperMac and Charlie George.

The largest crowd for the 1977 season witnessed an amazing game of football, with both two superstar drawcards scoring goals. Macdonald earned the plaudits with *Soccer Action* writing:

Macdonald's performance was so good that it earned him the first 10-point rating in the Yugoslav Airlines Player of the Year Award.

"What else could he of [sic] done? He committed himself in every attack, he fetched the ball and delivered it with pinpoint accuracy, he scored both of Hellas' goals and he twice hit the post.

It was also Charlie George's best game for St George-Budapest. He scored their second goal as the visitors ran out 3–2 winners in a game long remembered by everyone involved. George Harris said it was the only game in Australia that Charlie George got up for and Smith remembers his goal because of the celebration.

"When Charlie George scored in the FA Cup final a few years before from 35 metres he threw himself backwards on the ground to celebrate. He did the same celebration in the game against us."

The publicity generated by Macdonald's visit included a hastily assembled Thursday afternoon clinic for kids at Middle Park. Smith remembers how SuperMac adapted.

"It wasn't very efficiently organised. I picked him up and when we arrived there were 100 kids. No one had planned on how it was going to work.

"He looked at it and thought it would be nearly impossible, but then he organised a couple of pick-up games and he spoke to all the kids."

The sugar hit of the crowds and the momentum of Macdonald's visit didn't have the flow-on effect it should have. According to Smith, not much was done in terms of planning, be it coaching, playing or attracting kids and sponsors to the game.

"We didn't maximise the benefits of him being out here. I don't know what discussion or contact was made to him prior.

"He did run a coaching session with the first team, but it was pretty simplistic, not too much analysis. He probably wondered what he got into, the gap between where he was playing at the time and us was huge."

Smith does remember the attitude of Macdonald at training and how he willed himself to adapt to Australian football.

"Our delivery to him wasn't what he normally got of course. Macdonald's version was you put the ball in that spot and I've got to get there. If you try and hit me on the head you won't do it. Nine out of ten times it won't happen. It still sticks in my mind, as what we could learn from someone like that."

Former Socceroos player and coach Ange Postecoglou is a lifelong South Melbourne person who was a 12 year-old at this time. Many years later, in 2012, he wrote about the game not cashing in on the hype:

The short-term boost to the club and the game was never capitalised on and what should have been a foundation on which to build the game became an obsession with who could come up with the next gimmick that would get them the most headlines.

Ted Smith stresses that we don't use these international guests the right way when they are in Australia.

"At that time, the set-up for youth players was minimal, so we didn't get the benefits from SuperMac. The players that we import now, come for a longer period, I'm not sure how well we have or haven't used them either."

Macdonald's fourth game away against Canberra City didn't eventuate.

His playing impact with South Melbourne Hellas was such that SuperMac's three games saw him with the highest rating in the *Soccer Action* Yugoslav Airlines Player of the Year award. However, three games meant he didn't have enough votes to win the award outright.

Macdonald was forced to retire prematurely at 29 due to a degenerative knee condition. Turning to management he had stints at Fulham and Huddersfield Town before working in the football media.

The Australian connection would not quite be over for Macdonald. His partner Carol is the former wife of AC/DC lead singer Brian Johnson. AC/DC is an Australian rock band that was established in 1973 and which Johnson joined in 1980.

*   *   *

Kazuyoshi Miura: Sydney FC, 2005-06, 6 games, 2 goals

In December 2005 the FIFA Club World Championship tournament was to be held in Tokyo, Japan.

Qualification for any Australian club came through Oceania as Australia had not yet joined the Asian Football Confederation. The timing wasn't ideal as this was when Australia had rebooted and rebranded its domestic competition to the A-League and competition was yet to kick off. A knockout tournament was held to determine who would represent Australia as the Club champions to go to the Oceania finals in Tahiti.

The seven inaugural Australian A-League clubs (the New Zealand Knights were not included) competed in a knockout format held in early May 2005 to see which club would make it to Tahiti. Perth Glory, the team that had won the final NSL grand final 13 months previously, and who would roll into the new football competition, were seeded into the semi-finals.

Sydney FC won the knockout tournament, and even before all the hype of season one of the A-League, they found themselves off to Tahiti where they comfortably defeated their Oceania opponents.

Before a ball was ever kicked in the A-League, one of the new A-League teams had qualified for a tournament on the world stage, to be held in seven months' time.

It was going to take some creative thinking for the young club to make an impact at the tournament. Sydney FC had already created headlines by signing English Premier League sensation Dwight Yorke as their marquee player and German coach Pierre Littbarski, a veteran of three World Cup tournaments as a player, and a World Cup winner.

Prior to joining Sydney FC, Littbarski was coach of Yokohama FC in the J-League where he had been exposed to Japan's first-ever football superstar in Kazuyoshi Miura. Known globally as Kazu, he famously left home as a teenager to travel to Brazil to make it as a professional footballer.

Kazu played professionally for six clubs in Brazil before returning to Japan. His return coincided with the start of the J-League in 1990 and being selected for the national team. Playing for Verdy Kawasaki (now known as Tokyo Verdy), Kazu scored 118 goals in 197 games as their flamboyant forward. He also had a loan spell in Italy's Serie A with Genoa, becoming the first Japanese player to make it professionally in Europe. A short stint with Dinamo Zagreb followed, and a trial with Bournemouth, before returning to play another seven years in the J-League.

He was the national team's pin-up boy. Such is Kazu's popularity, there was a book released of him in 1995 modelling nude. Kazu retired from the national team, the Blue Samurai, in 2000. At the time, he was Japan's second highest goalscorer with 55 goals in 89 games.

In a perfect storm for the new A-League and Sydney FC, four-game guest contracts for marquee-type players were on offer in its first season.

Sydney FC's chief executive officer at the time was Tim Parker.

"The Japanese organiser of the Club World Championship was a company called Dentsu. Their sports marketing arm was charged with making the Cup a success and they had Toyota as a major sponsor but they had a bit of sense that it wasn't going to get a lot of traction locally with no Japanese clubs in it.

"So the idea popped up that Kazu would come to Sydney, play for Sydney FC and garner a lot of attention from a Japanese audience as he was still very popular in Japan. So that would get the Japanese focus on soccer in Australia as well as give them a club to 'adopt' in Japan whilst the tournament was on.

"From our point of view, I was happy because there is a very significant Japanese contingent in and around Sydney. If we could get them motivated, we could put a couple of thousand on the gate.

"It was a marketing ploy to boost the Club World Cup in Japan."

Joining Sydney FC in mid-November 2005, the 38-year-old Kazu arrived in Australia for four games in the A-League, before heading back to Japan with the Sky Blues for the FIFA Club World Championship.

Playing three games at home in his four-game stint, Kazu was off to a slow start, the team winning 1–0 against Queensland Roar before a 0–0 draw with Perth Glory. Kazu's star really shone at Hindmarsh stadium in Round 14 when he scored both goals for Sydney FC in a 3–2 loss to Adelaide United. With Dwight Yorke feeding Kazu his first goal, the professionalism of the two marquee players really shone through.

"They showed what it took to be a professional footballer. Kazu had to adapt pretty quickly to an Australian summer. He was so quick, it was quite extraordinary. It was a real boost at the time," recalls Parker.

With Kazu's last game in Sydney against Melbourne Victory, multicultural sports marketer Patrick Skene approached Sydney FC to help promote the game. Looking to target the Sydney-based Japanese community, Skene worked hard with Parker to ensure Kazu's final game in Australia would have a large Asian following.

The promotion to the Japanese community was for four tickets for the price of three. Skene and his company went to work with a promotional poster placed in over 500 Japanese shops and restaurants, as well as the three Sydney-based Japanese language newspapers and websites.

"The fish just don't jump into the boat, the Japanese media need to be fed. It was a huge success. As far as imports go there hasn't been anything like it."

Tim Parker was excited when 17,272 fans turned up for Kazu's last game. With more than 1,000 special offers taken up from Skene's promotion, approximately 5,000 Japanese fans were in attendance as Sydney FC won 2–1.

"I was quite surprised at the extent and availability of Japanese media in and around Sydney.

"The thing with the Japanese, when their attention turns to something they are the most enthusiastic supporters, which is just the sort of thing you want," said Skene.

Four games in the A-League, two wins, a draw and a loss along with two goals, Kazu's efforts in Australia were a perfect lead-in to the 2005 FIFA Club World Championship.

Sydney FC's first game was against CONCACAF champions from Costa Rica, Deportivo Saprissa. With more than 28,000 people in attendance, and many choosing to barrack for the Australian side, Parker said Kazu's recruitment was justified.

Hollywood actor and then Sydney FC Director and investor Anthony LaPaglia was in Tokyo for the tournament and told fifa.com what a selection boon Kazu was.

"One of the aims of the club is to branch out and qualify for the Asian Champions League. Signing Kazu was a stroke of genius because it's generated massive interest for us here and it's given the Japanese people someone to shout for."

A 1–0 loss meant that they were relegated to the 5th placed playoff against CAF side Al Ahly from Egypt which they won, 2–1. Brazil's Sao Paulo won the Championship with a 1–0 win over Liverpool.

Kazu reflected on his time with Sydney FC to fifa.com.

"A-League players are not living life on easy street, nobody is there pulling in six figures a week. Veterans and youth alike, they are giving their all, not for a big salary or a glamorous lifestyle but because football is what their life is all about.

"The work ethic is instilled in the way they train and that is the way I have played all my life. The players have a really tough mentality, which is something I hope all Japan, players and fans alike, will get to see ..."

The legacy of Kazu's time in the A-League is such that it was mentioned by Shinji Ono when he joined Western Sydney Wanderers in 2012, and by Keisuke Honda when he joined Melbourne Victory in 2018. Kazu was a trailblazer for Japanese players, but Asian import players have not been truly embraced by A-League clubs.

Parker is disappointed that Australian clubs haven't used the guest contract on Asian players more often.

"The whole point of Australia joining the AFC was to gain more traction. Australia hasn't really embraced Asia at club level, it still has its base in Europe. It surprises me since my time there has been very little use of the guest players in the A-league."

Kazu returned to his club side, Yokohama FC, after his games with Sydney FC and, in 2021 at age 54, continues to play games and score goals. He also played for Japan in the 2012 Futsal World Cup

*   *   *

David Villa: Melbourne City,
2014-15, 4 games, 2 goals

In 2008 English Premier League club Manchester City were bought by the Abu Dhabi United Group for Development and Investment (ADUG), a United Arab Emirates-based private equity company owned by Sheikh Mansour bin Zayed Al Nahyan, member of the Abu Dhabi royal family.

Five years later, ADUG established the City Football Group to manage global football interests, specifically targeting football clubs across the globe. The City Football Group's worldwide footprint began in 2013 with the establishment of New York City FC, in a partnership with baseball's New York Yankees. The club would start playing in the MLS in 2015 with a high-profile trio of marquee players being David Villa from Atletico Madrid, Frank Lampard from Chelsea and Andreas Pirlo from Juventus.

City Football Group's next club was in Australia when they purchased 80% of Melbourne Heart from its owners for $12 million in 2014. (The other 20% was initially being bought by a consortium associated with Rugby League team Melbourne Storm before the City Football Group bought them out one year later.)

New York City's first season in the MLS would begin four months after the rebranded Melbourne Heart would begin life as Melbourne City in the A-League. To generate some good publicity for the rebranding in Australia, City Football Group arranged for David Villa and Frank Lampard to play some guest games in Melbourne.

Both were set to play for Melbourne City in the 2014–15 season on a 10-game guest stint, as lead-in to the MLS season start in 2015, when FFA and the other A-League clubs moved to block both players joining the club as they feared an 'imbalance' to the competition. Rather than look at the media attention, crowds and interest it would create, FFA and the other A-League clubs feared they would create a superpower.

Journalist David Davutovic recalls: "I heard Lampard was a done deal and that would have been a season-long loan, or a much longer loan spell, but then the FFA and the A-League changed the rule.

"It's a bugbear of mine that we have to pander to the lowest common denominator, everyone was scared that they would become too good as opposed to the bigger picture. Think about what that would have done to grow the game with crowds and TV ratings."

Rather than both stars, it was Spain's 2010 World Cup winner, David Villa, who was brought out for a 10-game guest stint in a whirl of publicity to promote the new branding of Melbourne Heart to Melbourne City. Villa arrived in time to also be the face of City, filming all the promotions for the broadcaster Fox Sports.

Melbourne Heart had been run on a modest budget. They mostly made their money selling good young players overseas to help keep them afloat. For example, Curtis Good was sold to Newcastle United on a six-year deal netting them a transfer fee of $600,000 whilst Eli Babalj joined Dutch club AZ Alkmaar for a reported $200,000 transfer fee. It was at home where their lack of cash would stand out. Rather than ice baths for the players to recover, they would stand in wheelie bins whilst teammates would pour in bags of ice purchased from service stations, ice normally used to cool drinks at barbecues.

City Football Club invested $15 million to upgrade the facilities at LaTrobe University to be the best in the A-League and W-League, but the overhaul of the training facilities was not completed until 2015.

Villa arrived one week prior to the season opening in 2014/1—a player worth millions of dollars who was used to the world-class facilities of Atletico Madrid, Barcelona and Valencia, coming to train with the basic facilities of one of Australia's previously poorest professional football clubs. Adding further to what must have been quite a disconnect for him was his lack of English language skills. City player Jonatan Germano from Argentina was both teammate and translator during his stay.

Australian-born former Croatian international Joey Didulica was goalkeeper coach for Melbourne City and remembers well the facilities they had prior to City Football Group's wealth.

"Where we trained was next to this lake and long grass. It was a perfect haven for wildlife."

Australia is famous for its exotic and deadly animals, but they can be forgiven for not mentioning to Villa that their facilities had a brown snake problem. Didulica recalls assistant coach, Ante Milicic, almost stepping on one.

"We were walking out to train and he nearly trod on a brown snake. Right in front of us on the steps of the portable, he opened the door to step out and this brown snake is just sunbaking, catching some rays. He ran back inside starting to squeal. John Aloisi and I were going 'What the hell?' a bloody massive brown snake out there.

"There was a serious issue with snakes, I was petrified going into every changeroom, looking under for snakes. It was horrific."

Having to take matters into your own hands is not recommended with brown snakes. The eastern brown snake or common brown snake is the second most venomous land snake in the world. Adults grow as long as two metres and they are responsible for 60% of all snake bite deaths in Australia.

But that didn't stop one of City's players, according to Didulica.

"I saw Jacob Melling with my own eyes kill a brown snake with a wheelie bin.

"Then he held it by the tail showing everyone. I went 'What the hell? This is not normal!'.

"These are massive brown snakes, a deadly creature, a deadly reptile. Then we have David Villa arrive at these facilities, a €100 million player!"

Luckily David Villa didn't see any brown snakes in Bundoora. Didulica says he brought a professional approach to training with Melbourne City.

"I think for the younger players it was good to see how he was at training, the way he finished, and the way he wanted to do extras after training.

"Also for our sports scientists here who try and overtake football, who try and overtake sessions, count minutes etcetera. They saw that David Villa, one of the world's best, a World Cup winning striker, didn't want to go in after the session. He wanted to stay out there, wanted to get the goalkeepers and shoot some goals.

"This should show the sports scientists that this is how the best do it. I loved that about him, no one was going to tell David Villa to go inside, he wanted to get his eye in and shoot some goals."

Didulica says Villa also didn't agree with the emphasis on running and fitness, especially close to a match, that was favoured by assistant coach Luciano Trani.

"Everyone knows Luciano is a fanatic. It was a hot day and we were doing some patterns of play. He was getting Villa to run and to chase. David, being the professional that he was, did it the first time, he did it the second time, but by the third time he started looking around going 'Is this guy serious?.' Then Luciano didn't stop it was like fourth, fifth, sixth time, all this running.

"I remember thinking this was no good. And Villa asked Germano 'Is this normal, do you guys do this before a game?'

"He couldn't believe it, he didn't want to train like this, it was too much, crazy running the day before the game."

Melbourne City's first game under the new name was away to Sydney FC. In pouring rain at Sydney Football Stadium, City took to the pitch in their away strip, which was the old Melbourne Heart red-and-white stripes. In front of more than 25,000 people, Villa started on the bench before coming on in the second half. After going behind 1-0, Villa showed his class with an equaliser in the 63rd minute. Receiving the ball from Irishman Damien Duff, another high calibre City recruit with English Premier League experience, he smashed it home on his right foot. Simon Hill's commentary of that game summed up the feeling of the time.

"David Villa, there's the goal! That's why he's won a World Cup! That's why he's won the Champions League! And that's why he will be big! Box office! Right around Australia over the next couple of months!"

Melbourne City gained a point in a 1–1 draw.

In the four seasons of Melbourne Heart, they rarely pulled big crowds that weren't derbies against local rivals Melbourne Victory. At their home ground Heart only topped 10,000 four times and that included their first-ever game and when Alessandro

Del Piero came to town.

It was much anticipated that their first home game as Melbourne City, with David Villa in the line-up, would see them exceed these numbers for the Round 2 home game against Newcastle Jets.

"It definitely gave Melbourne City that real sugar hit, I remember that Newcastle game as I had been covering Melbourne Heart for the past four years," recalled journalist David Davutovic.

"There was a real hype and build up, the media department were really excited waiting and wondering if the top tier [of the stadium] would be open. I remember it might have been just before or after the game had kicked off that people were streaming through the little hole into the top tier, it was a great occasion!"

A crowd of 15,717 saw Newcastle Jets spoil the party by taking a 1–0 lead in the 62nd minute through a goal by Ecuadorian Edson Montano. Despite a rusty start to the season for City, Villa did read the script and managed to score the equaliser in the 87th minute. The game again finished in a 1–1 draw and the crowd got to see the world-class striker score.

Davutovic recalls: "They didn't play a great game, and because Villa joined late they were a bit disjointed and the ball movement quite slow. They didn't utilise him as well as they could have, but for that home game it was just a fantastic occasion."

With two games and two goals, the move to recruit Villa was looking like a masterstroke. The Melbourne Derby was next.

However, despite an early 2–1 lead they would be swamped 5–2, with a goalscoring masterclass from Besart Berisha (three goals) and Archie Thompson (two goals).

Villa struggled through this match and hardly touched the ball. According to Didulica, it was more to do with the Australian standard than the Spaniard.

"He made the right moves and the ball wasn't coming to him. I felt a bit sorry for him, you could see his level of play and his football intelligence, which is way beyond what we had.

"He was just on a different level and he saw the game at a different level then all of our players. He was more than one kick ahead of our guys, maybe two or three. He saw the game unfold before it unfolded, I think with David he couldn't get our patterns of play as they were unpredictable.

"In Australia, it's a totally different game and people don't understand that people of a high level may have trouble adjusting because it's a totally different league, especially a striker who needs balls to be fed in."

Villa's fourth game at home was another big crowd for City, their third highest home non-derby crowd in history as 13,083 saw City lose 2–1 to Adelaide United.

Despite coming on a 10-game guest contract and City promoting 10 games to attract members and crowds, Villa headed to New York after just four games and two goals.

Didulica says they were expecting him to play for longer until he joined training, when it became clear it wouldn't be for the 10 games.

"We were told minimum four, but possibly eight, but when he touched down and we started speaking to him it was going to be four maximum."

Coach of City at the time was former Dutch international John van 't Schip and Didulica said that the length of his stay didn't affect any of his planning.

"JVS is very nonchalant, very relaxed about all things. His attitude was David is here but if he leaves we move on. He wasn't really stressed, JVS doesn't stress on too many things."

John van 't Schip may have not stressed, but it proved to be a real letdown for both the City fans, football fans in Australia and the Australian football media.

Fox Sports broadcaster Adam Peacock reflected on only four games.

"That was one of the biggest disappointments I have seen in the A-League that this guy couldn't stay for the ten games. That left a bit of a sour taste in our mouth, it looked like we were taken for a bit of a ride down here after that.

"It was still a bit early with the new facilities being built at Melbourne City. I reckon if it had happened a year or two later they would have been a much better chance of hanging on to him for his allotted ten games."

It remains unclear why his guest stint was cut short. Was it Villa's decision, was it New York City FC or Manchester City deciding to save him for the MLS, or did he actually see a brown snake? David Davutovic believes it was the player's decision.

"I tend to think it was Villa. I know he was staying in a hotel in the city so it was quite a trip for him to Bundoora. A few of those things may have underwhelmed him.

"I remember seeing him at an Adidas promotional event in their Bourke Street store. There were probably 1,500–2,000 people there to see him. I knew he was a star but that hit home how big the guy was. Bourke Street Mall was absolutely packed. It was a pleasure to see someone in their prime of that calibre here in the A-League.

"That was a really exciting period for the game. In general there was a real buzz around. The 2012-13-14 years of the A-League were a real high watermark for the game, you add the Wanderers coming in and CFG had just bought Melbourne Heart and then Ange got the public to fall back in love with the Socceroos with some good performances at the World Cup.

"It was a great period for the game and just the excitement levels when someone of the calibre of Villa coming was quite extraordinary.

"I know at the *Herald-Sun* we really got behind it. He was on the front cover of the sport section following the Newcastle game and we had some Spanish words in there, and then the big double page spread. A genuine superstar still in the prime of his career."

Crowds higher than 10,000 have only happened 10 times in the years since Villa played for Melbourne City, none exceeding those two home crowds and one included a free family ticket of four offer with a McDonald's purchase. The Adelaide United game would turn out to be Villa's final game with Melbourne City.

"A lot of people were disappointed and underwhelmed [when he left early]," says Davutovic.

"People had bought memberships and season passes based on five or six Villa home games. I remember reporting it would be around the ten-game mark and that's what we were told. It was really disappointing when he departed prematurely."

Commentator Simon Hill reflected on Villa's time in Australia.

"Given he put bums on seats, it makes you wonder why Melbourne City haven't repeated that experiment.

"We want them to repeat that experiment because it worked. The problem was it didn't last very long, and within a month he was gone, and all those fans who had bought tickets, season passes were left short changed.

"He was supposed to be there for half the season. He only stayed for four games, which was really disappointing. There is no doubt that if he had stayed he would have been a big star in the A-League, unfortunately blink and you miss him.

"It makes you scratch your head why they haven't repeated that, because it clearly worked, it's not as if they haven't got the means to do it."

David Villa would be New York City FC's first-ever captain and continued his amazing goalscoring record, netting 77 times in 117 games.

Alex (Sandy) Young as
an Everton player, 1907

Peter Price for Gladesville Ryde, 1963

Takis Loukanidis challenged by Hakoah's Ziggy Spilarewicz at the Sydney
Sports Ground, 1968

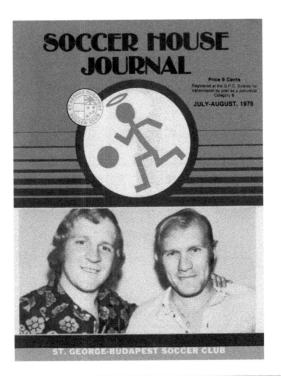

St George-Budapest
programme featuring
Francis Lee
and Socceroo
Manfred Schaefer,
1976

Mimis Papaioannou
takes a corner for
Heidelberg United
(then Fitzroy
Alexander), 1976

Charlie George for St George, number 7, was one of the first superstar guest players in the NSL era, 1977. Here he celebrates a goal against South Melbourne in the Queens Birthday clash at Middle Park.

Another match-day programme from St George-Budapest featuring Ray Clemence on the cover,1978

The match-day programme cover for Newcastle KB United vs Marconi featuring Bobby Charlton, 1978

18-year-old
Craig Johnston (right),
pictured with
Bob Mountford,
both playing with
Newcastle KB United,
1978

Peter Marinello (left)
is met at
Canberra Airport by
Canberra City coach,
Johnny Warren,
1978

Eamon Bannon played four games for Frankston City, 1979

… while Martin Peters (left) played five, also in 1979

Bobby Charlton arrives at Sydney Airport to be met by the coach of Blacktown City, Mick Jones, 1980

Martin Chivers for Frankston City with the Mayor of Frankston, Kenneth Mair, 1980

Bobby Moore for Inglewood Kiev (centre), 1981

John Sydenham (left) and Alan Ball at Floreat Athena, 1982

George Best drinking
a cup of tea at
the press conference
on arrival at
Sydney Airport, 1983

… and with his
West Adelaide teammates
in the same year

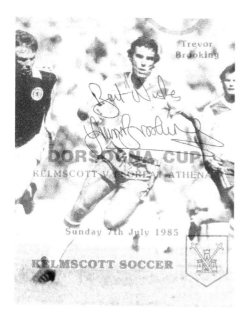

An autographed programme Trevor Brooking for the Dorsogna Cup, Kelmscott vs Floreat Athena (Perth), 1985

Davie Provan – happy to be free from autograph hunters in suburban Coogee in Sydney, 1985

Ossie Ardiles playing for St George-Budapest vs Marconi at St George Stadium, 1985

Kevin Keegan at one of the junior coaching clinics he conducted for Blacktown, 1985

Kevin Keegan for Blacktown is checked by Canberra City's John Mihailides at Gabbie Stadium, 1985

Another Wollongong City Wollactico, Alan Brazil pictured with his daughter Lucy, Laurie Kelly from the club, and promoter Harry Michaels, 1988

John Samaras celebrating his goal for South Melbourne, 1988

Paul Mariner (left), one of Harry Michaels' Wollacticos, heading the ball for Wollongong City, 1988

The third Wollactico, Trevor Francis for Wollongong City after the 4-1 flogging at the hands of Footscray JUST, 1988

Kosta Kouis for
Heidelberg United,
1989

Jimmy Case at
British Wanneroo (Perth),
1993

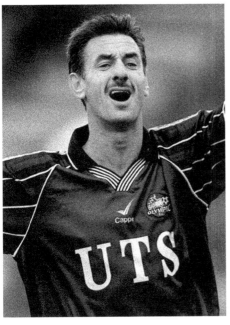

Ian Rush playing for Sydney Olympic, 1999

Kazu Miura playing for Sydney FC at the FIFA Club World Cup against Deportivo Saprissa, 2005

Buddy Farah (left) with Gianfranco Zola at a junior coaching clinic for Marconi, 2006

Mario Jardel arrived in Newcastle to high hopes but his 11 game stint in 2007-08 was disappointing - to put it mildly

David Villa plays the first of his four games for Melbourne City vs Sydney FC, 2014

Usain Bolt came on as a substitute in his first trial game
for the Central Coast Mariners, 2018

For the love of the game

The standard pathway for guest stars is to be offered a pile of money to appear in between jobs in Europe in the vain hope that that money would be returned to the signing club through a boost in gate revenue. However, there is a special class of guest star for whom money was not a factor. These players played, effectively, for free (with expenses covered), out of a sense of loyalty to a club or a diaspora of countrymen. Ultimately these players chose allegiance to football over lining their pockets.

Danny McGrain: Rochedale Rovers, 1987, 3 games, 0 goals

Danny McGrain is Glasgow Celtic royalty. The fullback was a mainstay of the Celtic side of the 1970s and 1980s, taking part in nine League championships, six Cup wins, and is fifth in the club's all-time appearance records (with 439). McGrain became Celtic captain in 1977, after he won the Scottish Football Writers' Association Footballer of the Year 1977, taking over as captain from Kenny Dalgleish.

However, a foot injury cancelled him out for most of that season, causing Celtic to go trophy-less in his absence and for him also to miss the 1978 World Cup with Scotland. Despite this, his 62 caps for Scotland has him 11th on the Scots' all time appearance list. He is also an MBE, in the Scottish Football Hall of Fame, and was voted by Celtic supporters in 2002 into their all-time Celtic XI.

That was, of course, the second great honour bestowed on McGrain by Celtic supporters. In 1987 at the end of his career with Celtic (he joined Hamilton for a season on a 'free' for the '87–88 season), the Celtic Supporters of Brisbane somehow arranged for McGrain to play three games in the Queensland State League.

Rochedale is a southern suburb of Brisbane, on the way to the Gold Coast. The local club, the Rochedale Rovers, evolved slowly in the early 1970s as a junior club but quickly expanded through local support to include senior clubs. By 1987 they were in the Queensland State First Division, and, improbably, fielding one of Scotland's finest ever players.

It is not clear how actively involved members of the Celtic Supporters Association were with Rochedale at the time (one tongue-in-cheek article in Go Soccer described the club as being "run by the Celtic Supporters Association"), but when McGrain's visit became a reality, Rochedale Rovers was the club selected. Originally reported as a four-match guest stint, McGrain actually only appeared three times in the league for Rochedale.

In fact, star football lightning struck more than once in Queensland in 1987. In some ways 1987 was a devastating year for football in Queensland, with no Sunshine State clubs competing in the National League for the first time since its inception. Perhaps to compensate, the QSF were eager to give local fans some taste of elite football. Only weeks before McGrain's arrival, Queenslanders were wowed by the appearance of England and Manchester United legend Bryan Robson, who suited up in maroon to play for Queensland in their annual interstate match against NSW. He was here on the QSF's dime for a 'paid holiday', which included an after-dinner speaking function and a variety of opportunities for autograph hunters.

Robson also appeared in an indoor soccer tournament. He didn't play any club games in Australia, but Bryan Robson's 1987 guest stint is one of the more improbable to date.

McGrain's guest stint with Rochedale started strongly, with a 2–0 win against Taringa, with the next game a predictable 5–1 loss to Brisbane City who had just been relegated out of the NSL.

His final game was at home against local rivals Mt Gravatt at Underwood Park.

Despite the result being another loss (2–1), McGrain lifted his game.

Sports writer Antony Sutton was there, and while the game itself didn't leave a big impression, he does recall McGrain being "accompanied on to the pitch by some bloke with bagpipes". Rochedale lost 1–2, but despite the poor points return (one win and two losses) the McGrain experience had been a positive one.

Eric Thompson, who was Queensland State Player of the Year in 1981 in a distinguished playing, and later coaching, career, described the McGrain signing as "a damn good promotion for the game".

"Rochdale fans obviously enjoyed playing alongside the great Scotsman and fans turned out to watch him play", was Thompson's assessment, who also praised the crowds for the Mt. Gravatt game. While he'd only led the Brisbane side to one win from three, Thompson's hot-take on the true value of the guest stint would be found not in memories in Brisbane, but those McGrain would take back with him to Scotland.

"We certainly aren't the hick outfit some in Britain have labelled us. McGrain is certain to go back and tell others that it is well worthwhile the trip out here."

Alas that didn't materialise. Like Bob Latchford, George Best and Alan Sunderland before him, McGrain's visit didn't lead to a stream of guest stars in Brisbane. He proved to be merely another in a semi-regular drip.

Ioannis (John) Samaras: South Melbourne, 1988, 1 game, 1 goal

South Melbourne Hellas are arguably Australia's most iconic club. They were only one of two clubs to compete in all 28 NSL seasons, won the championship four times (an equal record) and the NSL Cup twice. In 2010 they were crowned 'Oceania Club of the Century' by FIFA.

There is no grander name at South Melbourne than Samaras. The late Georgios Samaras helped establish the South Melbourne Hellas Football Club in 1952 after moving to Australia at the end of World War II. Ultimately, he would return to Greece with his family, including his Melbourne-born son Ioannis (John), 13 at the time, who had grown up going to Hellas games at Middle Park.

John developed into a successful pro in Greece with OFI Crete and Panathinaikos, and between 1986 and 1990 he played 16 times for Greece, scoring once in a friendly against Norway in 1989.

In 1988, the player with South Melbourne running through his veins was at the top of his game when he agreed to appear for free for Hellas in a single match, on loan from OFI Crete, against Greek rivals Sydney Olympic.

Then Federal Immigration and Ethnic Affairs Minister Clyde Holding, who happened to be the local MP, provided a ceremonial kick-off before the game. The pitch was so puddle-ridden that several groundsmen, and a few fans too, had to sweep the pools of water into glue-pits on the edge of the 18 yard box. None of that would have shocked Samaras who had seen it all before, unlike many international guest stars.

This was his local club and Samaras played the 1988 game for nothing. He repaid the South hierarchy with an infinite return-on-investment when he scored the second in a 2–1 win against Olympic. Over 4,000 people witnessed his delicate chip over Olympic's diving 'keeper from inside the six-yard box. His one-game cameo ended abruptly when he was substituted in the 72nd minute, but unlike Peter Beardsley in 2000 (who was embarrassed to be hooked), Samaras had called for it himself.

"I'm too tired, you know. This year I played 52 games—national team games,

Europe games—you know, I'm too tired. And I played only for the people of South Melbourne," he said after the game.

Hellas sought him out again in 1989, claiming in the football press that he would be back, but that deal never eventuated.

Ioannis's eldest son, born in 1985, bearing his grandfather's name Georgios, would go on to have an even more storied career, playing for clubs such as Manchester City and Celtic. He would also play upfront for Greece 81 times in an eight-year international career. While young George Samaras did not play for South Melbourne, he might be considered South Melbourne's greatest player to never appear for the club.

*　　*　　*

Jimmy Case: British Wanneroo, 1993, 3 games, 0 goals

Jimmy Case was a Liverpool local boy that made good. Born and raised on Merseyside, the apprentice electrician from South Liverpool made it all the way to the Reds first team in 1975, making the most of his 186 games with them, winning the First Division title four times as well as the UEFA Cup. Fearing his local roots would lead to trouble, manager Bob Paisley sent him to Brighton & Hove Albion in 1981, where he played in an FA Cup final with the Seagulls before over 200 games with Southampton.

It was these Southampton links that saw him head to Western Australia to play a guest stint with Wanneroo-British at Kingsway in 1993. When John Sydenham asked Case if he would be interested in a guest stint and Case said he was, the club set about raising money to make it happen.

Sydenham recalls how a Second Division club in Perth managed to get a professional footballer out for a guest stint.

"I was at a game at Southampton so I went up and had a chat with Jim there, and we organised to bring him and the family out for British-Wanneroo.

"We had to pay for all their fares. There were fundraisers and things on at the club to bring him over. We managed to raise the money and bring him out for a month. I was still playing at 50 but I didn't play with Jim as I started to have hip problems.

"Jim was a real pro though, he was great for them."

The Case family, comprising Jim, his wife and two daughters, stayed at the Sydenham family home for his stint in Australia. John's wife Jean says they were like a boarding house for soccer players the first 20 years they were in Australia.

Three home games in the Second Division in Perth against Balga, Swan Cracovia and Gosnells-Ferndale are hardly glamorous fixtures for someone who still wanted to be a professional footballer, but in Case's instance he still wanted to play. With most of his teammates being English expats, Case fitted right in, although communication proved to be an issue on the pitch as Case played with hearing aids.

Following his time in Perth, Case would rejoin Brighton & Hove Albion and in 1995 at the age of 41 he would become the oldest outfield player registered in the Premier League for that season, retiring in December that year after getting injured in the reserves.

In a 2006 worldwide poll '100 Players who shook the Kop', Jimmy Case was voted the 45th best Liverpool player of all time.

*　　*　　*

Kostas Katsouranis: Heidelberg United, 2015, 1 game, 0 goals

With the establishment of the A-League, the historic NSL Club Heidelberg United—like many others—were locked out of the top flight, destined to remain a State League entity. Their fate was to watch from afar as a new top-flight developed, co-opted the youngest generations of Heidelberg's fan base, and got the TV deals and crowds that many NSL clubs would have killed for.

But then in 2014 FFA opened a tiny window for clubs like Heidelberg when it introduced the 'FFA Cup'. The FFA Cup is as the name suggests; a national cup competition with 700-plus clubs eligible across the country.

It was a chance for big historic NPL (as the new State Leagues were called) clubs to take on the A-Leaguers and, where possible, make it personal.

In the first season of the Cup Heidelberg didn't progress to the national rounds, but witnessed several upsets including league and fellow Greek rival Bentleigh Greens knocking off A-League side Adelaide City in extra time in a Quarter Final. Bentleigh was beaten in the semi-final by Perth Glory 3–0, but the exposure was enormous for a side about which few football fans outside of Melbourne would have heard.

And so in 2015, when the Cup came calling, Heidelberg answered. They comfortably beat NSW NPL club Broadmeadow Magic 3–1, before getting over former NSL rival

Sydney United '58 2–0 in the Round of 16. A Quarter Final matchup against A-Leaguers Melbourne City awaited.

This was a good Heidelberg side. Not 'top flight' good, but the 'Bergers contained a handful of players who would get chances in the A-League (some specifically off the back of this Cup run).

Melbourne City, their next opponents in the Cup, had just completed their makeover to full ownership by the City Group. Aaron Mooy was their star player, and he was joined by new signing from Uruguay Bruno Fornaroli, who had scored on his debut for City in their big Cup win in the earlier round, a 5–0 against fellow A-Leaguers Wellington.

Clearly Heidelberg would be outmatched against their top tier opponents, but there was a fighting chance as Bentleigh had proven the previous season. The later rounds of the FFA Cup set the perfect scene for guest players where anything can happen.

With Greek pride on the line, the community reached out and found its champion.

Kostas Katsouranis is an icon of Greek football and walks tall alongside Heidelberg's previous guests Mimis Papaioannou and Kosta Kouis.

A special reverence is reserved for Katsouranis and the class of 2004. In the march toward their improbable Euro 2004 victory, Katsouranis had forced his way into the XI and was invaluable to the middle of the park in Lisbon in their 1–0 victory over the hosts in the Final. He represented his nation 116 times, is the third most capped player, and represented three of Greece's biggest clubs—AEK, Panathinaikos and PAOK—as well as several seasons with Benfica. As Greek footballers go there are few more revered.

As the tie with Melbourne City approached, the recruitment drive escalated. Contact had been made earlier to test the waters, but the deal was contingent on FFA approval. This became a formality when Daniel Heffernan was snapped up by A-Leaguers Central Coast Mariners for the 2015–16 season. With a key player removed from the Heidelberg squad, the FFA were obliged to approve the Katsouranis signing.

Heidelberg legend and Socceroo goalkeeper Jeff Olver was assistant manager in 2015, supporting manager George Katsakis. Olver recalls the move being orchestrated by director Harry Tsalikidis, brother of club chairman Steve Tsalikidis, who had built connections in Greek football and more widely in Europe. On a youth tour of Amsterdam with Heidelberg's under 14, to play against the mighty youth sides of Ajax, Harry connected to an agent based in Europe, George Kazianis.

Kazianis was born in Sydney of Greek ancestry, but had lived most of his life in Greece and professionally across Europe. The Australian connection helped, and while Heidelberg's Cup run continued the 'Bergers management quickly lay the groundwork with Kazianis. A little over two weeks after the win over Sydney United, Katsouranis signed on to join Heidelberg.

On Katsouranis's signing, Katsaskis told the club website: "When you start to put things into perspective, he played for Benfica, all over the world, to come to the Olympic Village for Heidelberg, it's amazing."

What was Katsouranis' match fee? Nothing. Several sources confirm that Katsouranis agreed to play for nothing, just like John Samaras in 1988. His expenses were covered, but they would be more than repaid to Heidelberg on the gate and through other appearances within the Greek community.

Indeed it seems the opportunity to connect with the Melbourne Greek community was the drawcard for Katsouranis. Manager Katsakis told the media when he arrived, "Being a servant of the Greek community, he's excited to see the patriotism that we have in Australia. He wants to experience it. I'm hoping he'll relate to the occasion and rise to it."

When asked directly about the fee involved, Katsakis said, "He's doing it to give something back to the Greek community."

Katsouranis' appearance for Heidelberg was, in essence, a celebration of Greek football and of Melbourne's rare and wonderful Greek identity following in the footsteps of Papaioannou, Nestoridis, Samaras and Kouis.

In the lead-up to the game Katsouranis put himself out there for the Greek community. His English wasn't great, but through an interpreter—former Greek national team sports scientist Yiannis Kotsis—he did his best to connect to fans. "He's very happy to be here, when you're ending your career, this is a wonderful opportunity to come especially because the Greek community is very large here," he told fans, through Kotsis.

There was a series of events set up by Heidelberg and the broader Greek community for Katsouranis. There was a mixture of appearances and drop-ins, like at the Greek Centre for Contemporary Culture where he announced the creation of football camps for kids. There were smaller, more intimate events like exclusive dinners for wealthy fans willing to drop four figures on a meal. A once-in-a-lifetime opportunity—a chance to share a meal with a living legend—and Heidelberg found ample members of the Greek community willing to pay anything for the experience.

But attention quickly turned to the match itself. As a PR exercise, signing Katsouranis was a masterstroke, but Heidelberg's objective was an upset win and a spot in the FFA Cup semi-final.

"I think what Kostas will bring to the table between now and next Tuesday will inspire the boys to lift another gear. I think that will transform onto the park come next Tuesday, and while there are two teams on the park, anything is possible," was the belief coming from manager George Katsakis.

Katsouranis may not have spoken fluent English, but he was fluent in football in a way that his younger teammates in the NPL Victoria were not. Olver remembers the sheer impact he had on the team, as a living embodiment of their elite level ambitions.

"Every time you bring in a quality player, players want to play with him. And as a coach you want to coach quality players. You know you're telling youngsters they need to be able to do X, Y and Z, and to play at that level that's what you've got to do. Then you have someone come in who's done it. So it's great to say 'Look at his first touch. Look at his body position, look where he plays the ball'."

By the night of the game an eclectic audience of new and old football fans were well and truly warmed up to Katsouranis's appearance. The scene was electric with 11,372 fans in attendance. Olver, who had played in derbies against South Melbourne, NSL Cups and NSL Finals at the ground, will never forget that night in 2015. It was a rare convergence of old and new football in Australia, with the Olympic Village pumping like it had done in the past at the height of the NSL.

"We used to talk about when Heidelberg was in the NSL and we'd play in front of 15,000. And the beauty of this game was, that night, that's how it used to be. So it was great for the community who might have been kids when they watched Heidelberg play, to bring their sons or daughters and say 'See this? This is how it was every week'."

Where NPL crowds usually max out at 1,500, it was an extraordinary return to the big time for Heidelberg.

"I know for a fact no other NPL club has drawn a crowd like that. It's still one of the biggest crowds for a Quarter Final since the inception of the FFA Cup. And that's why clubs want to get into the FFA Cup. Ok you've got the A-League. This is an opportunity to showcase the clubs who built the game up."

Hearts were pounding for Heidelberg once again after nearly 15 years outside the top flight, and with a Euro winning ball player in their side, the scene was set for an upset. A win on the night and Heidelberg were into an FFA Cup semi-final.

According to Olver, their game plan was to not concede and ease into the match in the first 15–20 minutes. Defend and get the pace of the game against Melbourne City, who were only in the middle of their pre-season. If they kept a tight ship, and if City weren't up for it on the night, or put off by the crowd, then a late winner was possible. Hell, with the hype around the game and Katsouranis at the wheel, a winner seemed inevitable if they could hold on and do the basics well like the Greeks had done in 2004.

The game plan worked perfectly—until the second minute when City's new striker Fornaroli scored. Mooy carved up the Heidelberg defence like rare lamb on a spit. His through ball was then cut back to the Uruguayan to tap home. Fornaroli would get a second near the final whistle, to bookend a Aaron Mooy second half hat-trick.

Mooy found the net twice from outside the box, and another was tapped in from a rebound. Mooy didn't get the memo that this was meant to be Heidelberg's night, and had a blinder. The game ended 5–0 to City, with Mooy taking home deeds to acres of real estate on the edge of Heidelberg's box.

"Mooy put a show on" was Olver's honest assessment. Katsouranis was good, but like a lot of his Heidelberg teammates he barely got near the ball. "When he had the ball it wasn't an issue. He still had the skill to take a touch and play, and read the game."

Once his shift was over Katsouranis left Australia. If Heidelberg had somehow managed a win, Katsouranis almost certainly would have stayed on for the semi-final (and beyond). There was also the expectation that he would return in March for the football camps he announced the opening of, but that didn't eventuate. George Katsakis commented when Katsouranis arrived that he would try and convince him to join for the NPL season in 2016, but that proved to be optimistic.

New football might have won the contest on the scoreboard, but this game was also a victory for nostalgia. It was a celebration of Melbourne's brand of Greek football, featuring one of Greece's biggest names, and a portal into the past when South Melbourne Hellas and Fitzroy/Heidelberg helped establish football into an Aussie Rules town kicking and screaming.

Some of That Old Premier League Magic

The English Premier League is the biggest football force in the world, full of clubs with more fans globally than the population of Sydney. The idea of dropping a former Liverpool or Manchester United player onto an Australian pitch to lure fans who hadn't yet given the local product a try wasn't new. But by the late 1990s when the Premier League was on the up, and featuring Socceroos like Harry Kewell in their prime, the NSL was in a terminal slide. The pressure to try anything to draw crowds became intense, and ageing stars from the 'home countries' became hot demand. Whether they were past or well past their prime barely seemed relevant.

Ian Rush: Sydney Olympic, 1999, 2 games, 1 goal

Ian Rush was 38 when he joined Sydney Olympic as a guest player in 1999. He was first approached by Sydney Olympic the year before when he left Newcastle United, but plumped for a season at Wrexham in England's third tier instead. As a Welshman he eyed a season for the Welsh club as a homecoming, but 17 games without a goal had spelled the end of his glorious career in the UK.

His silverware alone could fill the Sydney Opera House. He played over 400 games for Liverpool, scoring just under a goal every second game. He won five league titles with Liverpool, two European Cups and three FA Cups. He was Liverpool's top goalscorer eight times and was European Golden Boot in 1984. In 1987 he attracted a British record transfer fee when he joined Juventus for £3.2m.

In short, Ian Rush was a bona fide legend of the game and, on top of having an imperious reputation in the box, he was also one of football's universally loved statesmen.

"Ian Rush was a burning desire of the old Sydney Olympic consortium," according to player agent Tony Rallis who worked at the club when Rush was signed.

"One of our ambitions at the time was to raise the profile of the club to the broader community. While we respected the club's history, [we thought] let's try and put Sydney Olympic on the map. Nothing would be better than signing a high profile Premier League player who would hopefully make an impact."

By the late 1990s Sydney Olympic was facing an existential crisis. They had loyal, passionate (and some extremely wealthy) fans, but needed new focus and new leadership to steer the club into the new millennium.

The new leadership group became known in Sydney Olympic folklore as the 'Five White Knights', headed by the long-time Chairman of the Sydney Roosters NRL team, Nick Politis.

Rallis had prepped Politis about the commercial benefits Rush would bring. "We collectively came up with a plan and reached out to Ian Rush and paid him a fee of $50,000 for two appearances for Sydney Olympic and some commercial appearances outside of football."

Ian Rush was to be their talisman. Rallis claims Rush was the only player Olympic considered when they sketched out their plan to sign a global megastar. His global brand would have local Liverpool supporters salivating. In that 1999–2000 season Peter Beardsley would join NSL rivals the Melbourne Knights on a similar deal, but Beardsley doesn't quite breathe the same rare Liverpool air as Rush.

Another commercial benefit of Rush's guest stint was the goodwill generated for sponsors. According to Rallis, "At the time, we had something like $600–700,000 in sponsorships. That was a huge amount of corporate support. I was conscious of the fact that I needed to keep these people on the front and back pages."

Rush was also joining a side full of elite Australian talent. Future Socceroos Brett Emerton, Nick Carle, Jason Culina and Linsday Wilson were all in the shop window with Olympic. Having Rush at the club was bound to attract an influential eye or two.

So with the weight of the NSL's business model on his unsuspecting shoulders, Ian Rush boarded a flight to Sydney in November 1999 for a two-match guest contract with Sydney Olympic. His brief was to play two games in 15 days, in Rounds 8 and 10 of the 1999–2000 NSL season. The Round 9 clash was an away game in Melbourne against the Knights, and they wanted to keep Rush for the home games to maximise his gate receipts.

The media interest paid off immediately. According to Rallis, "the coverage was extreme. It was beyond my expectations. Rush, for the Australian media at the time, was huge."

A common theme in stories about Rush was that the move would probably be a commercial failure, but at least everyone would enjoy having a bona fide legend in their midst.

Manager Branko Culina was excited to have Rush on his team sheets. "He's very impressive. Players of his calibre have no problem settling into a team."

Rush's first appearance for Olympic was shown live on subscription TV, but also in front of 7,300 fans in a huge downpour that Tony Rallis believes cost Olympic a few thousand spectators. Their opponents were old local foes Marconi, and Olympic Golden Boy Brett Emerton opened the scoring in the 17th minute. A goal was clawed back for Marconi five minutes later. As though it was ordained by the football gods, the next goal came from Ian Rush.

"I remember him scoring it because I was sitting next to his agent and was jumping up and down. I vividly remember it. It was a snap shot on goal. Typical Rush. A sniper's goal," Rallis recalls.

Rush's opponent that day was a young Buddy Farah. Born in Sydney, Farah broke through with Marconi and was a member of the Australian Under 23 team before he was controversially cut from the squad before the Sydney Olympic Games. He went on to play international football for Lebanon and play in the Lebanon Premier League for Nejmeh.

Farah was only 20 at the time, and remembers the game fondly, despite being on the losing side. "It was quite a surreal moment because growing up watching Liverpool and being a Liverpool supporter, and then coming up against him at such a young age.

"I was hoping I'd be able to keep him [Rush] at bay. My first game in the NSL was against Damien Mori who was such a prolific goalscorer for Adelaide City. The week prior to that game [Marconi coaches] brought me in specifically to coach me on how to maintain Damien. We won that game 2–0 and he didn't get a sniff on goal. So I thought I might be able to emulate that when Rush came about, but unfortunately he was just too good for me."

Farah was a victim of Rush's veteran cunning. Rush surprised all that day with how quick and mobile he still was for his age. There are many centre backs in the English First Division and, later, the Premier League who can say they were outwitted and out positioned by Ian Rush. Farah is the only NSL defender who can—and it's a badge he wears with pride.

"He banged up against me in the box and within a second turned on the ball and put it in the back of the net. But it's something that will stay with me for the rest of my life. I'll be able to talk about that with my son as he gets older and starts to understand more of the game. "

Farah marked Rush the entire day and tried to extract everything he could from the experience.

"We had a good chat during the game. I was only young. I remember poking him in the ear to say 'I'm behind ya' but that's about it. He didn't react. I think he was used to all that. He was quite used to playing against guys like Vinnie Jones, so playing against a 20-year-old Buddy Farah back then was something that wasn't going to faze him."

Rush was hooked in the 78th minute for a well-earned rest. He had run hard on legs that everyone felt compelled to point out the age of. The press were ambivalent in their assessment of his debut. The quarter of the media who question the value of venerable imports had to eat humble pie after the goal, but still wouldn't stoop to genuine praise.

Keith Austin in the *Sydney Morning Herald* wrote in his match report: "Come on, hands up, who wasn't thinking, '50 grand a game for a bloke who's just turned 38— this is a joke?' Well, former Liverpool striker Ian Rush made his debut for Sydney Olympic in a local derby at Belmore Park last night and proved that when it comes to class, age is no barrier."

Austin reports Rush luring Marconi into a thrall by his sheer presence, which then opened up "too much room" for Emerton, Cardozo and Gabriel Mendez, especially for the opener where Emerton had acres to collect and beat the keeper.

Rush's second and final appearance was in front of 5,000 fans against Adelaide. This time it was a 2–0 triumph in a dour game with few chances in which Chris Kalantzis scored the opening goal. Rush was substituted in the 84th minute, no doubt worn out by the workload after a number of months off.

Rush himself, in a 2016 interview with FTBL.com.au, expressed his fondness for his time at Olympic, including the goal he foxed out of Marconi.

"Every time I've made my debut at a club I've never scored, that was the only time that when I've made my debut I've scored. It was also my last professional goal in football after that I retired, so my last professional goal was with Sydney Olympic."

With crowds of seven and five thousand, and a couple of wins on the board, did the Rush experiment pay off? After Rush had left town, manager Branko Culina was more circumspect about his impact. Later on that season, when Peter Beardsley was being lined up for the Melbourne Knights, Culina was asked about the Rush experience. "I would not do it again," he said.

"If you are trying to attract bigger crowds you have to get a current player. People nowadays can switch on the television and see the best players in the world all the time. It was different 20 years ago, when the names meant more because you weren't so exposed to them."

Culina conceded that he was a positive presence in the dressing room, but that by the second game Rush was spent.

Tony Rallis concedes the venture wasn't a big earner, but the indirect benefits were massive, at least by NSL standards.

"Money wasn't the only objective here. I was employed by the club at the time and while Sydney Olympic was one of the high profile supported and sponsored clubs with Thai Airlines and UTS as sponsors, we'd started to branch out into the corporate world, and we needed to re-invest in our corporates. So for me while I don't think we lost a lot, we definitely didn't make money. So do I think it was a good outcome for the club? Of course it was. History says Ian Rush played for our club."

The transfer deals executed by Olympic in the years after 1999 suggest that the Rush 'celebrity endorsement' may have also been beneficial. Emerton (Feyenoord), Carle (Troyes), Culina (Ajax) and Wilson (PSV) all joined top European leagues. Perhaps they were destined there anyway, but having Ian Rush as a teammate couldn't help but draw extra attention to Sydney Olympic and their crop of young stars.

*   *   *

Peter Beardsley: Melbourne Knights, 2000, 2 games, 0 goals

Peter Beardsley is undoubtedly one of the finest players of his generation. He was a nomadic wizard who propelled teams to greatness (or the best version of greatness they could achieve) with this skill and artistry on the ball. He was adaptable, could play anywhere in a front five, could both score and set up goals, and basically be where you wanted him to be.

At Newcastle, then Liverpool, then Everton and then Newcastle again he is revered. At the handful of other clubs he played at—with the exception of his 0 League games for Manchester United as a 21-year-old—he is also warmly regarded. He got Newcastle promoted, then helped get them to the brink of a Premier League title. At Liverpool he was signed to replace Ian Rush, and won two titles and an FA Cup in three consecutive seasons. He was in the PFA team of the year four times and was capped 59 times by England.

By the 1999 season Beardsley was 38. After hanging up the boots from the English scene he moved into a coaching role with old mate Kevin Keegan's England set-up. He was keeping fit training with the English senior and junior sides. And then, in February of 2000, after the clock had just ticked over into Beardsley's 39th year, he landed in Melbourne on a two-match guest contract with the Melbourne Knights.

Starting life as Essendon Croatia and developing one of Australia's early international stars, Eddie Krncevic, Melbourne Knights joined the NSL in 1984 as Melbourne Croatia and battled throughout the 1980s before losing three Grand Finals in four years from 1990–91 to 1993–94—two to Adelaide City—before claiming their first Championship (and a Cup double) in spectacular fashion in 1994–95. The following year they went back to back. The catalyst for this change of fortune was the indomitable Mark Viduka.

Viduka was 18 when he broke into the first team (who still went by Melbourne Croatia in 1993) and immediately became a household name. His transfer fee to Croatia Zagreb paid for the grandstand at Knights Stadium (still called the Mark Viduka Stand) and put the Melbourne Knights emphatically on the radar of European clubs.

In the years after Viduka's departure Josip Simunic, Danny Tiatto and Steve Horvat all followed Viduka overseas. Viduka himself would soon embark on a storied career in the UK, first at Celtic and then at Leeds, Middlesbrough and Newcastle United.

By the 1999–2000 season the NSL was in a parlous state, and most clubs were working like dogs to eke out new revenue opportunities. They tried to appeal to local Celtic fans to cash in on Viduka's celebrity in the green half of Glasgow, but it didn't stick.

So the club decided to roll the dice with Beardsley. The connection to Beardsley was brokered by Proactive Sports Management and its executive director and co-founder and former Manchester United winger Jesper Olsen. His man on the ground was John Grimaud who did the legwork and helped make the Beardsley deal a reality.

In February 2000, Beardsley was signed on a $40,000 two-match deal, with both games to be played at home in Rounds 24 and 26 of the 1999–2000 season. John Sigur, the Knights' Team Manager in 2000, remembers the hype around the deal at the time.

"It was excitement really, excitement that we were able to talk to a world name like Beardsley at the time. He was genuinely interested from the start, the fact that he knew the club's history, more so through Mark Viduka. Having him around the club was great and the excitement that generated around the club was extraordinary."

In the local press, Knights' Manager Vlado Vanis also talked up Beardsley's form. "He's fit enough, and he has still got great touch. It's clear he is a class player, and he can put several thousand on the gate."

The Knights Club News at the time was equally as ebullient about the deal. "Not only will Beardsley be great for everyone watching today at Knights Stadium, but he will be great for the younger Knights' players to learn all the soccer tricks of the trade.

As the stats will tell you, we truly have one of the greatest ever English footballers in our presence today."

He was reported to be "encouraging, cajoling and pointing things out to his squad" in early training sessions, and hadn't "stopped talking". It was his first time in the country, but was reportedly abreast of Australian football through playing against Harry Kewell and Mark Bosnich, and knew Mark Viduka by reputation.

Beardsley's debut at Knights Stadium (on Somers Street) on March 5, 2000 against South Melbourne (the previous season's champion) started gloriously for the club as the crowd assembled. A Knights record crowd of 11,415 crammed into the ground to watch a living legend at play.

David Davutovic remembers the crowd and its size as being something of a throwback. "It was a full house, which was something that you hadn't seen that season or for a few seasons. Derby crowds were decent but after those two finals wins in 1995 and 1996, crowds started dropping off, consistent with the rest of the NSL."

The crowd was great, the scene was great and the mood was electric. There was only one small problem. Beardsley was awful. He hadn't played since the previous season with Hartlepool (22 games and two goals), and hadn't lined up in a competitive match for over six months. It showed. Big time.

The Knights were routed by bitter rivals South Melbourne 4–0. And Beardsley was hooked after an hour.

Beardsley was livid with his substitution. He made no eye contact and didn't stick out his hand as he jogged past manager Vlado Vanic, offering a slightly more conciliatory hand to Vanic's assistant as he got to the bench. After the game he spoke to a TV reporter and didn't try to hide his disappointment.

"Vlado's made the decision … The people who run the football club, in terms of the directors as we would call them, I would have thought they would have a word with him. You know but obviously it's not my decision."

The uproar spilled over into next day's *Age* where "clear-the-air talks" between club directors and Beardsley were reported, with Beardsley apparently close to walking away from the deal entirely. Vanis was to be asked point blank why he subbed off the golden goose.

Club directors were reported as a mix of surprised and angry by the benching. "I was very surprised that he was substituted," Knights president Tony Karlusic told the press. "He was pretty upset about it, he believed he had a lot more to give in the game and he said that he hadn't come all this way to get embarrassed."

Vanic himself told the press, "I was trying to get us back in the game and he was not getting as much forward as in the second half. I thought he had been good in the first half and I was happy with his performance."

It seems incredible that the club would spend good money on a tourist attraction and then not give the tourists what they came for. What is more confusing is that when Beardsley was withdrawn, South Melbourne were only one goal up after taking the lead just before halftime. Literally a couple of minutes after Beardsley was removed South Melbourne scored again through striker John Anastasiadis, who was back in Australia after a 10-year career with PAOK in the Greek First Division. Two more goals followed and the Knights were cooked.

Star imports have been substituted before and have been substituted since. Some have been taken off injured, or exhausted after a full European season. But to sign someone deemed to be fit and healthy for $20,000 a match, and then remove him after an hour? Vanic was effectively pouring $6,000 down the toilet.

Beardsley ultimately didn't pull the pin on his contract and upheld his end of the deal. Most likely he didn't want to draw more attention to the scene of his embarrassment. Two weeks later, he got a full 90 minutes at home against Perth Glory. Perth would finish the 1999–2000 season on top of the table, but at Knights Stadium against a broken down Beardsley and a group of inspired kids, the Glory were sucker-punched in the sixth minute and would lose 1–0.

The crowd wasn't quite as spectacular as the earlier round. In the end 5,457 home fans caught their last glimpse of Peter Beardsley playing league football. After only 150 minutes, one win, no goals and over 30,000 eyeballs on the English great, Beardsley left town.

The Knights ultimately finished 12th that season (of 16), missing the finals by 10 points. Two of the clubs below them on the table went out of business the next season.

*   *   *

Gianfranco Zola, Marconi, 2006, 0.5 games, 0 goals
Gianfranco Zola, APIA-Leichhardt, 2006, 0.5 games, 0 goals

Sydney's Italian community was alive late in 2006 when a promotion for Italian athletic brand A-Line led to Gianfranco Zola coming to town for a one-off guest appearance.

The former Chelsea, Parma, Cagliari and Napoli striker played over 600 club games as well as 35 times for the national team. This included the 1994 World cup and 1996 European Championships. He is regarded as one of the best Italians to have graced the English Premier League and is a Chelsea fan favourite.

Former NSL player and now agent Buddy Farrah was instrumental in bringing Zola to Australia, revealing that it helped to launch his post-playing career.

"I was sponsored by A-Line when I played for the Lebanese national team. It was an Italian apparel brand and Zola wore the boots and was an ambassador for the brand.

"We were at the time trying to launch the brand in Australia and wanted to have a nice PR story behind it. We decided to bring him out here and include an exhibition match with a tribute dinner upstairs in the auditorium at Marconi."

Zola had a full itinerary in a whirlwind visit. He ran a training clinic at the home of APIA, Lambert Park, followed by the exhibition match and dinner and another clinic, this time at Marconi Stadium, within a three-day period.

Over 5,000 fans assembled at Marconi Stadium to see Zola play the first half for Marconi and then the second half for APIA-Leichhardt. It was his first competitive appearance for two years but early in the game it appeared that he had lost none of his touch, providing an assist to John Buonovoglia to help Marconi establish a 2–0 half-time lead. He also had a free kick hit the crossbar late in that first half.

The big crowd included former Socceroos captain Paul Okon, as well as Hollywood actor Anthony LaPaglia and a number of Chelsea fans who had travelled from around Australia for the chance to meet him.

At half-time he changed strips and played the remainder of the match as an attacking midfielder for APIA-Leichhardt. His tiring legs were unable to help the visiting team as Marconi scored twice again to win the The Apia Marconi Zola Challenge 4-0.

Around 1,200 people backed up after the exhibition match to attend the tribute dinner where Zola spoke about his career.

"He signed 1,200 autographs without flinching, he is one of the true gentlemen of football. He spoke at the dinner in both Italian and English. In fact he speaks English with a London accent after all the years he spent there," says Farah.

It was a big deal for the Italian-Australian football community, but it got even bigger in 2012 when Alessandro Del Piero arrived as a marquee player for Sydney FC.

*   *   *

Luis Garcia: Central Coast Mariners, 2015-16, 10 games, 2 goals

Even after the NSL had given way to the A-League, the notion of plugging in a Premier League name to lure crowds lingered in the boardrooms of the new franchise clubs.

One of the more peculiar recruitment strategies in Australian football was the A-League's recruitment of Spaniard Luis Garcia in 2015. The Central Coast Mariners recruited him straight out of retirement, from a Liverpool legends match. The Barcelona-born Garcia played for Spanish clubs Atletico Madrid and Barcelona before a 77-game career with Liverpool between 2004 and 2007. This coincided with their European Champions League victory in 2005.

After finishing with the Reds, Garcia played club football in Spain, Greece and Mexico before retiring in 2013. He was briefly lured out of retirement in 2014 to take up a marquee role in the newly formed Indian Super League with Atletico de Kolkata where he played 13 games before again retiring.

Garcia next surfaced for a Liverpool Legends team that came out to play a Socceroos Legends team in Sydney in 2015. Coached by Gerard Houllier, the Reds squad included Steven Gerard, Robbie Fowler and Ian Rush whilst the Socceroos included Mark Bosnich, Robbie Slater, Ante Milicic, Craig Foster, Craig Moore and Ned Zelic. Over 40,000 people attended this exhibition match, which Liverpool won 4–0, showing the pulling power of the world game, especially when it featured big names.

Needing some support staff for this game, Liverpool reached out to its former physio Dr Andrew Nealon, who was now working in Gosford for the Central Coast Mariners.

According to Mariners General Manager Shaun Mielekamp, because Nealon knew Garcia's body so well from his time at Liverpool and understood what shape he was in, there was an opportunity to get him for a guest spot on the Central Coast.

"'Nealo' got to have a close look at him first-hand when he was there and made a quick observation that Luis was extremely fit and his body was in really good shape. He had been taking care of himself.

"So it was a very unique opportunity that came up so we gave him a call and said 'What do you think? We know your body's right so why not?' It just became the perfect opportunity that happened very quickly for Luis to come in. It was a really tough season for us and it gave us a good spark.

"He scored some goals and got us some wins and gave the fans something to believe in. It was a really exciting moment plus he was a consummate professional so he added a lot to us off the pitch, from community events to scoring goals.

"The real unique part of it was that the rare opportunity that our physio was looking after the Liverpool legends and knew him and could tell where he was fitness wise. No other club in the world could have known that. All credit goes to Andrew Nealon on this one."

Commentator Simon Hill didn't like it at first, but his performances on the pitch changed his mind.

"He played pretty well in his short stint with the club. He probably put some bums on seats as well, they would perhaps argue that it was worthwhile. I think we have to be careful of respecting the competition and not just dragging players out of retirement.

"It's one thing to bring a Honda or a Del Piero whilst they are still active, but when you bring players out of retirement for a cameo stint, I don't know. The caveat against that is that he actually played quite well!"

Journalist David Davutovic agrees.

"I don't think it's a great one when you look at it globally in terms of credibility of the league. For your visa players, the last batch of signings, particularly the high-profile ones, become the reference point for the agents and players. Luis Garcia coming, having been signed from a Legends game having not played for a while, probably wasn't ideal."

Lifelong Liverpool fan and inaugural Central Coast Mariners member Keith Whelan remembers it well, and thinks Garcia gave the Mariners some credibility, although not initially.

"You didn't know whether to laugh or what. I went to that Liverpool Legends game in Sydney on a Wednesday and I remember getting a text on the Saturday about the breaking news and rumours. As a Mariners fan and a Liverpool fan it was if all of your birthdays had come at once. I went to one of his first training sessions and you could see his quality straight away. He stood out above everyone else.

"When he did start or came on, it was a marked difference to what he was used to. The legs weren't there at 37 but the brain was working brilliantly.

"He was fantastic with the fans. He knew what it was to be a professional footballer on and off the pitch. To have a Champions League winner at the Mariners was amazing.

"He was also a pseudo coach on the pitch and basically put his arm around the younger players to help them along. He relished that role."

Garcia scored two goals in his 10 games for the Mariners. They ended the season in last place with only three wins.

Something Extra For the Pension

Players leaving Europe at the tail-end of their careers to pick up some extra pay-days in the US, Asia or even Australia is common in football. The pace is slower, the pressures fewer, and fans are more likely to give you a pass for not pressing defenders if you pull off a moment of continental grade magic. For clubs the investment is also sound, on paper. A big name signing to excite existing fans, an experienced pro to set a standard on the training track, and just maybe some memories made on the pitch.

Dinos (Kosta) Kouis: Heidelberg United
1989, 4 games, 1 goals

The 1989 NSL season represents a turning point in Australian club football for multiple reasons. It was the last winter season before the move to summer to align to the European calendars for 1989/90. The 1989 season kicked off in January and had to be wrapped up by July to fit in the following season starting later in the year.

The timing of the 1989 season led to another quirk: an influx of rumours in the football media about guest stars. With the NSL finals run overlapping with Europe's off season, at various points Norman Whiteside, Peter Reid, Mark Falco, Georgos Togias and a return for John Samaras were reported as either likely or definite.

But only newly promoted Heidelberg managed to pull off a coup. With 11 matches to go, and rooted to bottom, the club announced that they had signed 33-year-old midfielder Dinos (Kosta) Kouis on a five week contract. Kouis was a legend at Aris Thessaloniki, arguably the club's greatest ever player. He is still the club's most capped and highest goalscorer with 141 goals in 473 games. Throw in 33 caps for Greece and one can easily place Kouis within the pantheon of Greek football.

Kouis was no stranger to fans of NSL import rumours. He was being lined up with a guest contract with West Adelaide in 1981. The deal looked done, with the player "due to arrive in Adelaide soon" until, a week later, he wasn't coming at all. Aris reportedly withdrew its permission for him to join.

Kouis also missed out on a multi-club tournament in Australia in 1983 with Aris, when the tour was banned by the ASF—primarily because dates kept shifting and the ASF wanted the four-team tournament to be played in September in the middle of the Greek season. When it was suggested that clubs might only send juniors or reserves players, perceiving a meaningless tournament on the other side of the world as less important than the league, the ASF got the hump and cancelled the whole thing.

At the halfway point of 1989 Heidelberg had won three, drawn one and lost nine games, including a humiliating 4–1 away loss to South Melbourne in front of 12,600 fans.

The club cycled through a number of players to try and find a winning formula, but nothing seemed to be working. Jeff Olver was lured back between the sticks from Melbourne Croatia. Garry McDowell, who had been signed from relegated Brunswick, was asked to make a call to his younger brother Paul, who was in his off season with East Fife in Scotland.

Club legend and former Socceroo Jim Tansey had been given the manager's role at the start of 1989 in his first full-time coaching role. By early April he was sacked and replaced by Miron Bleiberg.

Heidelberg needed something more to jump-start their season. They needed Kosta Kouis to drag them out of the bog, and Kouis got his debut in Round 18's relegation 'six pointer' away game to fellow cellar dweller Footscray JUST.

Heidelberg chalked up their fourth win of the season thanks to two goals from Phil Stubbins. Kouis's deal had him only playing games in Melbourne, to save his legs for paying Heidelberg fans, and so his second start was his first home match against St George in front of 4,000 fans. St George were in hot form and would end the 1989 season in second place, but in this game Heidelberg had Kouis, who powered home the only goal of the game, a bullet header in the 58th minute from John Stewart's cross.

Heidelberg was jumping. Kouis was supplying the magic at home, and was also somehow improving their interstate away form. Since his debut, the 'Bergers had four wins in a row and survival seemed just around the corner. With their tails high Heidelberg announced that they had extended Kouis's deal until the end of the season.

But almost immediately after announcing his extension it all fell apart. They were routed 3–0 by Preston Makedonia, and it soon emerged that something was amiss with Kouis's extension. He wouldn't be staying after all and, in fact, he would be leaving after their next game at Sunshine George Cross. That game was another loss, 1–0 with the late winner scored by Irishman Pat Morley, who himself was in town on a guest contract from Waterford United in the League of Ireland.

Kouis left after the Sunshine George Cross game to return to Aris, the extension on his deal proving to be more optimism than fact. It was cruel timing for Heidelberg. The week after his departure they welcomed South Melbourne. 5,320 fans watched a 1–1 draw in a game crying out for Kouis.

Heidelberg didn't win a game after Kouis left, finished bottom and were relegated. Like so many stories circulating in 1989, retaining Kouis for the rest of the season and potentially staving off the drop proved too good to be true.

*   *   *

Ciccio Graziani: APIA-Leichardt, 1988, 2 games, 0 goals

Francesco 'Ciccio' Graziani is an Italian legend. The forward played 64 times for the Azzurri including the 1978 World Cup, the 1980 European Championship and the winning 1982 World Cup team. He is equal ninth on the all-time scoring list for Italy, sharing that honour with an Italian with Australian links, Christian Vieri. Graziani played over 350 games for clubs such as Torino, Fiorentina, Roma and Udinese. He finished his playing career with a two-game cameo with Sydney club APIA-Leichhardt.

APIA, which stands for the Associazione Poli-sportiva Italo Australiana, was formed in 1954 by Italian migrants. The club was a powerhouse of NSW football in the 1960s and 1970s before joining the NSL in 1979. They won the title in 1987 before financial issues saw them return to State League competition in the early 1990s.

Graziani's first game in Australia was the Italian derby against fellow Italian-backed Sydney side Marconi to be held at APIA's home ground, Lambert Park, in the inner Sydney suburb of Leichhardt.

Television commentator Andy Paschalidis remembers the arrival of Graziani well, interviewing him at training during the lead-up.

"It was hilarious. You had this big Italian footballer turn up at Lambert Park. I went out to film his training session and there were more fans watching him training than I had ever seen at an APIA game. It was an amazing experience to see a player of his stature, and to watch him prepare."

Lambert Park only had a capacity of around 4,000 people, but 4,253 crammed in to see him play in a 2–0 loss to Marconi.

Along with Robbie Wheatley, Frank Farina was a goalscorer that day and remembers the game well.

"Lambert Park was a pretty small ground but it was full that day. It was huge for the Italian community to have a World Cup winner at Leichhardt."

Straight after the Italian derby, Lambert Park was again the venue on a Wednesday night as APIA-Leichhardt hosted Footscray JUST in a 2–2 draw in front of 1,988 people which would be Graziani's final game of professional football.

*   *   *

Andrea Icardi: Marconi, 1993–94, 8 games, 0 goals

Andrea Icardi began his professional career with powerhouse AC Milan in 1980 as a 17-year-old and quickly became a fixture in their midfield for their next six years. He put together 141 games for the Rossoneri, and picked up a handful of Italy Under 21 caps during that time.

To play 141 games for one of the biggest and most celebrated clubs in the world is no mean feat, and Icardi should be more of a household name than he is today. However, Icardi's exploits for Milan happened when the club were at rock bottom. Milan had been forcibly relegated at the end of 1979/80 after the 'Totonero' betting scandal. They finished third in Serie A, but president Felice Colombo and goalkeeper Enrico Albertosi were implicated in a probe into gambling on football matches in Serie A and Serie B. This was the same scandal in which Paolo Rossi was implicated, which forced his two-year suspension which ended, spectacularly, at the 1982 World Cup. It was Milan's first relegation since Serie A had formed in 1929.

Icardi left Milan when Silvio Berlusconi took over as club president in 1986 and brought some superstars to the club. Icardi joined Atalanta for two seasons, before another two seasons with Lazio relegated, before he joined newly promoted Lazio for another two followed by Hellas Verona (later Verona) for three seasons. When his contract expired at Verona at the end of the 1992–93 season, Icardi had played 14 seasons for 328 (mostly) Serie A matches and was aged just 30.

He was looking for new pastures and, with an eye on a coaching career, an offer from NSL champions Marconi-Fairfield came. It was a full-year deal promising ample returns.

Marconi had just won the NSL Championship in 1992–93, finishing second before knocking off Adelaide City in the grand final 1–0. There was a fantastic mix of young talent—namely a 21-year-old Mark Schwarzer fresh from winning NSL Goalkeeper of the Year and in his final season at the club before heading to Europe. There was also midfielder Steve Corica, who had just won the young NSL Player of the Year, and experienced strikers in Kimon Taliadoros and Andy Harper. Finally there was midfielder Ufuk Talay on its books to play back-up to Icardi and Corica.

Frank Arok was the Marconi boss, and he would have been licking his lips at the prospect of a seasoned Serie A pro joining his ranks.

Immediately on his arrival Icardi was slapped with the AC Milan label which, sadly, would come to fit him more like a yoke than a prestige. Marconi administration officer Frank Labbozetta—brother of President Tony Labbozetta—labelled Icardi the "buy of the year".

"He's a 29-year-old creative midfielder with silky ball skill …That's not all. He's played Serie A all his life, including seven years with league giants AC Milan," Labbozetta told the media. In truth he had turned 30 by that stage, had played a number of seasons in Serie B, and Milan were far from league giants when he was there; but the excitement was palpable and that mattered more than a few half-truths.

Marconi were obviously eager to leverage Icardi's marketing potential, and his brand adjacency to AC Milan. Milan were a hot brand in 1993 having just toured Australia in their off season, playing the Socceroos twice in front of more than 60,000 fans. And Marconi now had a Milan player on their books. They hoped they had another Roberto Vieri on their hands, and had many reasons to believe it.

Both Italian imports played on the opening day of the 1993–94 NSL season, a 2–2 draw away at Heidelberg. Arok was running a 4–3–3 with Corica, Icardi and Pelucchi in a fantasy midfield for Marconi's old-school Italian supporters, and those with longer memories of Roberto Vieri in his NSL prime.

But despite the hype and an away point on the opening day, the season started slowly for the reigning champions. Both Icardi and Pelucchi took part in Marconi's opening three games—a win, a loss and that opening day draw—before Pelucchi was dropped for Round four. The crowds were only 2,135 for Round four's scrappy win against Brisbane. Round five's local derby against Sydney Olympic was another omission for Pelucchi, but a fifth start on the bounce for Icardi. It would be a memorable one for all the wrong reasons.

Around this time the tag 'disappointing' started to be added before Icardi's name in press reports, and in Marconi's 1–0 loss to Olympic in mid-November, even opponents were picking up on it. Olympic midfielder Branko Milosevic reportedly sledged Icardi by telling him "If you could make Milan's top 30 [their squad], I'd be in their top 11".

Icardi didn't reappear until Round 11, coming on as a substitute in a 1–1 away at Morwell. Icardi came on again the following week in a 1–0 win over Parramatta. But then he wasn't seen for a couple of weeks, until he returned for his final start for Marconi in a 2–0 away loss at Sydney United featuring Tony Popovic and David Zdrilic. Icardi's performance was described in The *Sydney Morning Herald* match report as "totally ineffectual".

Not only did Marconi seem to lose with Icardi in the side, his omission coincided with better form and results, and allowed youngster Ufuk Talay to get minutes. In Round 18, two weeks after his last game, they turned around their early loss to Sydney Olympic by beating them 7–1. Icardi didn't appear again for Marconi, and by February 1994 both he and Pelucchi were gone. Icardi started six games, appeared as a sub in two more and scored no goals.

But despite the low return on investment, no bridges between Icardi and Marconi were burned. Frank Arok stepped aside at the end of the season and, to the surprise of some, Marconi appointed Andrea Icardi as their senior manager for the 1994–95 season.

That worked out just as well. There was an immediate culture clash of styles—despite not playing for him Icardi was from the Sacchi zonal school—and his former teammates struggled to adapt. Icardi decried his team's lack of organisation, concentration and their inability to read space around them. He brought in Angelo Colombo, who was at Milan in the golden Sacchi years and had been part of the European Cup teams. Admittedly he wasn't a big part of them, and was 33 years old when he joined Marconi and had been retired for two years.

Marconi finished 10th that season and Icardi's departure as coach was confirmed before the end of the season. His failed coaching tactics at Marconi would have been embraced with open arms in today's A-League, and he was probably a victim of being ahead of his time—or Australia being behind it.

While his time in Sydney as a player and manager was unspectacular, Icardi returned to Italy for 13 years before migrating to Australia in 2007 where he runs the AC Milan Coaching Academy.

*   *   *

Aljosa Asanovic: Sydney United
2000-01, 2 games, 1 goal;
Sydney United
2001-02, 2 games, 0 goals

The 1998 Croatian side that finished third at the World Cup holds a special place in the heart of Croatian Australians as it was not long after their country regained independence. Aljosa Asanovic was part of the 1998 squad and it was the Croatian-backed Sydney United that managed to recruit him for some guest appearances in April 2001.

Asanovic had a strong football pedigree, playing 62 games and scoring three goals for Croatia while playing club football across Europe in Croatia (Hajduk Split), England (Derby County), Italy (Napoli) and Greece (Panathinaikos).

The high-profile Croatian was used to some star treatment being a well-known footballer, so you can imagine his bemusement when the club overlooked the beauty of Sydney Harbour and tried to put him up in accommodation in the outer western Sydney suburb of Punchbowl. Former Sydney United captain and Socceroo Ante Milicic tells the story.

"We heard that they tried to put him in accommodation at the Croatian Club in Punchbowl. There was a little bit of a hotel there. It wasn't obviously up to his standard and they ended up putting him in a hotel in Double Bay!

"We remember hearing how he rocked up there and politely said 'This accommodation isn't for me!'."

Playing in the last two games of that season, Asanovic's class was on show when he had a hand in every Sydney United goal, as they defeated Sydney Olympic 3–2 in front of 5,124 people.

Francis Awaritefe was a goalscoring sensation in the NSL, the naturalised Australian becoming a Socceroo after scoring 123 goals in over 313 games for four clubs. His last-ever NSL game and goal came playing for Sydney United in Asanovic's cameo.

"The place was packed and it was a fantastic atmosphere. We won the game 3–2 and I scored. Asanovic created my goal and as it happened it was the last goal I scored in professional football.

"It was a cross from the right-hand side that he bent in, I just got my knee to the ball and threw myself at it and the ball went in.

"His left foot was unbelievable, his thinking was light years ahead of everyone. Lucky for me I could read what he was going to do, so that goal I just got on to the end of it."

Asanovic dominated that game, leading United from a 2–1 deficit to 3–2 winners.

In the final round of the 2000–01 NSL, Asanovic joined Sydney United as they hosted New Zealand side the Football Kingz. Asanovic scored from a penalty in a 4–2 loss, eventually replaced in the 71st minute by a 16-year-old Australian playing in his third NSL game, named Mile Jedinak.

Such was Asanovic's success in those two games, the powers that be at Sydney United brought him back the following season for another two-game guest stint in December 2001.

Socceroo Ante Milicic had returned from playing in Croatia to captain Sydney United that season and remembers his welcome.

"I remember when he came to the airport there were the Hajduk Split fans and banners and all that. He got a very big welcome, the community in those days was a lot stronger and a lot bigger than what it is now. So there was a huge buzz and it was a big thing."

The second coming of Asanovic was not nearly as successful. A year older at 36, the off season and semi-retirement had not been so kind; he was clearly carrying more kilograms as Milicic recalls.

"When he came, people were saying he was just a little bit heavier than what he was. He hadn't played a great deal of football but because of the success of the first time, they brought him out again.

"He didn't bring intensity but he did bring quality. His thinking was quicker than everyone else and his first touch was better than everyone else. Watching him at the end of training his left foot was incredible, it was outrageous. Taking free kicks at the end of training, it was quality for the boys to see what the top-level class players do."

His return saw him play two home games—the Croatian derby against Melbourne Knights as well as a game against Parramatta Power.

According to Milicic, a Croatian derby on the other side of the world was a strange concept to Asanovic but he wanted to contribute.

Milicic turned out to be the hero in that Croatian derby, scoring both goals in a 2–1 win against the Melbourne Knights; the first was from a penalty to level the scores. He remembers it well as he offered it to his star teammate Asanovic.

"I was near the 18 yard box and Aljosa was on the halfway line, I turned around and said to him, 'Here you go, you take it'. He just waved his arm in the air, it wasn't like he couldn't be bothered, it was more don't worry about it you take it, you're standing there. I sort of felt bad, I'm captain and you're a World Cup player, you take it, the people want to see you score.

"I thought 'I'll ask you once' but in the end I'm a striker I like scoring too. So I took it." Asanovic was replaced in the 75th minute and in his fourth and final game against Parramatta Power, he sat on the bench at the 59th minute in a 2–0 loss.

His stint with Sydney United made quite an impression on both the club and its fans, both Awaritefe and Milicic remembering him as a gentleman.

In 2017–18, Asanovic returned to Australia to manage the Croatian-backed Melbourne Knights.

Busted Arses

In interviews with former Socceroos, elite coaches and club administrators, there is one feature that they all agree a successful guest signing must have: they have to be able to play. Washed-up star names have circulated the hallways of NSL and A-League clubs throughout the years, names that clubs hoped would be recognisable to fans and who might still be able to do a job. But when the following names were considered, over-excited administrators were so preoccupied with securing their signature, they didn't stop to think if they actually should.

Nicola Berti: Northern Spirit, 2001-02, 8 games, 0 goals

In 1997 an NSL club was created to play in North Sydney called Northern Spirit. With the backing of high-profile returning Australian players Graham Arnold and Robbie Slater, the club was drawing on the game's broader appeal and trying to steer away from an ethnic base to the club. Australia's golden boy Harry Kewell was even roped in to help promote the club. As well as these high-profile Aussie players, in 2001 the Northern Spirit recruited a high-profile overseas player with some calibre in Nicola Berti.

Berti began his career at Parma before playing more than 200 games with Inter Milan. He then played in the English Premier League with Tottenham and in La Liga at Alaves. Berti was part of the Italian team that made the 1994 World Cup final.

He had quite the pedigree to be playing in Australia's top domestic league, but when he arrived, some might say he was a little out of shape.

Robbie Slater was an investor, shareholder and playing captain of the Northern Spirit.

"We say to this day it wasn't him. We say it must have been his twin brother; he was terrible.

"The amazing thing about him, it wasn't that long since he had been playing at the highest level, at Tottenham, Inter Milan. This is the guy that got voted into the team of the year at the World Cup. He played in a World Cup final!

"It was so disappointing. Look he was a lovely man but I don't think he took it that seriously. Nicola wasn't a highly technical player, so given he didn't have his fitness, it ended up a complete disaster.

"We used to laugh. I would sit with Ian Crook and Graham Arnold and we'd have a beer sometimes and Nicola would play or train or whatever and we would joke, we should check his passport, it's not him. It's got to be someone else."

*   *   *

Romario: Adelaide United, 2006-07, 4 games, 1 goal

"Romario was playing like a busted arse. He couldn't move so I hooked him."

So said Adelaide United coach John Kosmina, when reflecting on the Brazilian's four games in the A-League in 2006–07.

Romario arrived with much fanfare, brought to the club to pursue his 1000th career goal. His career began in Brazil in 1985 with Vasco da Gama, and saw him play at the 1988 Olympics, win the World Cup in 1994, and score goals in countries and leagues around the world such as the Netherlands and Spain. Romario even scored a hat-trick against Kosmina and the Socceroos at the 1988 Seoul Olympics, at a time when the Olympic football tournament was still an open-age competition.

Robbie Cornthwaite was then a young player with Adelaide United, just starting his career. He said it created a real buzz among the playing group.

"Although he wasn't going to be the player he was in his heyday, we were still incredibly excited to have a player of that quality come to the club."

It created some real excitement off the field also. Even in regional Gosford, where Central Coast Mariners had averaged crowds of 9,000, 15,000 people turned up when Adelaide United visited with Romario.

"He sold most of those tickets," recalls commentator Simon Hill. "Commercially you could say he was a success."

While Romario's guest stint was a major success with crowds and publicity, it quickly became evident on the training track that his pursuit of his 1000th goal was probably less likely.

Cornthwaite remembers his approach to training as something he was yet to see within a professional environment.

"We were in the middle of a passing drill and in the middle of it, Romario just walked off the pitch, sat at the side of the pitch and took his boots off without saying anything to anyone. He just left the training, sat down and just watched the rest of the session."

What also stood out for Cornthwaite was the entourage that Romario had, which included a personal trainer.

"This guy would literally hold his leg for him to stretch. Romario would be standing there, and this guy would be picking up his leg and stretching his quad. I mean Romario wouldn't even hold his own foot for a quad stretch. For me at that age and that time in my career, I thought it was so funny to see. Someone else was stretching every part of his body. It was hilarious."

As he mentions in Loukas Founten's book A Decade United, Kosmina clashed with his own officials when it came to playing the famous Brazilian.

They told me they'd invested too much in Romario and he had to play. I told them I didn't care if he's got the shits because he was killing the team. We had momentum and we'd lost it completely since he'd come.

From a media point of view journalist Dave Davutovic recalls the tension.

"There was clearly some tension between Romario and John Kosmina. A lot of these signings were not led by the coaches, they were led by the chairman or Board members who really pushed it through.

"The coach has certain ideas and views on the game and a guy like Romario comes in, and they would have had to tweak their game plan. I don't think Romario was in a physical condition to play a high pressing game or anything like that. I don't think he pressed all that much in any stage of his career, but he didn't need to do so in his prime."

Simon Hill talks about it ruining team balance.

"I know Kossie was very much against it as he felt it disrupted his team and more it disrupted his coaching as he had to select him. You have to be careful how you do it, off the field that was a success, but on the field probably less so."

The clearly unfit Romario played four games for Adelaide United and was subbed off in three of them. Simon Hill called his only goal, when he scored in the 15th minute against the Newcastle Jets. It was his final game for the Reds.

Successful or not, Romario's cameo in 2007 led to Adelaide United recruiting three

Brazilian players in 2008, albeit under a new coach after Kosmina was let go.

Cassio, Cristiano and Diego had all heard of Adelaide United thanks to Romario, and they helped lead the Reds to the Asian Champions League final in 2008.

"If you bring a player like Romario, it's going to put Adelaide United's name at the forefront in Brazil and then when players hear that Romario played there, it probably did help bring some more higher quality Brazllians, I'm sure that did play some part."

Davutovic says these players are reference points for the A-League.

"In my travels if you mention the A-League they won't know what you are talking about but if you mention Sydney FC they will know that's the club that Alessandro Del Piero played for and Victory is Honda's club. In terms of the evolution of the A-League, there have been as many misses as well as hits. These guys have all played an important role in the publicity of Australian football abroad, which is something that we really overlook a bit here, being so insular."

Adelaide United management say that because of Romario's signing they sold 250,000 Adelaide United shirts in Brazil.

*   *   *

Mario Jardel: Newcastle Jets, 2007–08, 11 games, 0 goals

Lessons on Berti were not heeded one season later when a unique scouting method saw the Newcastle Jets recruit Mario Jardel for a brief stint in the A-League in 2008.

Jardel was a Brazilian international with a penchant for spectacular-headed goals. He once scored 57 goals in a European season with Portuguese club Porto. His highlights are amazing and it was this highlight reel that saw him on the radar of the Newcastle Jets as he was scouted off YouTube. What wasn't taken into account was that the highlights reel was ten years old.

The shambolic nature of Jardel's time in Australia started when he arrived into the country on a tourist visa, so couldn't initially play the first few games until his sports visa was processed.

Gary van Egmond, who was the Jets coach at the time, said he didn't know about Jardel's recruitment until he was presented to the media.

The press gallery gasped and sniggered as a clearly large Jardel was presented to the media at least 15 kilograms above his playing weight.

"Obviously he wasn't in the best shape when he got here. There were also a few things going on in his life and that made it a little bit more difficult for him."

Simon Hill and David Davutovic are a little more direct when they talk about Jardel on the pitch, Hill calling his first game.

"He was just hopeless. I called his debut and he came off the bench and I remember thinking, gee his belly is bigger than mine! He was horribly out of shape and clearly not at the standard required because he wasn't fit.

"You look at his record in Europe, he scored a bagful of goals and was a Brazilian international. What an amazing CV, but they've got to be in the right physical condition, frame of mind, got to have the right attitude. Mario didn't."

Davutovic remembers covering his games for *The Daily Telegraph*.

"He looked like he swallowed a sheep, he literally had a beer gut. Luckily he had a loose fitting shirt. If they had one of those classic Italian Kappa strips like that it would have been quite embarrassing. I think he played less than 350 minutes, 11 games and no goals. He did almost score on debut, but Clint Bolton pulled off a good save.

"Jardel played ten times for Brazil in the era of Romario and Ronaldo. If you read his bios, missing the 2002 World Cup was the trigger for this life to spiral out of control. He came from Cyprus to the Newcastle Jets, he was not in the right nick to be playing professional football. If you look at his stats afterwards, he did score goals after Newcastle.

"But it will go down as one of the worst overseas recruits in A-League history."

The tension created between Van Egmond, Newcastle owner Con Constantine and Jardel was also obvious, as Davutovic recalls.

"There was some mega tension between Con and Gary van Egmond, but If they had done just a little bit of research into Jardel after missing the 2002 World Cup squad, his career and life spiralled out of control. He developed a cocaine habit and probably wasn't the right fit on and off the field in 2007 and 2008."

Van Egmond is more diplomatic. He says Jardel was a nice guy but it was never going to work, and even Constantine worked it out eventually.

"The language barrier made it difficult too. You saw flashes of brilliance and what he could do at training but overall he wasn't a big inspiration for the team."

Van Egmond recalls one of the glimpses of brilliance.

"We did a crossing and finishing drill at one stage, and the ball got knocked to him. He was outside the box and he headed the ball and it went like a bullet into the top corner. It was one of those moments when everyone just stood with their mouths just wide open."

Every cloud has a silver lining. Once Jardel was let go, the club recruited South

Korean Song Jin-hyung, and finished that year as A-League champions with Song starring in their grand final win over the Central Coast Mariners in 2008.

* * *

William Gallas: Perth Glory, 2013-14, 15 games, 1 goal

William Gallas was an outstanding French footballer who played 84 times for the national team including in the 2006 World Cup final. He won the English Premier League title twice with Chelsea, was appointed captain of Arsenal, and is the first and thus far only player to play for all three big London clubs in Chelsea, Arsenal and Tottenham. In season 2013–14 direct from the Premier League, Gallas signed with A-League club Perth Glory, and became the first Frenchman to play in the A-League.

In February 2014, Melbourne Heart had a game scheduled against Perth Glory to be played in Albury, a regional border town between NSW and Victoria about a four-hour drive from Melbourne.

Perth Glory are located in Western Australia and their shortest flight to any away match is over three hours. Add to that a four-hour drive to regional NSW, and you can understand they would be cranky before the game began.

Gallas would be playing this game in the middle of Australia's summer at 3 p.m. where it was scheduled to be 40 degrees Celsius at kick-off. Officials decided to postpone the game to a 5 p.m. kick-off because of the heat, and allocated two drinks breaks per half. A great idea in theory but it was still 39.8C at kick-off and got worse at half-time, reaching 40.8C.

Ben McKay was a journalist at AAP at the time, and he remembers the game well for a number of reasons.

"Gallas did NOT look like he was into it at all. He actually cost them the game. After a lost ball in midfield, Ben Garuccio for Melbourne threaded it through for David Williams. 'Willo' just left Gallas for dead, had an initial shot saved by Danny Vukovic but had enough time to get to the rebound and head home. Gallas attempted a goal line clearance but couldn't get there in time and his momentum took him into the net with the ball. God knows what he was thinking."

Perth were chasing a finals appearance whilst Melbourne Heart were sitting 10th, so a 2–1 loss for Perth was hardly ideal when there was a four-hour return drive to Melbourne Airport to catch the flight back to Perth.

McKay recalls the post-game process for journalists.

"When covering matches like this you usually file something right on the deadline and then wait for players and coaches and write some more. Except for this match Perth Glory coach Kenny Lowe was so steaming he went straight into the press room, sounded off, and then they got the bus running pretty bloody quickly.

"Melbourne Heart coach John van 't Schip followed in the press room and after a couple of little tinkers, I was done. I decided to do more writing when I got home to the air conditioning.

"Normally journos are the last people out of the stadium but today I hot-footed it. I stopped for a bite about halfway to Melbourne at Glenrowan."

Glenrowan is famous as the last stand of notorious bushranger Ned Kelly before he was arrested and subsequently hung. It also houses one of the biggest service centres in Australia. On the side of the Hume Highway they have a petrol station, with toilets, playground and eateries. When McKay pitched up for a bite to eat he couldn't believe it. There was William Gallas and Perth Glory, ordering burgers from Glenrowan Maccas.

After 15 uneventful games with the Glory, only nine of which Gallas completed the full 90 minutes, the 36-year-old Gallas retired, his Perth career a blip on a tremendous resume where his on-field gaffes far outweighed any real highlights.

* * *

Usain Bolt: Central Coast Mariners, 2018-19, 2 games, 2 goals

Usain St Leo Bolt of Jamaica is widely recognised as the greatest sprinter of all time. He has won a staggering eight Olympic gold medals, is the world record holder in the sprint double, and has won consecutive gold medals at three Olympics in both the 100 metres and 200 metres.

In Bolt's 2013 autobiography Faster than Lightning he gave his thoughts of a career after sprinting by writing about a dream switch to football.

If I can't race at the top level by 2016, then I want to turn my hand to another game—football, most probably, because I can play, and with enough effort I can get better. I might even get good enough to earn a pro contract. I know that sounds crazy, but the way I look at it is that a manager should take a chance on a player every now and then. I reckon I could add something special to a team in England.Imagine what I could do with a lot of practice.

It didn't turn out to be England, although the mad Manchester United fan did play in exhibition games there, but Australia gave Bolt the chance to live out his post track and field dreams of playing professional football.

After failed trials in Norway and South Africa, Usain Bolt arrived in 2018 to begin a pre-season in the A-League with Central Coast Mariners.

Player manager Tony Rallis thought the Mariners, one of the few regional professional sports clubs in Australia, was the perfect club to take on Usain Bolt, and he brokered the deal to have him trial.

"I thought Usain Bolt would be a star player. My agenda was the A-League, and what could we do to give the A-League a big boost. And I thought I could do it if we could get Bolt but it wasn't in Australia where we got the big boost. A consulting firm estimated the international coverage in the first two weeks was worth $22 million.

"I was able to prove to the FFA—who incidentally were spending $22m on staff costs—that I didn't need money to promote the A-League. And smack bang in the middle of the AFL and NRL finals we were on the front page, back page and middle page.

"We were on every radio show and every TV show here and around the world. It was about me proving out that we could promote our game without necessarily needing a lot of money. So that was my agenda.

"Bolt's manager was a reluctant participant but it was Bolt who wanted to give it a go as he believed he could be a player. After weeks of toing and froing I said to the FFA,

"We're going to do this with you or without you" and watched the fireworks that came out of it. Of course the FFA were happy to grandstand.

"I respect the Central Coast Mariners for what they did. But if it was Melbourne Victory or the Western Sydney Wanderers trying to commercialise this it would have gone a different way."

Journalist Tom Smithies broke the story with the front-page headline of 'Reggae League' saying that Bolt was coming to Gosford for a pre-season trial in 2018. It was greeted in different ways with most people seeing it was a publicity stunt.

As a football purist, Simon Hill disagreed with the idea.

"I was dead set against it. Nothing against Usain as a bloke, I've been told he's a very nice guy and a fantastic athlete, a world-class athlete but he wasn't a footballer, he never has been. Plus he was 31, he was a foreigner and he wanted big money!"

Shaun Mielekamp was General Manager of Central Coast Mariners at the time and recalls how Bolt made it to the club. He claims it was worth the punt.

"Usain was definitely wanting to focus on his football career and had a real passion for it, had been training and doing a bit with some clubs, and was in Norway for a stint. It was a passion for Usain. If he wanted to be treated like a footballer, then we would give him that opportunity."

A media throng, including many who had never previously covered football, descended on Gosford when Usain Bolt arrived for his first pre-season training session.

Football journalists knew after 15 minutes that Bolt was not going to make it as a professional.

Ray Gatt is a respected football journalist, now retired, and also a Central Coast Mariners member.

"The media attention was fantastic, dozens of cameras and journos there. But you could tell from the start it wasn't going to happen. At 31, he wasn't going to get any better.

"He had his hands on hips early, taking deep breaths. He struggled with his fitness, but his touch was terrible as well."

Bolt soldiered on regardless, staying in the area and working towards securing a contract. The media circus wasn't about to let up when it was revealed that Bolt was to interrupt his training to fly to France to appear in a commercial. Central Coast Mariners' management said they knew this was part of the deal.

Not long after Bolt's return from Europe it was revealed that the Mariners would play two pre-season friendlies against NPL teams. It was not unusual for such teams to play A-League teams in pre-season. However, the difference was that these pre-season friendlies would be televised.

Adam Peacock commentated the first game in front of almost 10,000 fans in Gosford. Central Coast Mariners' average crowd for regular season games is just over 9,000. He remembers it as a fun night out, but he also remembers Bolt's performance.

"That was a carnival atmosphere but he was playing a team of part-timers. He was plainly not up to it."

Wearing the non-traditional football number of 95, a nod to his world record 100 metre sprint time of 9.58 seconds, Bolt came off the bench at the 70th minute mark but failed to make any impact.

The second televised game was when things took somewhat of an awkward turn. The football commentary team was adjusted for this game, with former Australian Olympic sprinter Matt Shirvington added to the coverage to provide special comments, replacing regular football commentators.

The opposition were handpicked for the game and the Mariners were two weeks from the start of their season, so coach Mike Mulvey needed to get his strongest side on the park. He was on a hiding to nothing. He had to play Bolt to appease his club, the crowd and the television network but needed to start his strongest team, which included former Socceroo Tommy Oar, who had played in the 2014 World Cup, as well as former Scottish international, Ross McCormack.

Oar, renowned for his crossing, continued to feed Bolt in the early parts of the game but to no avail as Bolt's heading and football skills couldn't deliver. Then in the 57th minute Ross McCormack provided the pass that would lead to worldwide headlines, as Bolt ran on to the perfect through ball, evaded his opponent and hit it with his left foot across the keeper and into the net.

This made the score 3-0 to the Mariners and gave the crowd and the TV audience exactly what they wanted: an international superstar scoring for a professional football team.

Bolt even celebrated with his trademark lightning pose, complete in his yellow and navy Mariners gear.

In the 68th minute, a calamity of errors by the opposition saw the ball literally fall at Bolt's feet and he walked the goal in, his second and the Mariners fourth.

Bolt was withdrawn at the 75th minute to a standing ovation from the crowd of nearly 6,000 people at Campbelltown's Sports Stadium, with the score finishing at 4-0.

Following on from his trial games, the Mariners realised that they wouldn't be getting much from Bolt on the pitch, but were hoping to capitalise off the pitch so approached FFA for some marketing funds. The FFA were reluctant to dish out cash to a player that wasn't going to provide for the competition on the field. The Mariners didn't have much to play with, but still offered Usain Bolt a professional contract of $100,000 for the season. At the same time, a club in Malta also offered Bolt a contract to play with them in Europe.

For a guy who is used to earning millions of dollars a year, the six-figure offer wasn't enough, and his dreams to be a professional footballer faded very quickly.

Simon Hill reflects. "Did he actually want to be a footballer or did he just want money and publicity? You could argue it cost Mike Mulvey his job, I don't think it helped, it was a complete circus.

"I think the Mariners were genuinely trying to drum up some good publicity for themselves and for the league, but it underlined that mainstream media in this country see our league as a bit of a joke."

The image of Bolt striking a lightning pose in a Mariners jersey will be remembered for a long time in Australian football, Mielekamp telling me that there is a unique piece of sporting memorabilia somewhere out there.

"He never did give us the jersey back. He kept it, so I am sure it's special for him."

Despite the best intentions of the Central Coast Mariners, they finished the 2018/19 season in last place and coach Mike Mulvey was sacked prior to the season's end.

Part 2 :
Clubs Whose Identities Were Powered By Guest Stars

St George-Budapest the Original Bling FC

Francis Lee: 1976, 2 games, 0 goals

Charlie George: 1977, 6 games, 1 goal

Ray Clemence: 1978, 2 games, 0 goals

Ralph Coates: 1978, 11 games, 3 goals

Ted MacDougall: 1982, 9 games, 2 goals

Ossie Ardiles: 1985, 1 game, 0 goals

Decades before Sydney FC was given the moniker of 'Bling FC' in the A-League, there was a club in Sydney called Budapest, founded by Hungarian immigrants, who were Australia's original Bling FC.

The club was at their peak in the late 1960s and 1970s, NSW champions in 1967, 1971, 1974 and 1975 as well as runners-up in 1962, 1964, 1965, 1969, 1970, 1972 and 1976, before joining the inaugural National Soccer League in 1977.

One of the first international stars of note to play with St George-Budapest was former Celtic, Swindon and Scotland goalkeeper Frank Haffey.

Haffey played 201 games for Celtic between 1958 and 1964 and twice represented Scotland. He played 105 games across five seasons for St George between 1965 and 1969, including the 1967 NSW grand final against APIA. He also played for Hakoah-Sydney and later coached.

St George-Budapest was the first Australian club to have a full-time professional coach in Frank Arok. Former Socceroo Captain and Australian football identity Johnny Warren talks about the appointment in his biography, entitled *Sheilas, Wogs & Poofters*:

Frank had been working as a journalist at the 1966 World Cup in England when he had a chance meeting with Australian soccer writer Andrew Dettre. Frank expressed an interest in Australian soccer and the possibility of coaching out here so when Andrew returned to Australia he mentioned Frank to president of St George, Les Bordacs. Negotiations continued over the next two years until Andrew's then colleague at Soccer World Lou Gautier travelled to the 1968 Olympics in Mexico where Frank was working at the games and passed on the St George contract. The next thing the players knew, we had a new foreign coach, of whom we knew nothing, arriving to take charge of us.

It would be a turning point in Australian football. The combination of Arok with the likes of a visionary such as Johnny Warren shaped St George-Budapest into a powerhouse of Australian football.

Former junior player, club captain and Socceroo George Harris reflected on his time at the club and his formative years with Arok and Warren.

"When Frank Arok arrived, I had been a forward for a while and when he saw that I didn't like people going past me he thought my future may be more suited in defence.

"Frank Arok and Johnny Warren were St George and the reason why they were a success. Johnny pushed the idea of local players and Arok was fabulous too. I mean they mixed them with quality players like Atti Abonyi to the club, but with big local influences like Harry Williams.

"Harry and I came through the juniors together as wingers, and it was Arok who converted us both to full backs.

"I have so much time for Arok, but it was Johnny Warren in a managerial role, and then playing and coaching as well, who made such an impact. It was a fortunate situation for young Australian players to be there at that time, because they got that support at St George."

St George-Budapest have had such an influence on Australian football that, in addition to Arok, three other coaches led the national team at some stage: Joe Vlasits, Raul Blanco and Rale Rasic.

George Harris credits his 48 games with the Socceroos due to Arok and Rasic also being at St George.

St George-Budapest was one of the first Australian clubs to have an overseas tournament win when they toured Japan in 1971. Organised by Andrew Dettre, the tournament involved the Japanese national team, Japan B, and Danish First Division side, Frem. Two wins and a draw earned St George-Budapest the inaugural and only Tokyo International Tournament trophy.

When Pele toured Australia with his Brazillian club side Santos in 1972, it was at the St George-Budapest clubrooms where they turned up to socialise, mingling with the Sydney football elite for a meal at Soccer House after they had played against Australia at the Sydney Cricket Ground.

When Australia qualified for the World Cup for the first time in 1974, eight players in the squad had played or would go on to play for the Hungarian-backed club.

These included Warren, Abonyi, Williams, Adrian Alston, Ernie Campbell, Jack Reilly, Manfred Schaefer and Doug Utjesenovic.

In the very first edition of *Soccer Action* magazine in February 1976, it was announced that George Best would come and play four games for St George-Budapest. Club president Alex Pongrass was in the United Kingdom arranging the details. Best was to arrive for an undisclosed fee, would run clinics and install "professional methods into the club". The move fell through as Best joined the Los Angeles Aztecs in North America.

The spotlight on St George-Budapest as the pinnacle of Australian club football was further showcased through Johnny Warren's media involvement. Thanks to football journalist David Jack, Warren started a column in *The Sun* and he had a weekly guest spot on Channel 7's Today show.

Australia's first major domestic football competition, the NSL, began in 1977 following the Socceroos first appearance at the World Cup three years earlier. St George-Budapest's Alex Pongrass and Les Bordacs, along with Hakoah president and later FFA Chairman, Frank Lowy, were the initiators of the new national competition, starting discussions with other major clubs in 1975.

St George-Budapest were also pioneers of Australian football in the women's game. In a dominant spell from 1971–1977 the St George-Budapest women's team did not lose a game.

A mainstay of the Australian women's team, now known as the Matildas, was Julie Dolan. Dolan is Australian football royalty in much the same way as Johnny Warren. Dolan started her career in the St George-Budapest junior teams. At the age of 14 she travelled to Hong Kong with the NSW team, which unofficially represented Australia at the Asian Cup. She was the Matildas' first-ever captain when they played their first recognised A-international against New Zealand in 1979. Such was Dolan's influence on women's football in Australia that the award for the best player in the Australian domestic competition, the W-League, receives the Julie Dolan Medal.

*　　*　　*

Francis Lee was a famous English forward in the 1960s and 1970s who won league medals with Manchester City and Derby County as well as being capped 27 times for England including at the 1970 World Cup.

Averaging just under a goal every two games, Lee was famous for his ability to win penalties and amazingly in his 1971–72 season with Manchester City, 15 of his 35 goals were from the spot. He also held the record for most goals scored in Manchester derbies until 2012.

At the back end of his playing career in 1976 it was reported that Lee was coming to Australia for some guest appearances. First touted to be coming to the Rale Rasic-coached Marconi for a fee of $1,600, Lee's availability did not correspond with any of their home fixtures. Marconi's request to transfer home games was not met with any enthusiasm by the opposition clubs, so Lee joined St George-Budapest instead.

Lee was rumoured to be on $1,400 per game. According to *Soccer World* the total cost to St George-Budapest, including flights and accommodation for he and his wife, would be close to $7,000.

Former Socceroo and St George-Budapest captain George Harris remembers Lee's time at the club.

"I was there with Franny Lee, I remember him clearly. He was not like some of the other overseas players, he put in 100%. The thing about him was that he wasn't out here for a holiday, he was out here to play."

In his first outing for the club Lee failed to impress in a 1–0 win over Pan-Hellenic.

The hard ground did not help the Englishman with his style of play.

The next game was an away fixture to Newcastle mid-week to tackle local club West Wallsend, with Lee on the team bus. St George won 3–1 but the hard ground saw Lee hurt his hamstring and not have too much of an influence.

As was the custom with a two and-a-half-hour bus trip returning to Sydney from Newcastle, the boys had some beers. Stopping for comfort breaks when required, George Harris tells the story of the trip home.

"When someone needed to go to the toilet, we would just stop and wander into the bush. At one stage, we got back on the bus and it started off down the road, and only then we realised that Franny wasn't on the bus!

"We've got this English international player and the bus has taken off and he's stuck on the side of the road!

"We stopped only to see Franny limping along with his injured hamstring, trying to catch up."

Lee's hamstring injury—perhaps not helped by him limping along the highway—saw an end to his guest stint.

Rasic remembers how Lee handled the money promised to him.

"When he got his wages, he only got half because he was injured. He said to me 'Tell Alex (Pongrass) that I have more money than he has, forget about this cheque.

I'm going home.'"

Lee's post-playing career saw him become a millionaire, first as a horse trainer, then as a manufacturer of toilet paper.

In fact, he had so much money that he bought his former club Manchester City in 1994. Formerly known by City fans as 'Lee Won Pen' for his ability to win penalties, he soon became known as 'Super Fran the bog roll man!'

Despite appointing former England teammate Alan Ball as manager, Lee's ownership of the club was less than successful. The club was relegated after the first season, and Lee resigned as Chairman before City moved to the third tier in 1998.

*   *   *

Charlie George was a teammate of Franny Lee at Derby County when he signed to play a guest stint with St George-Budapest in 1977. George had previously had guest stints in Hong Kong and the USA.

General manager of St George-Budapest Soccer Club Les Bordacs said the club were looking to sign Arsenal's Malcolm MacDonald, but given he was only available for three weeks they went with Charlie George instead.

Rather than Derby County, George is probably more famous for being an Arsenal legend growing up a stone's throw from Highbury. He literally went from a hardcore fan on the terraces to the playing pitch for the Gunners. As a player, there were songs written about him such as 'The Charlie George Calypso' and 'I Wish I Could Play Like Charlie George'. He scored the winner in the FA Cup Final and helped them to the double in 1970–71.

St George-Budapest flew George, his wife and children to Australia. In his autobiography, *Charlie George – My Story*, he raved about the Hungarian goulash.

Five days after arriving in Sydney, FC Zurich in Switzerland made a £400,000 offer to Derby County for George, and he was required to travel to Switzerland. Ultimately, the deal fell through but it meant that George was required to play his first game after three long-haul flights in just over a week.

George played six games for St George-Budapest, only scoring once. Overall, his contribution did not help his team, as they lost twice and drew four times during his six games.

According to George Harris, "Charlie George came out for a paid holiday. His first game that he played for us was at the old sports ground and I remember we hadn't played all that well. The big story in the paper the next day was that the St George players had failed to find Charlie George with the ball and he was starved of possession up front!

"The real story from our point of view was that Charlie didn't want the ball and couldn't be found."

The big game for Charlie George was when he came up against Malcolm MacDonald who was making guest appearances for South Melbourne Hellas.

It was the only game where George scored. Harris believes that Charlie George only put in the effort in this game because of the big match atmosphere, a former Arsenal legend versus a current Arsenal legend.

"We saw a completely different player. Charlie George had a blinder that day and scored! Super Mac scored two goals for South Melbourne. Both of them starred, because of the occasion, the big crowd and the game.

"If you could pick one game that exemplified the benefits of bringing out those players, it was that game, because it was a real spectacle. I can't imagine anyone who went to see it or even played in it, who wasn't glad to be a part of it."

After his stint down under George had guest stints in the USA with Minnesota Kicks and for Hong Kong club Bulova. Returning to England, George joined Southampton before being loaned to Nottingham Forest. He only played four games for Brian Clough's Forest but one of those was the final of the 1979 UEFA Super Cup against Barcelona where he scored the only goal in the home leg.

George has now returned to his beloved Arsenal where he runs stadium and museum tours for the club. Such was George's football at Arsenal he is listed on their website as the ninth greatest Arsenal player of all time.

*   *   *

In 1978 England failed to qualify for the World Cup for the second successive time, which meant that goalkeeper Ray Clemence had time on his hands. He signed with the Australian Broadcasting Corporation as a guest commentator for the World Cup tournament that was played in Argentina.

Originally from Scunthorpe United, Bill Shankly signed Clemence for Liverpool in 1967 where he represented the Reds with distinction in the 1970s, winning the First Division five times.

Joining Clemence in the ABC commentary team to discuss the World Cup were well-known professional sports commentator Norman May and 1974 Socceroos World Cup coach Rale Rasic.

Rasic remembers Clemence as the utmost professional.

It was during Clemence's time in Sydney that St George-Budapest came calling again, arranging for Clemence to feature in two home fixtures as well as running a coaching session at the club.

St George-Budapest were battling that season. They had replaced their manager Ilija Takac after 12 rounds and had recalled 'Uncle' Joe Vlasits to lead the side the week before Clemence's first game in Round 13 of the National Soccer League. Vlasits was Hungarian-born and had previously coached the club in 1962, as well as leading the Socceroos from 1967–69.

It would be in the fourth minute in Clemence's debut game for St George against West Adelaide Hellas when he touched the ball for the first time, picking it up from the back of the net after conceding a penalty in Round 14.

Giving the game some international flavour, the goal was scored by former Greek international Con Kambas.

Kambas came to West Adelaide from Greece in late 1977; the centre back would play for them for a few more seasons as well as their championship year in 1978. West Adelaide teammate, Neil McGachey, remembers the game well.

"As part-time footballers we were fans in the first instance, in those days you could watch Match of the Day and see all these people. The excitement in playing against Ray Clemence was fantastic!"

The match remained 1–0. Clemence didn't have much else to do as St George-Budapest squandered their chances in front of 3,254 people at Barton Park. The match report in *Soccer World* referred to the missed penalty with the headline 'Wrong way Ray!'.

Two games later, St George-Budapest added another high-profile recruit, when Ralph Coates, the Tottenham midfielder with the second most famous comb-over in world football, joined the team.

Coates had previously toured Australia in 1976 with Spurs and was coming to the end of his career. The four-time capped Englishmen played over 200 times for Burnley and when they were relegated in 1971 he joined Tottenham. In 2010 he was voted in the top 50 Tottenham players of all time.

After a troubled start to the season, 'Uncle' Joe Vlatsis and Coates changed the club's fortune. In Coates' 11 games they won seven and drew two, with the winger scoring three goals in the process. Captain George Harris remembers a professional approach from Coates.

"It was always disputed who had the better influence (Ralph or Uncle Joe) as we had been going poorly but we won seven of the next 11 games whilst Ralph Coates was there.

"It turns out Uncle Joe was an amazing inspiration and you didn't want to let him down, and then Coates put everything into every game that he played.

"Coates wasn't one who said a lot, but he showed a lot through his continuous work rate.

"He chased and wanted the ball. That had a marked effect. It showed the boys that they wanted to play."

Coates and Clemence combined for one game together, their second for St George-Budapest when they hosted Adelaide City at Barton Park in Round 17. A crowd of 2,452 saw St George-Budapest come back from a 1–0 deficit to win 2–1.

At 1–1 in the 43rd minute, Adelaide City earned a penalty and Clemence would again be called into action. Taking the penalty for Adelaide City was former Motherwell, Celtic and Scotland striker Dixie Deans. Deans was one of the most high-profile recruits in the National Soccer League having scored more than 150 goals in Scotland.

Clemence would need to be on his toes, but Deans' strike went wide. Coates went off injured early in the second half and it was his replacement Peter Hensman who would score the winner in a 2–1 result for St George-Budapest.

George Harris could not have been more complimentary of Clemence's two-game cameo.

"He was a fantastic person who set the example.

"At St George Stadium there used to be a big southerly that came up in the afternoon. The wind was coming from behind our goals and someone put a cross in. Ray came out and called out 'my ball' . He didn't get within five metres of the ball. Someone had a shot, but luckily one of our players headed it off the line.

"He made such a point of going to thank him.

"As a defender, playing with Ray Clemence was special. He spoke to you all of the time. If you achieved something, like make a tackle or concede a corner and you would go back to your post, he would always acknowledge what you've done. He would say simple things before the game, but you would listen and he would always mention good things as they happened during the game."

Clemence ran a coaching clinic at St George-Budapest on the Sunday after one of his games for the Sydney football community and what impressed Harris the most was the effort that he put into training.

"I remember he started his spiel and started to show a few drills and then said that when he would do them he would be physically sick.

"He did the drills and sure enough, he had to wander off and be sick. It was a real lesson to see someone who had played a lot of international football, who was doing a coaching session, and the effort that he put into training in making himself physically sick. It gave us an idea as players what was required to be successful.

"It is exactly what we wanted at that time in Australia, in becoming more professional.

"Having people like him, Lee and Coates was great. They showed you what was needed for you to be successful at the highest level."

Clemence played over 450 times for Liverpool before heading to Tottenham for another 200 plus games. He represented England 61 times and retired from football in 1988.

After his guest stint with St George-Budapest in the 1978 season, Ralph Coates finished his career with three more seasons in London at Leyton-Orient.

St George-Budapest finished seventh of 14 teams in the 1978 National Soccer League.

*   *   *

Centre forward Ted Macdougall played seven times for Scotland and had an incredible career in England. Famously scoring nine goals in an FA Cup tie, for Bournemouth against Margate in an 11–0 win, he went on to represent other big clubs such as Southampton, Norwich City and Manchester United. He won the English First Division golden boot in 1975–76 with 23 goals for Norwich City.

His Southampton connection with former player John Sydenham saw him sign a two-year deal with Floreat Athena in Perth, Western Australia.

MacDougall had a hard time in Perth. He only scored once from open play for Floreat Athena when his great friend Alan Ball put it on a plate for him. A subsequent falling out with the assistant coach saw MacDougall pack up and head east looking for another opportunity.

He was set to sign with South Melbourne Hellas, then coached by fellow Scotsman Tommy Docherty. However, Hellas had already filled their quota of four overseas players so they couldn't sign him. Frank Arok signed him to play for St George-Budapest instead.

With nine games and two goals at St George-Budapest, MacDougall formed a potent front three with veteran Dez Marton and cheeky youngster Robbie Slater as St George-Budapest made the grand final and defeated Sydney City 3–1. But it was off the pitch that he made the biggest impact on the young and impressionable Slater.

"Ted MacDougall changed my life. I was a kid, I was still in school. He was this flamboyant guy with a great CV, Rangers and a Scottish international. He had the hair, which at the time was all the go, the curly sort of mullet.

"Why I say he changed my life, well he was actually bought to replace me. I was only 17, so they wanted me to play off the bench but that only happened for a few games, and then it was me and Ted starting and firing on all cylinders from memory.

"He grabbed me and said 'What is this haircut you've got?'. I had the old bowl cut as a spotty 17-year-old kid. So he made me change my hair, got me new clothes. He kind of made me his apprentice in lifestyle.

"I still remember him showing me shirts and taking me shopping and to the hairdressers to change my hair, which was then changed forever. He did have a big impact on me."

Apparently Arok wanted MacDougall back for the following season, but it didn't happen. Slater thinks he had achieved all he could in the National Soccer League. "His mission was accomplished, buying me gear and getting my haircut."

*   *   *

In 1985 Tottenham Hotspur toured Australia again, and St George-Budapest went to work, trying to find a suitable Spurs player to guest with their team. They hinted as such in their own publication *Soccer House Journal* with the following snippet:

When St George play Marconi on June 10th they could easily have in their line-up one of the biggest names in world soccer. The Club's officials are doing everything to sign one of the most illustrious names in British Soccer for four to five games.

Because Tottenham is one of the visiting teams, it is not hard to speculate on names and one would expect one of the next four names - Chidise, the Ethiopian star winger; Crooks the outstanding centre forward; Hoddle – one of the most skilful but unrecognised English geniuses; or Ardiles.

Any of those players, especially the last two would be a bonus for our spectators, and all the soccer lovers in Australia. That game will be on Monday 10th June.

So it was that the Argentine Osvaldo Ardiles lined up for St George-Budapest for one game in 1985. Also in that St George-Budapest side was Robbie Slater.

"He was class. I do remember being a little bit in awe of him, but what a lovely man."

Ardiles was part of Argentina's 1978 winning World Cup Squad. Following the tournament, Ardiles and fellow Argentine Ricardo Villa moved to England to join Tottenham Hotspur.

Ardiles and Villa have been recognised as trailblazers; they were one of the first few non-British or non-Irish players to move to England and have an impact. They helped Tottenham win the 100th FA Cup in their third season, Villa scoring twice in a 3–2 win over Manchester City in 1980–81.

When England and Argentina were at war in the Falkland Islands, Ardiles deemed it too difficult to play in England and chose to be loaned out to Paris-St Germain for the 1982–83 season. Ardiles returned to Tottenham and helped them win the 1983–84 UEFA Cup.

But in 1985 the presence of the Argentine didn't help St George as 4,380 people watched them go down 1–0 to Marconi-Fairfield.

After his playing career, Ardiles moved into management. His career started in England with Swindon Town in 1989. He eventually took over his beloved Tottenham in 1993–94 before coaching in Mexico, Japan, Croatia, Syria, Argentina, Israel and Paraguay. He was inducted into the Tottenham Hotspur Hall of Fame in 2008.

*   *   *

St George won the NSL Grand Final in 1987 and made the semi-finals again in 1989. The club's last season in the NSL was 1990–91. They were omitted due to the NSL's restructure, when they reduced the number of Sydney and Melbourne-based clubs.

They have had mixed success since, combining some local success with lean times, but they have never been lower than the NSW second tier.

In 1997 the club made the decision to close down their famous social club Soccer House. Speaking to Michael Cockerill in the *Sydney Morning Herald* after that decision, president Alex Pongrass made it clear it was a commercial decision.

The links between soccer and the migrant Hungarian community were diminishing as well. As Pongrass told Cockerill,

"The people who started it all are either old or dead. The second-generation Hungarians are not involved. One can only try to maintain the traditions. But what can you do when no one is interested?"

Venture Capital: Canberra City's Search for Name Recognition

Adrian Alston: 1977, 9 games, 3 goals
Peter Marinello: 1978, 11 games, 1 goal
Ian Callaghan: 1979, 9 games, 0 goals

When the NSL was conceived and implemented in 1977, it was intended as an invite-only collective of the biggest and best supported clubs (on the eastern seaboard) in Australia. But while the NSL was in its infancy one club stood out as different: Canberra City.

Canberra City was one of the first clubs established to appeal to a broad cross-section of the community. It represented the demographic reality of Australian football fans: passionately diverse. If you were in the nation's capital and liked the round ball, this was your team.

Former Socceroo captain Johnny Warren was the coach and Aboriginal activist Charlie Perkins, a renowned former player in his own right in Adelaide and Sydney, was the vice president. Perkins brought a rich pedigree in both administration, as a key and public figure within the Department of Aboriginal Affairs, and football.

The city itself would produce Ned Zelic, Josip Simunic, Andy Bernal and Tom Rogic (to name a few), some of the finest players ever to kick their first ball in Australia. But producing international superstars seemed light years away for the Canberra City Soccer Club of the late 1970s.

To kick-start an identity, Canberra City invited Australia's 'Mr Football', Johnny Warren, to be its inaugural manager.

But the start wasn't quite the success the football-keen city had hoped for. In Warren's autobiography he writes about the club's beguiling early culture of enthusiasm and naivety.

Everywhere I went people were excited about getting into the national competition and making a real go of it … there was a real buzz about the place.

But while everyone was so positive in Canberra there was one big problem … there was simply no money.

To help pad out his contract Warren was also given the role as the technical director for the Australian Capital Territory.

Halfway through the 1977 season the real threat of relegation hung over Warren's Canberra City. With only two wins and five draws in their first 17 rounds, Warren had sent out an SOS to his old Socceroos teammate Adrian 'Noddy' Alston who was playing in the lucrative North American Soccer League.

The English-born Alston played a starring role in the 1974 World Cup under Rale Rasic. Alston famously performed an evasive manoeuvre whilst in possession against East Germany. This skilful move was five days before The Netherlands Johan Cruyff did the exact same thing against Sweden in what is now incorrectly referred to as the 'Cruyff-turn'. According to Alston, Cruyff was doing his homework.

"I tell you he was in his hotel room watching that, five days before, I know he did. He was working on it for five days and then he did the famous one."

Alston's performances at that World Cup attracted the attention of German clubs Hertha Berlin, Hamburg and Eintracht Frankfurt, but Alston returned to England where he joined Luton Town for a season. Despite the Hatters getting relegated that season Alston was the joint leading goalscorer with eight. He then joined Welsh club Cardiff City, winning the Welsh Cup with them in 1976. Following on from here the lucrative North American Soccer League came calling and Alston joined the Tampa Bay Rowdies.

In 1977 Canberra City and the Australian Soccer Federation arranged with Tampa Bay for Alston to return to Australia on a 10-game guest stint. The ruling that guest players were not to arrive after a certain date that year was waived by the league as they saw it as an opportunity to have Alston available for the World Cup Qualifiers for the 1978 World Cup. Alston saw it as a favour for the coach and his great mate Johnny Warren.

"Johnny and I being as close as we were, he was coaching the Canberra team who had a very young side with Danny Moulis and Stevie Hogg.

"It was difficult times and the bottom team got relegated, so it was important that Canberra stayed in there. They were struggling a little bit. Johnny Warren asked me to do that, which I did. I had to sacrifice my wage at the club and Johnny was trying to get enough to pay me back from a couple of newspaper articles that he asked me to do and stuff like that."

Danny Moulis was the youngest player on the pitch at only 16 years of age in the inaugural NSL game between Canberra City and West Adelaide, played at Manuka Oval. Moulis is perhaps better known today as a football administrator, including holding board positions with the FFA after kicking on with a law career after football. He remembers Alston joining Canberra City, and the natural ability he had.

"He was a superstar who really thrilled the crowds and the fans loved him. A tall, lanky forward who was good in the air. Fast feet, really fast feet. In a small area he could move really quickly, turn well and shoot well."

Alston played 10 games for Canberra City and scored three goals. Despite his obvious influence on the field that season, it was some of his personality traits and support as a teammate that Moulis reflected on.

"He was a fantastic influence on me, friendly, helpful and encouraging. In fact he was in the same mould of Johnny Warren, always encouraging us and protecting us from the harder opposition players.

"He was always supporting the younger players in the team, he would always have a kind word. If things were not going well, he would always come over and encourage you or be quick with a joke."

For Alston and Warren, their main job in those last 10 games of 1977 was to avoid relegation. A key Round 21 match away to Brisbane City at Perry Park saw Warren make a special offer to Alston and their goalkeeper Ron Tilsed. Tilsed was an ex-England youth international who was on the books at Arsenal and played senior football at Portsmouth.

"Johnny said to me and Ron, if you win this game boys, we will stay in Brisbane and have a weekend away and I'll pay for everything for you two."

This was quite the incentive for two renowned social animals. It turned into the Tilsed-and-Alston show when they conjured up a late winner to take the game 1–0. Alston tells the story.

"It was the 85th minute, Tilly got the ball, kicked a half volley over the stoppers head, I took off, went round the keeper, slipped it in and I ran straight off the pitch into the shower."

That win over the mid-table Brisbane City certainly helped Canberra City with valuable late-season points and Warren's wallet took a beating as Tilsed and Alston enjoyed the spoils in the sunshine state.

A further win and two draws, including against the table-topping Sydney City, was enough to ensure Canberra City avoided the wooden spoon. So much so that in the final game of the season when they took on bottom side Mooroolbark, they knew they wouldn't finish last and were able to take their foot off the pedal. They may have been relaxed too much as they were flogged 4–1. Alston's job at Canberra City was a success.

"Excellent times at Canberra, I came for one reason to help Johnny out (avoid relegation) and I was more than happy to do that."

Alston wasn't selected for the Socceroos in those qualifiers, but his short-term influence on the young players at Canberra City shouldn't be underestimated. Alston reckons his availability was an afterthought and the Socceroos coach Jim Shoulder didn't know who he was.

"There was no chance, they couldn't afford to bring me back and accommodate me and provide airfares.

"There were no finances (for the Socceroos) to bring people, fly them around the world and accommodate them in those days. They couldn't afford to bring me back really.

"Johnny Warren was the complete instigator of my return.

"By the time I returned the Socceroos had played five games. I watched them play one of the games, from the stands as I wasn't in the squad.

"All I remember is they had players of the calibre of Jack Reilly, Jimmy Rooney and Atti Abonyi on the bench and I was thinking 'what the fuck is going on?'

"Our best players are on the bench!"

After the highs of 1974 the Socceroos failed to make the 1978 World Cup, and wouldn't qualify again until 2006.

Alston was the first Socceroo to return from overseas to our national domestic league, but he certainly wasn't the last. Socceroos finishing their careers back in Australia would become a feature of the National Soccer League and A-League for many years to come.

* * *

Peter Marinello was known as the Scottish George Best, a label that would haunt him for most of his football career. The Edinburgh boy burst onto the scene as a teenager in the late 1960s, the slight winger impressing enough in his first 45 games for Hibernian to earn a call up to a Scotland squad that would include Frances Burns. Burns, of Manchester United, Southampton and Preston North End fame would later emigrate to Australia and form part of the Western Australian football scene as a coach in the 1980s.

Still shy of his 20th birthday, Marinello's stellar form in Scotland earned him a £100,000 move to Arsenal in 1970. This represented the largest fee that Arsenal had paid for any player and their first-ever six-figure signing. The Hollywood-style script for Marinello continued when he scored on debut against Manchester United at Old Trafford in a 2–2 draw.

The sky was the limit for Marinello and the London lifestyle and fame was ready and waiting for the Scottish George Best. Marinello appeared as a guest host on *Top of the Pops*, wrote pop reviews in *Melody Maker*, was into fashion wearing all the right clothes, visiting the hottest clubs and discotheques, theatres, the West End, Soho, he wrote a column for the *Daily Express*, had modelling and advertising contracts and was even offered a recording deal, something that fell over when it was apparent that he couldn't sing! All of this coupled with Marinello's penchant for a drink didn't help him translate this potential to the pitch.

Marinello was touted to join the likes of Charlie George and Eddie Kelly as the young guns on the rise, but he only managed three games in Arsenal's 1970–71 double-winning campaign. Injury cruelling the start of his career, a combination of injuries, drinking and the London lifestyle led to Marinello transferring to Portsmouth after only 51 games in three seasons with the Gunners.

At Portsmouth Marinello would rejoin ex-Arsenal teammate Ron Tilsed, a central figure in getting Marinello to Australia later in his career. Another combination of squandered potential and a heavy drinking lifestyle saw Marinello return to Scotland after 95 unfulfilled games with Pompey to run the wing at Motherwell.

Australian football doyen Johnny Warren brought goalkeeper Ron Tilsed to Australia and in 1977 when the NSL commenced, Tilsed was in goals for Canberra City in the first-ever National League game.

Tilsed's relationship with Marinello would see Motherwell loan him to Canberra City for a guest stint in 1978. Marinello was keen to come to Australia as his wife's family had immigrated here. He and his young family stayed on the top two floors of Johnny Warren's four-storey hilltop home as he joined Canberra City as a sponsored player.

With airline Qantas paying to fly him and his family over and Avis paying his wages and accommodation, the Marinello family viewed it as a paid holiday, Marinello just needing to help out Warren with some school football clinics.

Three weeks after playing Rangers in front of 40,000 at Ibrox, Marinello was lining up against Marconi in front of 8,000 at Bruce Stadium in Canberra. Former Socceroo Danny Moulis was a teammate at Canberra City and remembers Marinello's first game against Marconi.

"It was the first year that we moved to Bruce Stadium, which the British players thought was such a lark, as did I.

"Monty Python was very popular in those days and the Bruce skit with all the Australians called Bruce, and here they were in Australia playing at Bruce Stadium."

Socceroo Ray Richards was playing for Marconi and Moulis remembers his response to the wiry Scot.

"Marinello ran Ray Richards ragged. Ray started kicking him and the crowd didn't take too kindly to it and gave him the bird. Ray then abused the crowd.

"It was very unlike Ray Richards, he then wrote a letter of apology to Canberra City which was published in the next home program for Canberra City.

"I have never seen Ray so flustered."

In Marinello's 2007 book *Fallen Idle* he says that Qantas gave them open-ended tickets to return from interstate games, which meant sometimes it would be as late as a Tuesday when they returned from a weekend game, especially if the opposition clubs in Adelaide, Brisbane, Melbourne or Sydney offered great hospitality. Having Ron Tilsed as a drinking partner obviously spurred him on.

Marinello ended up scoring once in his eleventh and final game for Canberra City before returning to Motherwell. Although Marinello likened the Australian standard to the English Third Division, Moulis remembers a real talent that was on display for Canberra City.

"He came out here and was such a great player individually.

"He was mesmerising on the ball. He was fast, he would pop up on the right wing, he would pop up on the left wing, even though he didn't have a lot of stamina he worked pretty hard. He even came off in a few games when he couldn't go anymore.

"He was slightly built, he was a bit injury prone and he'd get cleaned up by these big defenders. You can imagine what Peter Wilson would do.

"He didn't come inside as much as you might have hoped. Because he was such a famous forward from the UK, people thought he was going to be good and he was going to score goals for us, well that assumption was incorrect. He didn't see himself as playing inside the box, he did see himself as an out and out winger where he had room, where he could run at players, where he could get crosses in."

He would end up finishing his career in 1984, adding Fulham, Heart of Midlothian, Phoenix (USA) and Partick Thistle to his playing resume.

*   *   *

After two seasons Canberra had finished second bottom on the table twice and Warren vacated the job by mutual consent. The crowd numbers were reasonable by NSL standard, but the output wasn't there and the squad mix of British expats and young locals wasn't working.

By 1979 the club needed something—anything—to correct the ship. Star player Tony Henderson had split and joined Marconi. Warren was gone, but Argentine import Vic Fernandez, who had played with Warren throughout the 1960s and been his assistant, was offered the top job. The young team was a year older, sprinkled with experienced heads and the odd expat like Jimmy Cant (Hearts), Roy Stark (Aston Villa), Isaac Farrell (Motherwell), and John Brown who had been on the books with Hearts and St Mirren before bouncing from South Africa to Canberra.

Along with young Danny Moulis at right back, they had striker Terry Byrne who was 20 in 1979 and was an up-and-comer having put in nine goals the previous season. John Davies, born in Liverpool but raised Canberra, was also a key figure in Canberra's midfield.

But the fledgling club needed something more. With a pretty raw squad, Canberra needed a player who could lead on the pitch and not just off it, and they got that in Liverpool club legend Ian Callaghan.

'Cally' played at Liverpool for 18 years, appearing in a club record 857 games (640 in the league), over 120 more than the second player on the list, Jamie Carragher. From 1959 to 1978 Callaghan helped steer the Reds back into the First Division (inconceivably today they were relegated in 1953/54), drove the side on into the title in 1963/64 (the club's first in nearly 20 years), an FA Cup the following year, and another First Division crown the year after that. He would win another title and FA Cup under iconic manager Bill Shankly, and a UEFA Cup in 1972/73.

Under Shankly's ward Bob Paisley he won two more First Division titles, was player of the season in 1973/74 and won two European Cups, being selected on the bench for the 1977/78 final victory over Club Brugge at Wembley.

Callaghan was a World Cup winner in 1966, playing the full 90 minutes in England's final group game against France. He wasn't used in any of the other matches, but received his Winners medal when FIFA moved to include squad members among the medal recipients in 2009.

At the end of the 1977/78 season, at the age of 36 Callaghan took a call from Liverpool teammate John Toshack who had just taken the job as player-manager of Swansea City.

Swansea had just been promoted to Division Three, and with Callaghan in midfield—who was still actually training with the Liverpool first team—they were promoted and then promoted again into the First Division in 1981/82.

It was a fairy-tale rise that allowed Callaghan to continue his career into a venerable age. Swansea City also opened up other exciting new options for Callaghan: guest contracts. He had given his life to football and had earned the right to travel, see the world, and maybe pick up some extra money doing what came naturally to him.

His first tour of duty was with Fort Lauderdale in 1978. He took the contract to play over the English off season with the blessing of Paisley and Toshack while his transfer to Swansea was being worked out. He played in Florida for five months with Gordon Banks in goal while sharing a place with George Best. It was peak NASL: exotic locations, superstar players who had just crested their peaks but were still capable of magic and real money on the table.

Next up was the surrounds of Lake Burley Griffin. Callaghan signed with Canberra City on a guest contract for 1979.

Callaghan was walking into a club with some raw talent but in desperate need of someone to pull them together. And if Australia's Mr Football couldn't do it, then perhaps Liverpool's could.

The Canberra press were immediately onto the Callaghan story, announcing his arrival in May with a quote from Charlie Perkins, who by 1979 was the club president, defining him as "One of the major signings in Australian soccer", and that his "vast experience will obviously be of great benefit to our young side".

The logic of signing Callaghan to a guest contract was infallible and would be repeated multiple times with Keegan, Rush, Beardsley and Fowler. Add a Liverpool legend into the mix and more eyeballs than ever before will turn to the club, and if a bit of First Division magic rubbed off on the youngsters—like John Davies—then more is the better.

However, Callaghan didn't sign the normal run-of-the-mill guest contact. In multiple reports Callaghan was said to have signed a two-year deal.

Indeed on Callaghan's arrival he told reporters he would be with the club for "two years at the least". The deal was most likely a one-year-plus-one deal, which *Soccer Action* described as a try-before-you-buy deal and that Callaghan was "interested in settling in Australia and will make his mind up after his stay with Canberra".

Club president Charlie Perkins told the press that Dunlop Footwear was involved by underwriting the deal. While in Australia Callaghan was to promote the new Liverpool boot, which had been designed by Bobby Charlton, and which would be adopted en masse in the 1980 NSL season and also by the Socceroos. John Kosmina, who was with West Adelaide in 1979 and on the cusp of becoming one of the NSL's biggest stars, was already wearing the boot.

Callaghan's first taste of capital football was in a home NSL Cup Quarter Final against fellow NSL club Footscray JUST. Callaghan arrived in the city three days earlier, and suiting up was the best PR move Callaghan could make to validate his positioning as a tough, uncompromising elite pro.

"For a man who has travelled about 20,000 km to play for City and whose formidable reputation would have excused a touch of the prima donna syndrome —or at least a certain irritability after battling jet lag—Callaghan showed the tough-minded dedication and sportsmanship for which the English fans love him," wrote one journalist.

Vic Fernandez, after a mere amuse-bouche of Callaghan at training, described his marquee as "beautiful … fit, keen and he's got a great shot".

Callaghan's debut did not disappoint. Canberra walloped Footscray 4–1, turning around a 3–0 league loss to the team from Melbourne a month earlier. In a match report, Callaghan was lauded for his link play alongside young tearaway Johnny Davies. "Certainly his presence lifted each and every one of Canberra's players. It was a great team victory."

Fernandez, on multiple levels, was rapt to have Callaghan in his side. As a player Fernandez had been a short, hard-working midfielder with a deft and wide range of passes. To have Callaghan in the side was almost like selecting a younger, but more highly credentialed version of himself. Fernandez was only in his early 40s and immediately struck up a great professional relationship with Callaghan.

Callaghan's combination with Davies in central midfield would also characterise his performances for Canberra. Danny Moulis remembers their combination of work rate and finesse. "For a guy that age he was really tough and he was quick. He'd intercept the ball regularly. He'd distribute well. He'd win the ball and distribute and then he'd do it again! He had a really good relationship with Johnny Davies. They sort of played off each other. Johnny Davies was probably not as robust, but equally if not more skilful on the ball, and Cally was the hard working, direct, hardman in midfield."

After that win Canberra's marketing team went into overdrive putting together a number of social appearances with Callaghan.

Off the field Callaghan was agreeable to appearances for the club, but they must have been hard work for him. Famously humble to the point of shyness, Callaghan didn't do a lot of social mixing with his mostly younger teammates. He was a quiet presence in the rooms, mixing occasionally with the older players in the squad and Fernandez, but in keeping with the professional standards he set on the field and at training.

"He was a pretty private guy," Moulis recalls. "He just had a sole focus on his performance on the field. He was a team player because he was a team player on the field. But he was a quiet player. He just went about his business."

Callaghan's League debut was away at Rale Rasic's Adelaide City, featuring the mercurial former Celtic striker Dixie Deans. The match ended in a 1–1 draw after a goal to Moulis for Canberra and 16-year-old substitute, Charlie Villani, for Adelaide City.

Callaghan's first home game arrived the following week, when 7,510 fans crammed

Bruce Stadium (then half of its capacity) to watch Callaghan face Brisbane Lions. It was the season's biggest crowd and only agonisingly short of the 8,000 record set the previous season.

It wasn't only the numbers that were big. In attendance and drawn in by the Canberra City marketing machine was the then Governor General Sir Zelman Cowen. While they weren't present at the game Prime Minister Malcolm Fraser and Opposition Leader Bill Hayden (a Queenslander) got in on the act too, sending 'telegrams of congratulations' to their respective sides.

The PR around Callaghan's arrival was quickly eroded. "Sparkle, but not on the field" was the assessment of match reporter Peter Windsor—a club employee—which turned out to be the most generous line in his report.

"Frankly, it was an abominable display—by far Canberra's worst of the season! And ominously, it was at a similar stage last year that Canberra began to tumble down the table."

It was a stark and prophetic assessment from a man normally motivated to put a brave face on the club. Canberra couldn't break Brisbane's rear guard defence, lacking the spark to do so, and gave up a winner to Brisbane in the 87th minute. It ended 2–1, with Callaghan spinning plates all across the midfield.

Round thirteen was away against powerhouse Sydney City, and another 2–1 loss, this time conceding a 40th minute lead. Round 14 was back at Bruce Stadium and another choke, this time against a paltry 3,220 fans, as Canberra gave up an 83rd minute equaliser to St George to draw 1–1.

Since his scintillating arrival in the Cup, Callaghan's Canberra had taken just one point in four games and could have had seven (when a win was worth two points). Something wasn't working, and they were running out of games.

At an official welcome luncheon put on by sponsor Dunlop Footwear at their factory in Blacktown, Sydney, Callaghan was obtuse with his answers to journalists' questions at times. When asked if he intended to play on, he said "I was going to give it up. But I still enjoy playing and feel that I could play another season or two."

Question: "Will you play till the end of the season with Canberra City?"

Callaghan: "I am not contracted to anyone, so I see no reason to return to England at an earlier date. I have a small business, an insurance broker's firm, but my partner is doing fairly well on his own at the moment so I can stay and enjoy my game. My family is quite happy, which adds to our present mood to stay for as long as possible."

So was it 10 games? The rest of the year? An option for a second? Callaghan was running around the Australian football media like they were German opposition in Europe in the early 1970s.

What did Callaghan make of the quality of football in the NSL? "It is a fraction slower than in England, which gives me that extra inch in which to turn or pass, but it is far more skilful than I had expected."

He didn't have long to wait for an opportunity to bathe in the local skill level. The next match was at home to South Melbourne, who were having an uncharacteristically poor season. It was a massive chance for Canberra, who just could not close out games and keep out goals. Vic Fernandez was at a loss and was willing to try things, so he played his wildcard. Callaghan was to play up front against the Greek boys from Melbourne.

"I'm willing to try anything," Fernandez told the press. "He's got a great shot and with his experience I'm sure he'll play well up front."

Callaghan's positional change came with a change of formation. The 4–4–2 was out, and replaced with a 4–3–3 with Callaghan being partnered by the in-form Terry Byrne and a 21-year-old Scot who had recently made Australia his home after trying his luck in the US. He was Donald Maclaren, father of modern-day Socceroo Jamie.

South Melbourne arrived at Bruce Stadium featuring star striker and former Liverpool teammate of Callaghan's Alun Evans, whom Hellas had signed for $15,000 from Walsall in 1978.

Fernandez wanted goals, and goals are what he got. A dwindling crowd of 2,225 saw Canberra City reverse their form and come back from 2–1 down to win 3–2. The goals all came from Callaghan's new offsiders Byrne (two) and Maclaren, cancelling out an early Evans goal in the second half that put South Melbourne in front.

A week later Canberra travelled to Footscray, who Callaghan had helped slay in the Cup, and also reversed a one goal deficit to win 2–1 with goals from both Maclaren and Byrne in the second half.

Whatever the Callaghan front three was doing, it was clearly working—but it wouldn't last. The following weekend on the road to West Adelaide, Canberra lost 2–0. A home goalless draw against Brisbane City in front of 3,378 followed and the sudden burst of inspiration seemed to have dried up.

Then, unexpectedly, Callaghan announced he was going home. His ninth league game, the rearranged Round 15 game midweek against Marconi, would be his last for the club, a 1–1 draw.

A 19-year-old Eddie Krncevic in his first NSL season plundered an 83rd minute equaliser after Terry Byrne had opened for Canberra.

The announcement that Callaghan was leaving came as a surprise to many who believed that he would play out the NSL season.

President Charles Perkins outlined the reasons why the Liverpool legend would be heading home. "Ian asked the club for permission to return to England in order to straighten out private business commitments. As Canberra City now seems out of contention for a final four position, the Board has decided to allow Ian to return to England."

It was a remarkably amiable decision for the club to make about their star import. While any hopes of a high finish were indeed dashed—the club ultimately finished third bottom that season—to let their star asset slip through their fingers seems benevolent to a fault.

In hindsight the club likely weighed up a couple of options and decided letting him go was actually in their best interests. Callaghan had agreed to help broker a partnership between Liverpool FC and Canberra City. The first manifestation of this would be Vic Fernandez visiting Anfield when the 1979 season was over to study coaching and training methods, which he did and also caught up with his new friend Callaghan while he was there. Callaghan also agreed to act as a scout for Canberra City while he was back in the UK.

Outside of his debut, Callaghan wasn't pulling huge crowds for the club and they didn't really have the players around him, or the set-up, to get the most of his abilities in 1979. Canberra football journalist Herb Hild described Callaghan's performances as "moments of individual brilliance which at times seemed to put into an unfavourable perspective the ability of many PSL [Phillips National Soccer League] players in general".

Most of all, Canberra City were motivated to accept Callaghan's return to England because they thought he'd be back for the 1980 season. Perkins told reporters when his exit was announced: "He will be coming back to Canberra to complete the remainder of his two-year contract. The club has been most impressed with Ian's attitude to the playing and promotion of soccer and looks forward to his return next season."

The problem was Callaghan didn't return. He played the 1979/80 season with Toshack at Swansea City in the Second Division, broke Bobby Charlton's FA Cup appearance record, then didn't appear at all in 1980/81. He played a handful of games in 1981 in Ireland with Cork City and then at Crewe Alexandra when, by his own admission, he was "finished".

For Canberra City in 1979 he was a star who shone too brightly—too brightly for his teammates to fully handle—and then burnt out never to return.

With Callaghan in the League they won three, lost three and drew three. A very median outcome, but they also threw countless points away late in matches.

After the 1979 season was over Vic Fernandez wrote candidly about his side in

Canberra City's Annual Report, listing everything that had gone wrong.

Harry Williams was injured. Roy Stark and Jim Cant didn't fit his team—physically or tactically—and Stark ultimately became a distraction and was expelled from the first team. Many other players weren't fit enough for his system and he had not been consulted on transfers.

Sensationally, he names Ian Callaghan as an example. Ian was a great player, Fernandez is quick to add, but then adds, "When Ian arrived I found out that he was not the player I had been told he was." Quite remarkably, Fernandez was led to believe Callaghan was a striker, and had to move too many pieces around to accommodate another midfielder. In fact he played Callaghan up front for a while because he had developed plans for boom-recruit Callaghan the striker. "He did not want to play up front, but later agreed to do that for me, mainly because everyone thought that he was a goalscorer."

It seems absurd that either Fernandez, or the coach and backroom staff didn't know who they were getting when they signed Callaghan. His reputation preceded him: there were 640 Liverpool games worth of data to figure it out.

"His individual performance was good, but his team performance was not because we could not blend in with him in such a short time," regrets Fernandez about the man he had struck up a personal friendship with. Fernandez didn't throw all the blame on the club's decline on the Callaghan signing, but at the time he does cite it as part of the problem.

Moulis, on the other hand, considers Callaghan to have been a stabilising force, and that other factors contributed to the 1979 season's ultimate decline.

"Cally actually fitted into Vic's (high passing high tempo) style well. He had good distribution and sideways vision, and Vic acknowledged that publicly. To be completely truthful, the core squad members—the British players who had been with the club for a while—put up with Vic's intensity for a while, and we got great results. But the style of play didn't stick and the attitude of some players disrupted the team harmony and the implementation of Vic's playing strategy."

So, like a prototypical Marcelo Bielsa, Fernandez's methods demanded a lot from his part-time professional—some of which like Stark and Cant didn't ascribe to the same philosophies—and the performances suffered as the season progressed.

The years that followed suggest that the lack of cohesion within Canberra City was never really overcome. Canberra City's best result in an NSL season was fifth. They lost 45% of all their matches over the years and were nearly always in the bottom half. It was a squad assembled by different coaches, for different styles, for a club that lacked a clear and persistent identity.

In 1986 when the NSL sought guidance on how to remove their conference system and reduce the league from 24 to 14 teams, they sought advice from existing clubs. The option proposed was that expulsion would be based on historical performances. In early 1986 Canberra City voted in favour of this historical points-weighting that would have (and did) certainly relegated them. The Canberra Times called it a "fatal error of judgement".

It was a sad, but somehow inevitable fate for a club that had hosted some living legends in the boardroom, in the dug-out and on the pitch. But no matter what they tried they just could not get out of the bottom half, or build a lasting identity. Signing its own execution papers was an outcome that started from the outset.

Frankston Goes to Hollywood

Martin Peters: 1979, 5 games, 3 goals
Eamonn Bannon: 1979, 4 games, 2 goals
Martin Chivers: 1980, 2 games, 0 goals

Martin Peters, Martin Chivers and Eamonn Bannon are among the finest British footballers in the post-War era.

Between them they won a World Cup, multiple English FA Cups, a Scottish League title, a European Cup Winners Cup, a UEFA Cup and a European Cup semi-final. Between them they have over 100 international caps for England (Peters and Chivers) and Scotland (Bannon). Peters broke the English transfer record, and Bannon the Scottish one.

All three also played in the Victorian State League.

Recruiting three of British football's most illustrious names to play in a State League is one of the most amazing feats of sports management ever achieved in Australia. To put this into context, in the 1979 football season, Ian Callaghan—who appeared once in the 1966 World Cup for England—was playing in the NSL for Canberra City. But Frankston City managed to convince Peters, an essential cog in Alf Ramey's system and who scored in the World Cup Final, to join them and play at the level below.

So how did they manage this? What was in it for Martin Peters? And, perhaps the most compelling head scratcher of all, who the heck were Frankston City?

Frankston, the place, is simultaneously a suburb of Melbourne and the gateway to the Mornington Peninsula, the eastern tip of Port Phillip Bay which has Melbourne at the top and Geelong on the west.

Throughout the years, Frankston has represented accessible housing prices on the edge of beach land, adjacent to wealthy suburbs like Mount Eliza, and a kind of satellite city drawing in the south east of Melbourne. Frankston's sporting teams have tended to try and be a focal point for the entire region. Rich, poor, multi-generational local and recent migrant: Frankston represents a bit of everything and everyone.

It was in this image of Frankston that the football club, Frankston City, was built. It had the guts and gumption to reach for some international stars and then, like many ships dotting the coastline, disappeared from sight forever.

Frankston City had humble beginnings, formed as the 'Heart of Oaks Soccer Club' in 1950, so named after the British Migrant Club in Frankston of that name. Proximity to the Naval base at HMAS Cerberus provided a steady stream of both players and fans. When the Victorian State Federation was formed in 1963, Frankston Town, as they were then known, was admitted into Division Three and changed its name in 1966 when Frankston, the area, achieved City status.

They were catapulted into the Victorian First Division in 1977 after the NSL was formed and South Melbourne, Footscray JUST, Mooroolbark and Fitzroy United joined it. Frankston finished fifth in their inaugural First Division season, and comfortably mid-table in their second season.

Their home, Centenary Park, is more famous today for its adjacent golf course and nearby sculpture park. It had been a garbage dump before the local council allocated Frankston City the site in 1977.

For the first two seasons in Victoria's top flight the club built its social club, sodded its pitch and, effectively, developed from scratch into a pro-ready club.

Frankston City modelled itself as a little piece of the home countries on the Mornington Peninsula. Ex-pats were drawn to the club, and brought all their connections from home to the boardroom.

The club had a clear plan. They represented a regional fanbase, a new stadium and, above all, ambition. From the moment they were promoted into the Victorian top flight, they turned their attention to a coveted spot in the NSL.

In the early NSL, promotion and relegation was decided based on submissions of interest. A team could finish last and be retained in the national competition if their submission was solid: lots of fans, the potential for on-field success, and a good business model. Similarly you could be promoted by the same criteria. It helped if a team from your state was relegated, but the NSL was forever thinking about expansion so interested State League clubs just needed to keep their house in order.

By the end of 1978 the club officially kicked off their official interest in joining the NSL by frequently discussing it in the media. They hadn't won anything, but they had a business plan and a grandstand which put them ahead of a lot of alternatives. The goal was to be considered by the NSL for entry into 1980, and they had one season to prove their worth. You didn't need to finish top to be admitted into the NSL, but it certainly helped your case.

Their problem was, they had a mid-table squad. At the advent of the 1979 season, club secretary Lee Smith admitted they needed a boost, having played "some awful football last season".

"We spent a lot of time on our new ground last season," he said. "And tended to neglect the team. But this season we have signed some very good soccer players."

In 1978 they signed a certain Scottish migrant Ged Bannon from Brunswick Juventus, which turned out to be a PR masterstroke. Ged was joined in 1979 by his brother Vince Bannon, who had been playing with their other brother, Pat, at Fitzroy United in the NSL. Pat was still at Fitzroy (who had just moved to Heidelberg), and built a career there as one of the NSL's toughest defenders. All three Bannons had migrated to Australia after their careers at Hearts (in Edinburgh) never got going. When they moved to Australia they left one of their name behind, the youngest boy of the quartet who showed too much talent on the ball for Hearts to let him go.

Joining the Bannons at Frankston City in 1979 was 27-year-old fullback Tony Young, who had spent the last two and a half seasons with York City. But only three years before, Young was playing at Old Trafford for Tommy Docherty's Manchester United where he appeared 83 times over six seasons.

Frankston picked up a number of other handy Brits and Irishmen willing to make Australia home. They signed Noel Mitten, who had also chosen to emigrate to Australia after a solid career in Ireland with Bohemians after not quite making it as a Manchester United trainee.

But to properly kick-start the project Frankston City needed a lightning rod and one hell of a storm. To be considered for an NSL spot they needed to make a statement. They needed a player that would make the football world (or at least the backrooms of the ASF) and Frankston's mainly Anglophile fans take notice.

That player was Martin Peters.

Peters was one of the darlings of England's triumphant 1966 World Cup. He was 22 at the time, and came from nowhere to become an essential component of the side. Peters had been hidden away by manager Alf Ramsey, along with his winger-less 4–1–3–¬2 formation, until they were both unleashed mid-way through the tournament. Ramsey described Peters as "ten years ahead of his time," and a "modern multifunctional soccer player".

He may have been 10 years ahead of his time, but 13 years later he found himself in a time warp on park grounds across Melbourne.

Frankston City defied all sense of the football order by signing Peters. By February 1979 it was all a done deal, and when Norwich City's (his club at the time) season ended, his Frankston City season could begin.

Frankton Chrysler, Singapore Airlines, Dandenong Tourist Bureau, A home Away and the Eastern Suburbs Building Society, who was Frankton City's major sponsor, all chipped in to make the offer a reality.

Club vice president Del Lines flew to England to personally negotiate with Norwich City, where Peters was playing alongside his old Spurs teammate Martin Chivers. Peters was now 35 and could see the twilight approaching. He was being offered a bit of money and an all-expenses paid trip for him and his family to Melbourne, all during English off season.

The amazing part of the deal just was how they made the connection in the first place. Frankston vice president Del Lines was a "personal friend of Peters", according to reports in Melbourne. But just how did this suburban administrator and owner of Delcor Carpets of Mornington become tight with a World Cup winner?

Before emigrating to Australia, Lines owned a pub outside Upton Park. He knew the West Ham old boys because they all drank in his pub. On his recruiting drive to England he stayed with Frank Lampard (senior) before "popping in" to see former Hammer John Bond, who was manager of Peters at Norwich City.

Lines closed the deal for $8,000 in appearance fees. It was $5,000 from the club ($1,000 a game for five games) and the other $3,000 from sponsors to cover his flights and accommodation. Not sheep stations for England's first £200,000 transfer, but a nice little earner for the boy from Essex.

Not only did Norwich endorse the deal completely without a loan fee, according to Lines it was their idea. "I was in England for a holiday and popped into Norwich. I was telling Peters and club manager John Bond, another former West Ham man, about Frankston City.

"They suggested a big-name Norwich player could play as a guest with Frankston to help the club along. I was thrilled. I had intended to ask the club if something like that could be arranged but I didn't have the nerve!"

Lines pulled other remarkable coups while he was involved with Frankston City, including booking Tommy Docherty to host a sportsman's night in the club rooms. For a time, Del Lines must have been the best connected administrator in Victoria (and possibly the country). All because he had owned a pub opposite Upton Park.

In 1980 while the England team were in Australia to face the Socceroos, Lines flew to Sydney to hang out with Frank Lampard (senior). His rolodex featured a 'who's who' of British football and pulling off the Peters signing showed a level of connectedness that many NSL clubs at the time lacked.

"There are a lot of British migrants in the Frankston area," Lines told *Soccer Action*. "Most would remember Peters as one of the biggest names in English soccer. If we can get a big crowd to watch our home games featuring Peters, the club has a great chance of keeping those people interested and so increase membership."

Lines summed up the gambit perfectly. "If we can't draw a decent crowd with Martin Peters playing, we never will."

The 1979 season opened at the start of April, and buoyed by the Peters' announcement and the new crop of signings, Frankston City shot out of the gate. They led the table after five games, winning them all, scoring 11 goals and conceding three. All this before Peters had even arrived in the country.

Off the pitch, an ugly spat started brewing between the club and the ASF over their marquee man. Lines had done such a fantastic sales job of Australian football that Norwich City were keen to see it for themselves. Lines connected Norwich to the ASF and a club tour at the completion of the First Division season was quickly assembled. Norwich would play state rep teams from across Australia and New Zealand, including Victoria.

But Peters soon became a problem. He was Frankston's player, but the ASF wanted him. What was the point of inviting Norwich to tour if their big drawcard Peters wasn't playing (instead honouring his contract with Frankston)? The ASF had scheduled Norwich's opener against the Victorian state team for May 10. Peters first game for Frankston was set to be their Round six game against Croydon City on May 13.

The ASF's response was a threat to cancel the whole tour. To save face with Norwich, and to not rock the governing body's boat, Frankston begrudgingly agreed to let Peters line up for Norwich, as long as he avoided the long-haul flights to Western Australia, New Zealand and Queensland.

Peters was probably hoping for a relaxing family holiday with a bit of football thrown in. He was now booked to play six games in 14 days, so not only were Frankston City losing the unique selling point of the only place to see Peters live, they were also now losing out Peters' fitness for the tail end of the contract.

Peters ultimately did line up for Norwich against Victoria. With no Frankston players in the Victorian squad, jumped to a two-goal lead in front of 8,000 people at Olympic Park in Melbourne. But it was fool's gold as Justin Fashanu—who liked Australia so much he would return for his own guest stints in Adelaide—would get a goal back in the 77th minute, before Peters himself scored the second and fourth in a 4–2 win. It was a rip-roaring game and few of the fans will have left disappointed—not least because now they could cancel their plans of travelling to Frankston to see Peters in the League.

Frankston could only shrug and move on, and focus on making sure Peters' debut for the club was a raging success. To make this happen they hit the streets. 10,000 pamphlets were dropped in local mail boxes, offering local kids under 16 free entry during Peters' home games.

Football clubs in the region, from Dandenong to Doveton and Baxter, were all given four free tickets, while Peters' signed balls would be given out to kids before the game.

To top it off, a pipe-band would welcome him onto the pitch.

It was a bold and aggressive promotion, and Frankston were betting the existential future of the club on Peters working. "This is probably the biggest promotion taken on by a State League club, and if it doesn't pay off then we may as well go amateur," said Les Smith.

The stakes were massive for Frankston. Pull a big crowd for Peters debut and they could point to a working business model for the ASF. Doing that would take them a long way toward promotion into the NSL. If the Peters promotion flopped then the club would be seen as not fit for the NSL.

Their prayers were answered in front of 2,500 home fans as Frankston City and Martin Peters brushed aside Croydon City, 4–0. Frankston officials were thrilled with the outcome. It was an exponential uplift on their usual crowd numbers, which before Peters were reported in hundreds.

Peters, on debut, had a muted game—he was "shadowed" by Croydon City's "rugged midfield destroyer" Duncan Smith, according to the match report—but did contribute to two of the goals, including an assist for the fourth goal, deftly chipping Croydon's back four for striker Noel Mitten to run on and power home.

After the game, despite the lopsided result, manager Freddie Bunce decried the home side's poor touch while announcing that Peters would take training during the week.

"At first, Martin was a bit apprehensive about taking the training session," said Bunce. "He said he didn't want to tread on my territory. But Frankston may never again have a player of his ability at the club. It's a once-in-a-lifetime experience for us and so we will try and make the most of (it)."

During the days Peters was also running training of another kind, supporting junior soccer clinics in the May School Holidays in both Melbourne and Frankston.

His second match for Frankston was another 'home' match for Frankston against Prahran Slavia, who were asked by the VSF and Frankston to shift the Prahran home game to Centenary Park to help Frankston maximise their investment on Peters.

It was a generous gesture from Slavia to allow Frankston to have the home game. Slavia were a nomadic club and so the move was unlikely to cause a riot among the 10s of regular Slavia fans.

The result, another win to Frankston thanks to a late 1–0 winner from another

English import, Bruce Young, is overshadowed today by who was lining up for Slavia.

It is certain that Martin Peters wouldn't have realised he was facing a future Socceroo captain, but the Frankston crowd (which is not recorded) got a bonus dose of football royalty as 17-year-old Paul Wade ran out for his second-ever start as a senior player.

"Just the fact that I was playing at a ground with a stand around it. It wasn't all the way around it but before then I'd been playing on fields with picket fences, in fact some of them not even fences at all," said Wade on his reflections on that game and facing World Cup legend Martin Peters.

"I was probably too young to realise what a legend he was in world football. I was more focussed on this beautiful stadium. I probably would have been in awe of him if it happened tomorrow. [But it] was as much about my adventure onto this senior stage."

Wade concedes that he was probably so worked up about the game itself, in front of an actual crowd, that everything else skipped his attention.

Like many other debutants, Wade recalls the pace of the game being a step ahead of what he was used to, and that Peters was at the heart of that.

"I remember the speed with which the ball moved. Especially when he got it. It was like 'hang on a minute, I haven't even taken two steps to try and close you down and it's gone'. For him to be at that level it was probably really slow. But for me it was like 'wow, how quickly is he getting rid of this ball?' But it was only in hindsight because he knew what he was going to do with the ball way before he got it."

Peters got on the scoresheet in his third game, a 3–3 home goal fest against St Kilda Hakoah. It was Frankston's first dropped point of the campaign, and Frankston had to come back three times to level the score. Peters scored the second of Frankston's three just after half-time.

Peters' fourth game was away to Preston Makedonia. Preston were a big club in Victoria, with their own stadium, and were eyeing off the same NSL position as Frankston. Both clubs had tabled submissions for promotion into the NSL, and fate was presenting them both with a realistic chance. South Melbourne Hellas were having an uncharacteristically poor NSL season in 1979, and were staring down the barrel of relegation. A Victorian club going down would help Frankston or Preston's chances of promotion enormously.

It was a crucial game for Frankston, against a large and symbolic opponent at their home ground on the other side of Melbourne. The winner would be catapulted ahead in the reckoning for an NSL spot should one open up. To make sure this game went their way, Frankston played their trump card.

Eamonn Bannon was the youngest and most talented of the brothers, and had stayed behind in Edinburgh to forge a career with Hearts when his brothers moved to Australia. Bannon's persistence paid off, and he broke into the Hearts side in 1976. In February 1979, he was sold to Chelsea for £220,000 to help his boyhood club pay off a debt.

Bannon's time at Chelsea was an unhappy one. He'd stepped into the void left when Ray Wilkins joined Manchester United, but overall Chelsea were a poor side that season. Unthinkably Chelsea was relegated at the end of the 1978/79 season. In October 1979, age 21, Bannon was sold to Dundee United for a then Scottish transfer record of £165,000 after he had fallen out of favour with new Chelsea manager Geoff Hurst.

He kissed goodbye to £440 a week at Chelsea to accept £225 from Dundee United. But before then he said hello to Frankston City. It was a three-match deal, with another two as an option. Their sleeper agent signing of older brother Ged Bannon had paid off spectacularly, and enabled his younger, more talented, brother to want to relive the playground as adults.

On 10 June 1979, Chelsea star Eamonn Bannon suited up with two of his three older brothers and Martin Peters, as Frankston City snuck past Preston 1–0.

Bannon landed in Melbourne six hours before kick-off and still put in a 90-minute shift. He was named in Frankston's best players. Peters also comes in for some credit for his "good distribution"—and older brother Vince Bannon, energised by his illustrious brother's arrival, "overshadowed" Preston's striker Gary Ward.

Bannon played a part in Frankston's win. Bannon took a corner in the fifth minute, early enough in the game for the adrenaline to be suppressing his jetlag, and his inswinger was flicked on by Noel Mitten for defender Bob Adams to head home. From there Frankston hung on and secured the win.

Preston manager Tony Vrzina was livid with having two British stars amongst the opponents. "Our soccer must be unhealthy if the champion team [Frankston] wins games by defending for 85 minutes and using rough play," said Vrzina. "Soccer fans will very quickly lose interest if this physical style of soccer is allowed to prosper."

It takes an extremely pragmatic coach to sit back and defend in a game when you have two English First Division players in the starting 11 against Preston Makedonia. With a jet-lagged Eamonn Bannon and a completely worn out 35-year-old Martin Peters on the pitch, parking the bus probably made a lot of sense.

The Bannon deal was a masterstroke by Frankston, and was probably no more complex a task than asking Ged and Vince to put in the call. Bannon had had a rough time at Chelsea, and was eager to spend his off season with family. Why not pick up a game or two, and enjoy playing with his siblings while he was here?

In the next game, Frankston City took on Altona City in a game that should be etched in the annals of Victorian football. Again, both Martin Peters and Eamonn Bannon ran out for Frankston City hoping to continue the club's invincible season, but found themselves 2–0 down after 12 minutes. It looked like being a miserable finale for Peters until Altona keeper, Hans van der Poel, remembered the occasion and fumbled a corner in the 35th minute, allowing Peters to poke the mistake home. It was his second goal for the club, but he wasn't finished repaying Frankston City's investment.

Early in the second half Frankston won two penalties in the space of five minutes, both won by both Peters and Eamonn Bannon as they were hacked down in the box. Bannon converted both to bring the score up to 3–2, before Peters knocked home the fourth after Altona were reduced to 10 men. It was a 4–2 comeback, sparked by both marquees Peters and Bannon, where both stars got a brace. It could not have been a better scripted farewell to Peters, who returned to England after that match to complete his final season with Norwich City.

Before he left, Peters chatted with journalist Peter Desira from Soccer News about the state of football in Victoria. "The main problem is with the youngsters. Victoria has to get the game going through the schools like they have done in the USA so that at the age of 17 or 18 when they leave, the youngsters want to play soccer rather than anything else. The sport must switch from bringing players to bringing top coaches from overseas to organise schoolboys and soccer youth level."

As well as foretelling the next 40 years of debate about youth development in Australia, Peters shared his thoughts about his experiences on the pitch. "I thought the standard might have been better," he said, comparing the standard of the Victorian rep team he faced for Norwich as akin to the English Third or Fourth division. And the State League he was playing in was closer to non-league football in both skill and experience. "I was warned beforehand that attendances average around the 1,000 mark."

Peters was blunt, but he wasn't unkind in his assessment. He acknowledged that the "professional" version of football that Englishmen took for granted was in a "building stage" in Australia and he was more than happy to spend time coaching local clubs and talking to the small number of enthusiastic journos that followed him around.

Irrespective of the impression the Victorian State League had on Peters, Peters had a big impact on Frankston. Their membership doubled during his time at the club (albeit to 400), and the gate receipts allowed the club to "almost break even", according to officials.

Bannon stayed on with Frankston and played in two more matches before he was recalled by Chelsea. His third game was the crucial tie against title contenders Essendon Croatia (now known as the Melbourne Knights), which was billed as the most miserly defence (Essendon) against the free-scoring Frankston. It was top billed and it didn't disappoint. Frankston came back twice from a goal down to draw 2–2, with Croatia's legendary striker Tommy Cumming getting a brace.

Bannon played once more before he waved goodbye to his brothers and returned to London. A 4–1 drubbing of Juventus with Mitten getting two was a fitting farewell to the youngest Bannon.

In the seven games that Martin Peters or Eamonn Bannon (or both) played for Frankston City they won five and drew two, and those draws were both away to top of-the-table rivals. Between them they scored five goals and added their experience to a side now destined for the top.

Frankston's ambition to submit an entry for the NSL seemed vindicated, and Les Smith spruiked Frankston's suitability. "We hope to have a permit for full licenced clubrooms by November. And the local council has indicated it will turn our new ground at Centenary Park into a stadium, should the club gain entry to the Phillips League."

Smith also claimed to have a sponsorship deal in place with a "national company" should their bid be accepted.

When bids were formally submitted only Frankston and Preston made their applications official, as did Footscray JUST and South Melbourne to be retained. Frankston already had Preston's measure on the league table and in July and August many reports described Frankston's promotion as inevitable.

There was only one problem. The club slumped in the second half the season, going on a five-match stretch without a win, With a few rounds to go they slipped behind Essendon Croatia on goal difference (Frankston had conceded nine more goals), and couldn't make up the ground as both sides kept winning. They finished second that season and, humiliatingly, conceded the double to Croatia after losing to them in the final of the Dockerty Cup (the State cup competition in Victoria).

Suddenly, Frankston were no longer being discussed as potential NSL candidates. Now only Preston were being considered when the 1979 NSL season ended with South Melbourne Hellas in last spot. Ultimately South Melbourne didn't go down; they were a huge club and, coincidentally, their president Sam Papasavas was also the NSL Chairman. Sydney Olympic were sent down instead, despite finishing second last, and were replaced by another Sydney side, Blacktown City.

1979 turned out to be Frankston's only window of opportunity for NSL admission.

There was another, bigger problem at play for Frankston that likely spooked the

ASF and NSL. They were $100,000 in debt. The money invested in the squad, as well as the new club rooms and the new surface, was covered by overdrafts that needed to be repaid.

Recognising the gravity of the situation, the club hired a firm of accountants to take charge of their finances, consolidate their debts and set up a repayment scheme of $2,500 per month. Frankston City bragged of revenues of "a quarter of a million dollars per annum", but the bulk of that money was going on wages, and so costs had to be slashed.

Frankston stopped covering their players' contracts, and an exodus began. Eight of their first team players left before 1980, including both Bannons—kissing goodbye to any hope of a repeat trip from Eamonn. Noel Mitten did the unthinkable and joined Essendon Croatia.

Like so many clubs in Second Divisions, Frankston bet on the perceived riches of promotion and, when promotion didn't happen, their reality became debt.

*   *   *

Before Frankston could take a step back, reassess their financial position and forge a new sustainable path it had one more bullet in the chamber they were intent on using.

Martin Chivers had been an option 12 months earlier when Peters agreed to join and in 1980 they rekindled the connection to see if Chivers was still keen. With $1,000 a game still the going rate, enthusiasm from both parties was high.

Chivers was one of the top marksmen of his generation. He had come through the system at his local club Southampton in the early 1960s, gaining promotion to the First Division before being scouted by Tottenham, where he would inspire Spurs—with Martin Peters in midfield—to two League Cup and UEFA Cup victories in 1971–72. He is fourth on Spurs all-time scorers list, just behind Harry Kane, and is 12th on Southampton's all-time scorers despite only playing six seasons. He was Spurs leading scorer for four consecutive seasons in their League Cup and UEFA Cup seasons and also scored 13 times for England in 24 appearances in that time.

By 1980 Chivers was 35 and wrapping up an unfulfilling single season spell with Brighton & Hove Albion. He only managed five games for Brighton before joining non-league Dorchester Town for another five games.

When Chivers was announced, Frankston City weren't going quite as well as previous seasons. They were on the high side of mid-table but had struggled to put sides away. Chivers, a legendary English striker, seemed the obvious tonic.

When Chivers arrived, Frankston City didn't quite make the first impression they hoped for. When Chivers was shown his new "state of the art" dressing room his reported response was "the boot room at Tottenham is bigger than this".

However, on the pitch Chivers made an instant impression. "Chivers all class!" read the match report of his first game, a 3–0 win over the struggling Western Suburbs. Chivers was "strolling about in complete control" in front of a handful of supporters who braved the weather to see the First Division star. In the last 20 minutes Chivers "toyed" with his opposition by holding on to the ball, daring his opponents to come at him.

The third and final goal was unlocked by an assist from Chivers who "strolled past three opponents" before unleashing a pass down the right for Kevin Wall, who collected, cut in and shot truly inside the near post.

Stratos Tzanoudakis was an injured player with Western Suburbs that day, and was in the club's entourage to support them. His memories of Chivers are of a colossal figure in both name and presence. "I remember him coming out and he was huge. A big, big man. [One of my teammates] who played in the game was a mad Tottenham supporter and he was starstruck on the pitch. He kept looking at him thinking 'I'm playing against Martin Chivers'."

Frankston fans, reporters and enraptured Spurs fans had to wait a couple of weeks for another dose, and a visit from Brunswick Juventus featuring former Scottish international Frank Munro.

It was another win for Frankston, this time a controversial 1–0 scoreline after a Juve goal was disallowed for offside which caused "irate Italians" to "start spitting and threatening [the linesman] so severely that the game had to be held up until Juve coach Manny Poulakakis, keeper Jack Reilly and striker Bobby McGuinness walked to the distraught Juve fans and quelled the outburst."

Frankston went on to score and seal victory. The final lines of the match report capture the change in fortunes for Frankston's star import: "Martin Chivers was a failure as a midfield playmaker."

The hype around Chivers met a muddy end in advance of his third and final fixture against Preston Makedonia. Melbourne's notorious weather left a bog at Centenary Park, and a forlorn photo from *Soccer Action* of Chivers with Del Lines watching his investment sink into the mud is both symbolic and portentous.

That match didn't go ahead, but Chivers did his part around the club with an event for kids from local clubs, packed to the gills, followed by a Sportsman's Night in the clubrooms where Chivers appeared with former VFL player and media powerhouse Lou Richards and former Test fast bowler Ian Meckiff.

Chivers played two of his potential three games before the heavens intervened and he didn't score, in part because he was playing in midfield. When the final game against Makedonia was abandoned, Chivers returned $500 of the grand he was owed. He then returned to England to retire outside of a handful of games in Norway and the lower leagues.

It was only a month after Chivers' departure that the wheels fell off at Frankston.

By August they were skint, pouring all their money into paying off the overdraft of 1979, and started delaying payments to players.

There were other casualties. Del Lines was forced to resign along with long-time president, Hans Gussenhoven.

Del Lines claimed in *Soccer Action* that his resignation had more to do with another signing, that of once capped Irish player Jimmy Dunne of Fulham and Torquay. Lines had arranged the transfer and relocation, but the upheaval at the club saw the deal rejected by the Frankston transition board. Lines got the hump and quit. He called it an "embarrassing situation" and walked away from official duties even though he stuck around in an unofficial capacity. Lines' wife, Doreen, was manager of the Social Club so he was never too far away. Dunne joined Green Gully instead, and poetically scored the winner in a fixture against Frankston that season.

Before the end of the 1980 season the players were in open revolt. A senior player wrote to the VSF demanding intervention.

"The wages due to me have not been paid for eight weeks. Secondly, the signing-on fee agreed in the contract has not been honoured. Therefore, as I have fulfilled my part of the contract (i.e. turning up for training and for the games), I feel that the club is up for breach of contract. Therefore, I would like your decision on the matter as soon as possible."

The VSF intervened to hand free transfers to twelve players. If Frankston had met their obligations they might have been able to sell those players, and their combined value was estimated (in an article in *Soccer Action*) at the time at $40,000. Those fees could have paid down some of the debt. Instead, the losses compounded and $40,000 was allowed to walk out the door.

On the pitch Frankston actually did okay in 1980 for a club no longer paying its players. They finished sixth behind champions Preston Makedonia, who were accepted into the NSL for the 1981 season.

The NSL moved to a conference system in 1984 and admitted a swag of new clubs from the Victorian state First Division including Melbourne Croatia (formerly Essendon), Green Gully, Brunswick Juventus and Sunshine George Cross.

But by that time Frankston was out of the picture. They'd bet the farm on promotion and lost. The fans didn't come. Their average attendances dropped to around 200, and needed committee members to guarantee loans.

They returned for the 1981 Victorian State season with a threadbare side. Their one bright note was a young Scotsman named Charlie Egan who scored 20 goals in 22 appearances in 1981 and won the league Player of the Year award before being sold to South Melbourne. He won two caps for the Socceroos, scored 90 NSL goals and is the last example of Frankston's ability to find and nurture British talent.

By March 1983 they were gone. They wrote to the VSF to withdraw the club from the league. In their death notice in *Soccer Action*, writer Craig Mackenzie was poetic and maudlin, as Frankston City withdrew its membership of the VSF. "Frankston City burned itself out last week. It didn't die, just condemned itself to obscurity. It decided to fade away."

Harry Michael's Wollacticos

Alan Brazil: 1988, 12 games, 4 goals
Trevor Francis: 1988, 3 games, 2 goals
Paul Mariner: 1988, 2 games, 0 goals

The Wollongong City season of 1988 is the most implausible and bonkers season in NSL history.

For a fleeting moment, Wollongong became a destination club for the world's finest players. The cream of the English First Division were drawn to the NSL, and while around 10 huge names signed, three genuine superstars did: Paul Mariner, Trevor Francis and Alan Brazil. Newly promoted Wollongong and its illustrious ring-ins went from State League sloggers to top of the NSL in one season. It was all down to the vision, persistence and money of one man: Harry Michaels.

There are a wide range of impressions of Harry Michaels within Australian football. Some see him as some kind of agent provocateur, pushing football toward some personal agenda that goes against the history or culture of the game. Others call him a driving force behind the NSL—and Australian football more broadly—for the last 40 years. As much as he is a football man, he is a television man—and Michaels directed and produced the NSL for television from the mid 1980s to the mid 1990s (before it was hidden behind C7's paywall), opening it up to viewers like never before.

He won a Logie in 1998 for his coverage of the devastating World Cup qualifier between Australia and Iran at the Melbourne Cricket Ground. Fans still talk in sombre tones about the scenes captured on television that night after full-time. He has covered international football, league football, European football, and was awarded an Order of Australia Medal in 2004 for his services to football and to the media.

His journey into football media was as improbable as his 1988 Wollongong side. A life-long football fan, Michaels started his professional career as an actor on the long- running and popular TV soap *Number 96*, before following his passion into producing, directing and ultimately football.

Michaels produced light entertainment like *Greek Variety Show*, and is most famous today for being the brains behind *Aerobics Oz Style*. But in the late 1970s he moved sideways into football. Channel 10 had the NSL rights for its first two seasons, before dumping the product when it didn't rate. In the 1980s Michaels' production company bought the rights themselves, and put the package together for SBS.

As director of the games, Michaels was on the broadcast trucks putting the TV programme together in real time. It is a role that requires a knowledge and appreciation for football. One has to know the sport intimately to express the unique drama that connects football to the fans.

Michaels had strong ideas on how the game and its management could be improved. The game had not grown since the establishment of the NSL, and various efforts at tinkering with league structures through conferences and club numbers hadn't worked. League football in Australia was stagnating, and just wasn't connecting with fans. Like all entrepreneurs, he knew he had to become the change he wanted to see, and chose the only logical path.

At the age of 38 he invested in a club so he could put his money where his mouth was. "Football is in my blood. It's a madness. It's a disease, which caused me to go to the extreme. I thought I was a Berlusconi. I must have been dreaming," Michaels confesses, on reflection, but is then quick to add that the comparisons with the former Italian prime minister begin and end with club ownership. Michael's parties at the time were a lot more wholesome, he explains.

Like Berlusconi's AC Milan, Michaels sought to build a team of brand-name stars to awe and motivate closet football fans. It was to be a New York Cosmos on the Pacific. A 'Galacticos' of the Illawarra. A Wollacticos.

The most cynical take on Michael's plans was that he was using Wollongong as a billboard to drive up the value of his TV product. Every player signed—out of his own pocket—was a marketing investment he could write off. But football means more than that to Harry Michaels. It wasn't just a TV drama. Football needed visionaries, and it needed them fast.

"Everyone knows that soccer in this country has never been organised and packaged the right way," Michaels told journalist Michael Cockerill in 1988.

The seeds of the Wollacticos concept were sown in 1985, when Keegan swept through Sydney for his two games with Blacktown City. Michaels was there in his TV capacity and saw first-hand the magnetic appeal of big British names.

When Michaels conceived of his team of British All-Stars, he first approached Sydney Olympic and also sought out Frank Lowy to take over Sydney City (who ultimately withdrew from the 1987 season before it started), but couldn't find traction. So he turned to Wollongong.

Wollongong City had been relegated from the NSL at the end of the 1986 season when the Conference system was exorcised. They went back to the NSW State First Division, regrouped, and won the title and promotion back to the NSL for 1988.

Wollongong is a working class city, 100 kilometres or so south of Sydney on the Pacific coast. The city represents the nexus of wondrous coastline, big city vibes but small town intimacy. It is the perfect picturesque home base from which to launch lures for Brits to bite on.

In 1988 clubs were member organisations and franchises with investors weren't permitted so Michaels devised an ingenious workaround. He would take over the running of the club in exchange for a loan of $100,000 to Wollongong interest free to boost their budgets, with the money due to be repaid to Michaels after two years.

A key part of his proposition was that he would dip into his personal funds to pay for his guest stars, with the hope that he would see that money back through the gate and through a boost to his TV product. When his stars appeared he would get 40% of the gate on their debut, and 30% for subsequent appearances.

The marriage brought the wealthy, entrepreneurial actor and TV personality together with a working class club from a working class city, whose directors mowed the pitch and painted the stands—and whose chairman was a sitting Labor MP in NSW.

"I approached the Chairman of Wollongong, [the Honourable] Lawrie Kelly. He was also the Speaker of the House in NSW, he said 'we'd love you to come and take over the club', which I did."

Englishman and club legend John Fleming was Wollongong's manager. As a coach he was straight out of the Graham Taylor school (he had played for Taylor's Lincoln City in the 1970s): fight and run harder, get it long, compress the space, trap the ball in the forward half. Fleming took the Wolves coaching job in 1987 and, like Taylor, led his team to promotion.

Fleming reflects on that 1988 side and their dynamic with real fondness. "We had our own little unit and were fighting everyone. It was us against the world. They were a driven bunch of guys, [and many] were born and bred in the Illawarra. I don't think at any stage the players got the credit they deserved."

Despite being a promoted side, Fleming and his team had a singular and bold focus to finish the season first, which they did. His dedication to success was something that would have immediately struck a chord with Michaels.

At first, Michaels was welcomed heartily by the coach and players. "We won promotion from the State League and got informed that Harry Michaels was going to be involved in the club and was going to bring overseas players. Absolutely brilliant.

Great. So we went along with it," was Fleming's recollection of the early days of the experiment.

In 1988, Fleming confessed to having some role in the signings, albeit from a specific angle. "Every name that Harry comes up with, I check my contacts in England. Most of all I want to know if they're the sort of players who will come out here and bludge."

Michaels was also mindful of lifting standards for the existing squad. His vision was to see his team be fully professional, and that included the players who had come up in promotion. He procured memberships to the 'Golden Wing Club' for the entire squad, which entitled them to eat, drink and relax in hotel lounges on matchday. Michaels also treated his team to hotel stays in Sydney before games, and frequently took the team out together for meals.

But there wasn't always a consensus between coach and Michaels. Some big name NSL additions were approached but—reportedly—knocked back by coach John Fleming. Žarko Odžakov, who dazzled for Sydney Croatia, and Olympic's Peter Katholos were approached but ultimately not signed.

A bit of NSL experience does not an all-star team make. Michaels' pipeline to UK stars didn't turn on overnight, so he sought a local star, Danny Crainie, to get things going.

Crainie was lured to Wollongong from South Melbourne, where he had spent the last two seasons after a year with Brunswick Juventus. Before he landed in Australia he'd come through the system at Celtic, winning 27 caps with the Bhoys before hitting a ceiling and joining Wolverhampton. He made 64 appearances for Wolves before trying his luck in Australia.

By 1988 he was an experienced NSL player with a nous for getting crosses into the box. He also had a reputation as a bit of a party boy, and like a lot of party boys he was extremely well connected to boys who attended the same parties. It was Crainie who helped Michaels connect directly with players in the UK at a time before player agents were commonplace.

Top of Michaels' shopping list was Alan Brazil. Conveniently, Brazil and Crainie had been in the Celtic academy together, albeit a few years apart. Crainie helped Michaels with the introduction.

Alan Brazil was by now a journeyman footballer, a role forced on him largely by injury. He made his name spectacularly with Bobby Robson's Ipswich Town, playing a key role in their UEFA Cup win in 1981, and powered them into second place in the League in 1982. That season he was only just pipped by Kevin Keegan for the Golden Boot, and scored five times in a match for Ipswich against Southampton.

After Ipswich, Brazil moved to Spurs where he won another UEFA Cup, before Spurs flipped him for a profit to Ron Atkinson's Manchester United. There he struggled for fitness and game time, and a degenerative back injury started to set in. He moved to Coventry City midway through the 1985/86 season, and then joined QPR on a free in 1986. He only managed four games in 1986 before his English top flight career ended.

In his 2008 autobiography *Both Barrels From Brazil*, Brazil describes his retirement in early 1987 as being a directive from specialists. His back was too far gone and, at the tender age of only 27, he risked serious injury playing on. "So that was it." Brazil writes. "My football career was over."

Except, of course, it wasn't. A year later he was jetting into Sydney to play for Harry Michaels in the NSL.

Conveniently for NSL fans following Brazil's literary career, his 2007 autobiography *There's an Awful Lot of Bubbly in Brazil* doesn't repress all memories of his time in Wollongong.

Brazil recalls the introduction with Michaels coming from a former Yugoslav player. "He asked me to go to Australia and play for a team called Wollongong. It sounded like an Aborigine name to me, but as everybody had had a lot to drink I thought it was just pub talk so I said 'OK,' then forgot all about it. I must have given him my number because a few days later, at 2.30 in the morning, the phone rang and there was Harry Michaels."

When he landed, Brazil told journalist Ray Gatt, then with the *Sydney Morning Herald*, "I'm not here for a holiday." Brazil's attitude would change, but when he first landed in Sydney he said and did all the right things for Michaels' new side. "This is not about Alan Brazil. It is about the club [Wollongong] and helping them to win games."

Brazil quickly became the beacon for Harry Michaels' Wollacticos dream. "Maybe some of my critics will start to believe that I will deliver what I have promised," Michaels told reporters at Sydney Airport when Brazil landed..

Manchester United's 32-year-old striker Norman Whiteside was announced to be arriving in June, and fellow United legend Bryan Robson—then only 31—was also in advanced talks. Robson had been in Australia in 1987 to play in an indoor soccer tournament in Queensland—and, well, if he was willing to do that then, surely he'd be up for anything.

"There is more to come ... believe me," Michaels promised reporters.

It was around this time that tensions with the ASF started to simmer. Before the season kicked off, at the Annual General Meeting of the NSL, Michaels lobbied hard to increase the number of guest stars from one to infinity. While he won that vote—enabling him to have the option of many simultaneous guest contracts—the matter wasn't universally embraced.

Michaels recalls the toxic relationship with the Federation manifesting in multiple ways. "Soccer Australia were against the idea and I couldn't understand the reason.

Arthur George [ASF President] said 'why do we allow a guy like Harry Michaels to bring all these has-beens from overseas to Australia, and stop our young up and coming stars from getting a fair go?'.

"Finally I said: 'That's very very harsh, what you're saying, and you don't understand the game. It's no different to television, it's no different to films. If you want to put bums on seats you need a star. Doesn't matter how good your script is'."

The 1988 season got underway in the NSL Cup, with a trip to Brisbane to face the Lions. Wollongong lost that game 5–2 with Brazil in the game, still shaking off his jet lag.

The League season kicked off a week later, and despite the heavy loss to Brisbane in the Cup, Round one of the NSL season could not have been better scripted for Michaels' side. Brazil opened the scoring in a 3–1 win. He blasted home after a mis-hit from Crainie who had cut in from the left and sliced his shot straight into Brazil's lap.

The following week, in the roaring heat of February, was a more subdued 0–0 draw at home to Preston Makedonia. The official crowds for the first two games of the season at Brandon Park were an uninspiring 1,969, and 2,140. This was Brandon Park's debut season after being constructed brick-by-brick from donations from throughout the 1980s, with fans and committee members alike toiling to build up the stadium. It saw its first football in 1988 after first being trialled with a Midnight Oil concert in 1986. Its capacity was 20,000.

Club historian Malcolm Rowney recalls the crowds being on the low side, despite the matchday promotions within the local paper the *Illawarra Mercury*. As the editor of the Wollongong matchday programme, Rowney published his assessment of Round 1 as "a disappointing crowd in attendance".

Harry Michaels, however, is suspicious about 'official' NSL crowd numbers. "We [had] about eight to ten thousand people. I was happy with that. A lot of the numbers that were given out were wrong."

"Official attendances", as described by Michaels, were often a simple calculation of the gate receipts divided by the ticket price. The accuracy of this calculation is wholly dependent on the money from the gates staying put.

While there will always be debate about attendances, no one could doubt Wollongong's form. Round 3 was their first away trip to Adelaide City, and a final outing for Brazil on his initial month-long contract. Brazil and Wollongong had started hotly, and Michaels was eager to extend Brazil's deal. Michaels had set Brazil up in a house in Wollongong and Brazil was enjoying his football. An offer of a $200,000 season-long contract (pro-rated for the games he'd already played) was offered.

Adelaide City used the official program to throw serious shade on Brazil and Michaels' side. The president's message doesn't mention Brazil at all, and a welcome message from the editor, after the obligatory greeting, adds, "Unfortunately, Alan, City have reached their signing-on salary cap for 1988, which would make it a bit difficult to raise the $200,000 for your signature. However, best wishes to you and your family during your stay in 'Aussie.'" The program might have seemed funny in Adelaide, but Wollongong and Brazil had the last laugh with a 3–2 win.

With that Brazil returned to the UK. Whether the offer was as generous as $200,000 or not, Michaels wanted Brazil to return. He did about a month later. While he was gone injuries started to bite and Michaels needed more than just bums on seats. He needed bums on his bench.

Michaels' PR machine returned to churning out names like pallets in a battery hen farm. At the end of February, Robson and Whiteside were announced (again) to be on their way at some stage in the 1988 season, and Aberdeen's Charlie Nicholas would be joining them.

"Harry's been a breath of fresh air," manager John Fleming told reporters, in a rare show of solidarity for Michaels' vision. "He's got a lot of new ideas and has played a big part in our early success."

In a more sombre tone, Fleming added, "Harry's constantly giving me names but I've turned down a lot because I've felt they wouldn't contribute … I think it would be a retrograde step if we looked at making money rather than getting points."

Opinions vary on what happened next.

Michaels claims he always had the season-long deal in place in Brazil—and not a $5,000 per game rolling deal—and allowed Brazil to return home temporarily to take care of some personal business. Brazil recalls the situation differently. The dates are a bit off, but in his 2007 autobiography *There's an Awful lot of Bubbly in Brazil*, the Scottish marksman tells an incredible version. Brazil had been "celebrating" back in the UK, and football was the farthest thing from his mind:

A week after we got home, the phone rang again at 2.30am. Only this time it was not the calm, composed businessman I had come to know. Harry was panic-stricken. His centre-forward had broken his leg and his right-winger had been struck down with a virus. He begged me to return to Australia. On Saturday the team were playing the dreaded Sydney Olympic. My brain was scrambled. I couldn't even remember what day it was. But I was already starting to rise to the challenge of my round-the-world rescue mission. The only problem was Harry had implored me to find a winger to take with me. And I had to fly within two days.

The next part of the story can barely be believed, and makes Ali Dia look like, well, George Weah. Brazil continues: "The fog started to clear in my mind and I suddenly remembered an old pal I had met in a pub a couple of months earlier for the first time in a year. His name was Bruiser Keys. I've never known his first name, I've always known him as Bruiser."

"Bruiser"—whose actual name was Paul—Keyes needed little coercion to take an all-expenses paid trip to play football in Wollongong. He was working as a roofer when Brazil made the call, but as a junior he had spent time with Luton. While not a complete novice, he hadn't kicked a ball in years.

In the Sydney Olympic programme Keyes isn't mentioned on the team sheet—no one really knew what to expect from Keyes, or just who would be getting off that plane. "We were both exhilarated at the speed and drama of events and on the flight we gratefully accepted a few glasses of champagne. Then a few more. The cabin crew must have thought we were medically dependent on bubbly because the bottles just kept coming."

On that trip, Brazil and Keyes made the Australian Test Cricket team look like the quakers. On arrival in Sydney, after 40 hours of uninterrupted drinking, Brazil and Keyes—the roofer-cum-winger—reunited with a horrified Michaels. Both players were due to kick off against Sydney Olympic in five hours.

This was not some ordinary game. This was Sydney Olympic. This was the side that had rejected Michaels' advances despite Michaels, Greek-Cypriot by birth, being a long-time supporter and benefactor of the club. Here he was bringing his all-star team into their home. And his all-star players were a roofer called "Bruiser" and a striker with a crook back, both in the middle of a four-day bender.

At this point, only Brazil himself could supply the match report.

When we ran on to the pitch the adrenalin really started pumping. After five minutes I realised that, luckily, Sydney Olympic were not as good as I'd feared. Bruiser was burning up and down the right flank like a madman. We'd filled him full of energy drinks and it seemed to be working. Midway through the first half he fired over and I met it with my favoured left foot. One-nil.

Michaels was ecstatic. He was desperate to beat Olympic, and would go to any lengths to do it: including offering a $12,000 bonus payment to the players if they won. He brought the money in cash into the changing rooms as a visual incentive. "I was very annoyed with Sydney Olympic because they never wanted me. Because they thought I wanted to take over the club but not do the right thing by the ethnic supporters or that I wanted the glory," Michaels describes.

At full-time Brazil collapsed on the pitch, unable to move. He couldn't move for most of the second half, in fact, and camped in midfield pinging passes around the pitch. According to him his vision blurred and the energy drained from his body. Luckily, when the whistle blew, the Wollongong bench arrived to carry him off triumphant.

Paul Keyes—the second greatest roofer ever to play (after Wynton)—only played two matches for Wollongong, and though it was probably two too many, they were both games Harry Michaels will not forget.

The following week, after the necessary recovery time, Wollongong flew down to Melbourne to take on Sunshine George Cross. Michaels had been labelled a troublemaker by the establishment, and this ran deep with opposition fans, especially when results went against them. So when Pat Brodnik scored in extra time to clinch a 1–0 win, the Sunshine fans were not amused.

"They thought I bought the game," Michaels explains. "So I'm coming down and I was surrounded by six or seven people, and they said to me 'you fucking paid the referee' and I said 'no I didn't'. And I turn around and this guy that was asking me punched me. He fucking punched me, gave me a black eye.

"And when Alan found out, the whole team ran out to really start a riot! I said 'Guys, come on, don't do that.' But [Brazil and Keyes] and Danny Crainie came out as I left and they made a circle to protect me. They just said 'no, you're not going to do that to Harry'."

Brazil played three more matches in that run: two wins against Brunswick away (where Brazil scored), and South Melbourne at home, as well as an away draw at APIA. After eleven games, and two spells from Brazil, Wollongong had won seven, drawn three and lost once.

*   *   *

Brazil had been a success on the pitch, but Michaels needed another big name to create a trend and he was working feverishly to do that. He kept topping up his investment; it was all money that he wasn't really expecting to see again.

"If everything goes against me it will cost $250,000. If I walk away losing [only]

$100,000 I will be a very lucky man, and a very happy one," Michaels told the *Australian Financial Review* at the time. "Soccer has to go for names because Australia's pretty faces cannot make the game entertaining," he added.

Brazil had become Harry Michael's playmaker both on and off the pitch. While Paul Keyes wasn't a recruiting triumph for Wollongong, Brazil was willing to help Michaels connect with other big stars.

So Brazil opened his little black book and picked out Paul Mariner who had been Brazil's strike partner at Ipswich for seven years where, together, they scored over 150 goals. From Ipswich Mariner joined Arsenal, and then wound down his career with Portsmouth. He won 35 caps for England, playing alongside legendary English strikers Kevin Keegan, Trevor Francis and Bob Latchford, and played upfront with Francis in all of England's 1982 World Cup games, including scoring in the 3–1 win against France.

In 1988, with 34 years and 15 football seasons behind him, he answered the call to join Harry Michaels' Wollacticos. It was a $10,000 deal for two matches—at home against Sydney Croatia and away at Preston Makedonia—but when he signed he flagged the option to extend the deal further.

"If things go well there's no reason why I couldn't stay on until the end of the year," Mariner told reporter Jason Dasey who opened his piece with the rather unsympathetic assessment 'Old British soccer players never die: they just make huge money from guest appearances in Australia'.

Mariner had been in Australia before, representing England B in 1980 in the Centenary match against the Socceroos, and the first-ever meeting of the two fierce sporting rivals. While the A side prepped for the European Championships, a team of top English pros descended on the SCG where 45,000 spectators gathered. Mariner scored in a 2–1 win that always left an impression on him.

"I sort of fell in love with it," said Mariner 40 years on from the 1980 tour. "I thought 'wow this is an amazing place'. It was a short trip. We flew into Sydney, maybe a day to prep, and played at the Sydney Cricket Ground. Then we were taken around Sydney Harbour to look at the Opera House and look at the Bridge. And I thought 'Oh my god this is a beautiful place'. So when the opportunity crops up for me to come out again it wasn't even a discussion. I just wanted to do it."

Mariner had just finished up with Alan Ball's Portsmouth, who had just been relegated from the top flight, and recalls both Alans being involved in the deal with Wollongong behind the scenes. Ball himself had had a successful football dalliance in Perth in 1982, and along with Alan Brazil, Australia came with a fine recommendation.

With Mariner booked, Michaels' PR recruitment drive went into overdrive.

Wollongong became continuously linked with big names. Whiteside and Robson were linked again, and this time Mark Hughes, Glenn Hoddle, Ray Wilkins, Nigel Clough and Trevor Francis were also added to lists in the media as either "on their way" or "possible guests". John Fashanu was also keen, but was stuck in England attending to the pesky matter of the FA Cup final against Liverpool—a famous win for the Crazy Gang.

Then, breathtakingly, Wollongong started to be linked with a name that would have blown everyone away, one that seemed the most ludicrous of this most improbable of seasons. Just before Brazil left the second time, Michael Cockerill broke the headline 'Wolves snap up Platini'. Platini was, according to multiple sources, all but booked to make a $5,000 single appearance in Wollongong, in a game in early July against the Brisbane Lions.

It didn't happen. "We had Platini coming," reflects Michaels today. "But it didn't happen because of something happening back in France. He had an unexpected commitment. But we nearly had him. He nearly came out."

Michaels' insistence on guest stars started to take its toll on coach John Fleming, who told reporters he took objection to the "constant sniping at the team's ability", in a not-so-thinly veiled rebuke of Michaels' push for name reinforcements.

"Brazil has been a tremendous asset and has earned the respect of everyone at the club. But he has earned that by being a member of the team, not an individual star," Fleming told the media.

Wollongong were in top spot in the league, and according to Fleming it was the core squad that was behind their success, not the marquee stars.

The football gods disagreed, and St George beat Wollongong 2–1 in the fixture played between Brazil's departure and Mariner's debut.

"I am excited about coming out," Mariner told the *Sydney Morning Herald*. "It's not out of the question that I'll end up living there. Europe is saturated now and Australia would be the ideal place to get a fresh start."

Mariner's signing emboldened Michaels, who never missed a chance to present his vision for the game. A Michael Cockerill Day in the life piece on Harry Michaels, published just before Mariner arrived, ran with the headline 'Soccer Bosses must go, says Michaels' which would have turned a few heads at head office.

Before the ASF could load their weapons, Mariner squeezed in his debut in Round 14 against Sydney Croatia, in front of 4,755 fans at Brandon Park. It was the Wolves' best home crowd all season, helped along by the popularity of the opponent. But the excitement around the game quickly dissipated after kick-off. Robbie Slater ran rampant in a 3–0 win for Croatia, and Papua New Guinean striker Manis Lamond scored after five minutes, to set the rout in action.

Mariner started upfront and was marked mercilessly all day. He took a ball in the channel midway through the first half, tried a Cruyff turn and had the ball taken off him. His 34-year-old legs looked like they were stuck in the mud.

Mariner did have a couple of good moments. He forced a fantastic save from a volley at the top of the box late in the game. He also laid off a ball for Jeff Ainsworth to shoot and curl it just wide. But it wasn't enough.

The following week Mariner was to play his final game with Wollongong in this short-burst two-match deal. Mariner had a gig lined up in June leading a tour group through the European Championships in West Germany, but if he enjoyed Australia as much as he had in his previous visits he had a mind to return to Wollongong after the Euros ended.

By this time, Brazil had returned for a third time. On this occasion, Michaels signed him as a visa player (not a guest), with the intention of parachuting him in immediately for Mariner's last game.

However, after riling up the ASF with his comments in the press, the governing body was in no mood to do Michaels a favour. Before the match in Preston, Harry Michaels took a phone call in an office at the Preston ground.

"I got a call from Peter Russell—he was the ASF CEO at the time—he said 'Harry you've got a problem. There was a complaint from Preston management. You can't play Alan Brazil.' I said 'Why?' He said 'Because he's not legally here. It's not legally accepted. You can't play him.' That's what Peter Russell told me."

Brazil's paperwork apparently wasn't in order.

Even 30 years later, Michaels becomes animated in the retelling of the exchange. "I told him I was going to play him.

"He said 'You know what that means you'll be fined and you'll lose the two points.' I said 'Why are you victimising me? I'm someone putting his money where his mouth is who loves the game. It's people like you, bloody public servants, who are destroying the game. You're just a paper pusher.'"

Peter Russell started to protest. Michaels dug his heels in. "I said 'Peter. You are the cancer that's ruining this sport. You're a horrible person. Instead of appreciating what I'm doing in trying to promote the game, you guys are telling me that I'm cheating. Well thanks so much.' I hung up on him."

According to Michaels, the Wollongong players, including Mariner and Brazil, witnessed Michaels' side of the entire conversation in the adjacent room in quiet disbelief. Fleming disputes this but ultimately, despite Michaels' insistence to Peter Russell that Brazil would play, the decision was made by Fleming not to select him as he would not risk losing points.

As the players ran out, Michaels had another, more immediate problem. He started getting pelters from the Preston crowd, and was forced to retreat into the clubrooms, on police advice. Michaels' soon realised that he wasn't the only victim of the Preston abuse.

"So I'm watching the game somehow from the dressing room, and from the corner of my eye I see somebody giving Paul [Mariner] kicks and punches. So Paul who is a pro and a tough bastard, allowed them to. As the referee moved away Paul gives his opponent an elbow: eight stitches."

Mariner copped savage treatment from the Preston defenders all day. Fleming confirms the Mariner treatment and was proud of how his player stood up for himself and his teammates. "He was getting targeted from the start, and he looked after himself. It was that simple. He [Mariner] didn't have an ego, he was a quality young man and a quality player, and he looked after himself during the game."

The match finished 1–1, with Pat Brodnik scoring Wollongong's goal. But none of the visitors were pleased with the point taken away from Preston's raucous home.

"Everyone in the side was very upset with the result and with the standard of the refereeing," Fleming reflects today.

Paul Mariner returned to England shortly after the Preston game and never returned. Today, Mariner doesn't remember the incident at the home of Preston Makedonia. Nor does he remember much about his short, but incident-packed playing career for Wollongong.

Rough tactics in a glittering career that spanned Non-League with Chorley FC to the World Cup with England weren't new or novel to him. His reaction was, however, probably more a learning experience for his Preston opponent.

While Mariner can't pinpoint memories of playing for Wollongong City, he fondly recalls the City of Wollongong. "No ... I don't [remember], to be honest. I wish I did but I don't. It's all passed me by. I remember the city being a wonderful place. Not many people would know where Wollongong is but it's a really spectacular spot. It really is."

The same night as the Preston game after returning to Sydney, Mariner, Brazil and Michaels descended upon the Cauldron nightclub in Kings Cross. Mariner needed replenishing after his bruising match, and replenish he did. They ate dinner, with drinks, until 3 a.m.

*   *   *

When Mariner left town he tagged his old England strike partner Trevor Francis. As the star names shared with the media slowly started to recuse themselves—Robson had changed his mind at the last minute, Platini had business in France, Fashanu was celebrating his FA Cup win back home, and Nigel Clough was due any minute but never arrived—it was Trevor Francis who this time crossed the pond to join Brazil. Francis was offered a little more to sweeten the deal: $7,000 a game as opposed to Michaels' standard offer of $5,000.

The deal was done and Trevor Francis, the third of Michaels' Wollacticos, was on his way.

Like Mariner, Francis was 34, and was at the tail end of a magical career that had seen him go from Birmingham City to Nottingham Forest as Britain's first million-pound player and scored the winner in the 1979 European Cup Final.

Like Brazil, Francis had something of a journeyman club career, but his England career is somewhat more revered. He earned 52 caps between 1977 and 1986, including being top marksman in the 1982 World Cup which was a fine return in the era of Keegan, Mariner and Latchford.

Memorably Francis had toured Australia with England in 1983 on a three-game tour. In the first game of the series (and Frank Arok's first in charge of the Socceroos), in front of 28,000 at the SCG, Francis missed a penalty in a 0–0 draw.

In addition to a little more pay, Francis had another demand for Michaels. Unlike Brazil and Mariner, he didn't want to stay in Wollongong. He was determined to stay in Sydney with his wife and son.

"I refused to stay in Wollongong which was an hour and a half from Sydney, so we stayed in Sydney itself. I knew my fitness levels were good enough to fulfil my contract so I trained alone rather than making the three-hour round trip to Wollongong."

Fleming was not impressed by Francis' decision not to base himself in Wollongong. "I didn't see him ... He was here on holiday. I thought he was quite unprofessional."

A mere week after the fiasco in Preston, which saw Wollongong slip to third on the table, Michaels was hoping to experience his finest moment. Alan Brazil—papers now intact—and Trevor Francis were to start up front in Francis's debut, with record crowds predicted at Brandon Park.

But Michaels' finest moment could at best be described as bittersweet. Only 2,539 fans showed up on a bright sunny afternoon to watch both Francis and Brazil score in a 2–1 win.

In his match report, Michael Cockerill described the game as an "anti-climax", where Brazil and Francis carried the Wolves over the line in a game where few of the other 20 players showed up. Francis—who had landed in the country the day before and had had just four hours' sleep—brought with him the ability to match his billing.

"His pace, vision and skilful first touch and his eye for goal … have hardly dimmed with age," Cockerill wrote.

The following week both Francis and Brazil headed for Melbourne, with an away day against Melbourne Croatia on offer. It was a rare chance for Melburnians to see two football giants. Just how many Melburnians did that at Olympic Park is another point of departure between Michaels and the official stats. "There were about 14–15,000 people that day. That was a big one," Michaels recalls. Officially, the number was 1,851.

The fans in attendance caught another vintage Francis display, with Brazil also in hot form. It was 1–0 win to Wollongong, with a late winner powered home from Francis, that took Wollongong back to second on the table.

"Trevor Francis has the nonchalance of the soccer aristocrat. Scoring goals is second nature to him, so his expression hardly changed when he sank Melbourne Croatia at Olympic Park yesterday," wrote Laurie Schwab in the *Melbourne Age*.

Off the pitch the media started to become wise to what they increasingly perceived as Michaels' Wollactico end-game. While he wasn't the official owner of Wollongong, he desperately wanted the option to become it, and added his face to a growing movement to turn the league into a set of franchises that could be bought and sold.

In mid-1988, the NSL Chairman Stefan Kamasz had resigned his post to fight for franchising. Michaels found an immediate ally in Kamasz and quickly joined forces with him to back the proposal. Television commentator, Les Murray, in the *Sydney Morning Herald*, told readers that Michaels was "not the only, and not even the most heavily, stacked businessman ready to knock on soccer's door".

It was a delicately worded piece, but Murray, who knew Michaels well through SBS, was willing to back change. Like so many frustrated Australian football fans before and after 1988, Murray wanted to see change of any kind to shake football out of what he called "stagnation".

The NSL did start to tinker with private ownership after this time, allowing Footscray JUST to be purchased by a consortium which included their star player Oscar Crino. But Michaels wouldn't be the beneficiary of these changes.

By midway through the season, Michaels' interest in the project was waning, in part because the constant battles he was fighting wore him down. Wollongong were also distracting him from his other business interests, including producing the NSL as a TV product.

Michaels' frustration reached its limit in Francis's final match, a symbolic home game against the soon-to-be-privatised Footscray JUST. Footscray, who were in the bottom half, took Wollongong apart 4–1. In a bog, which should have played into Fleming's hoof-ball tactics, Wollongong were taken to school by the fit, active, short-passing Footscray.

It was Francis's last game for Wollongong, and he jumped on a plane and left Sydney that night. He had a shot tipped over the bar, and was brought down again in the box to no avail, but had failed to keep the Wolves in the game. True to form, Australian referees and their poor officiating of penalties had let him down again.

"If the score was a source of concern for coach John Fleming afterwards, so too must have been the poor contribution from his regular players. It was left to Francis, and to a lesser extent Brazil, to provide the only meaningful resistance," wrote journalist Michael Cockerill in the *Sydney Morning Herald*.

The week before his final match, Francis cast a searing assessment of Australian football to the local press. "Australian players battle hard. They are physical, but technically they are not particularly good. This time I've seen only three club teams, and all I can say is nothing has startled me."

While he may not have been a huge advocate on the quality of the NSL (or its referees), Francis did leave the door ajar for a return. "I would like to come out here and play out my last few years. I love Australia, and I fancy the idea of coming back."

That didn't occur. In the first few months of QPR's 1988/89 season, Francis was appointed player-manager which sparked a 15-year career in management in the English top flight.

By this time, the Wollacticos experiment was effectively over. Brazil had tested Michaels' patience, and would appear in only one more match. That was an away 1–1 draw with Marconi, in front of just under 3,000 fans at Marconi Stadium. It was a far cry from   Keegan's 15,000 at the same venue.

Brazil did not return, and nor would any other British big names. From this point, Fleming would have to make do with Australian players. Fleming is unflattering in his memories of Francis, but is quick to praise his other guest stars. "Alan Brazil and Paul Mariner fitted with the lads like clockwork. They were total professionals."

In a final act of canny recruiting—and to exact further revenge on Sydney Olympic—Michaels signed Socceroo striker Marshall Soper on loan from rivals, Sydney Olympic. Soper had fallen out with coach Eddie Thomson and was desperate for new pastures. With his stars gone, Soper's availability was a fantastic bit of luck for Wollongong.

At this point the relationship between Fleming and Michaels became untenable. Fleming wasn't happy with aspects of the Soper signing, and wasn't eager to use him straight away, preferring that he earn his place in the side. Michaels wasn't having it.

He walked away from the club around this point and had little to do with his experiment from then on.

The club took to their matchday program to put forward their side of the breakup with Michaels. According to the club Michaels had tried to move some games to Sydney to boost attendances. He sought a price hike of $3 on matchday tickets. For Brazil's third incarnation he was signed as a visa player, and not technically a guest player, but Michaels still wanted his 30% share of the gate. The piece also called out the incident over Brazil in Preston.

"Harry wanted John Fleming to play Alan and argue about his eligibility later. Club officials and John decided against this."

Michaels today describes the cause of the breakup as "board meddling".

"When you're investing your own money you have demands. You see it through your eyes, a different game to what they see. They're there for the politics and the barbecues and dinners and to carry-on like it's their own club. I decided I wasn't putting up with it when they crossed the line."

In spite of the chaos in the boardroom, matters on the pitch started to pick up. Even though he wasn't being used as much as Michaels had hoped, Soper was slowly integrating into the side, and started his first game against the Brisbane Lions

This was the 'Platini game', sans the Platini. But in the end Platini wouldn't have made any difference. Wollongong didn't need him or his Ballon d'Ors. They routed Brisbane 6–1, and Soper made a mockery of Fleming's doubts by scoring four times.

He may not have been English, or a First Division star, but Soper was white hot. He corrected the Wollongong ship and found a way to gel with his teammates.

The season's end was a nail-biter. Wollongong faced Sydney Croatia, who were level on points with Wollongong in second going into the final round. Top side South Melbourne went down to Adelaide City to open the door for either side to finish ahead of them.

The 1–1 result was enough to clinch the Premiership for Wollongong on goal difference. Wolves defender Mike Hollifield, the last defender, pulled down Robbie Slater who was through on goal just outside the box to prevent a certain goal. In 1988 that only warranted a yellow. 11 man Wollongong hung on at Croatia.

Soper didn't play in the final round (he was suspended) but his six goals in four starts were enough to drag Wollongong over the line on goal difference. Symbolically, Wollongong finished with six more goals than second-placed Croatia who also jumped above South Melbourne with that draw.

"Whatever happens now doesn't matter," John Fleming told the dressing room after the game—seemingly forgetting that they had a final series to come. "We're the most consistent side in the league over 26 rounds and that makes us the best side in the league no matter what the NSL says."

It was a bold strategy to write off a finals series on the eve of the finals series, and, inevitably, it backfired. Wollongong lost to Croatia on penalties in the first week, and by virtue of finishing top earned a second chance in a semi-final against Marconi. They lost that game 2–0, and Marconi went on to win the Grand Final and take home the title.

Commercially, was Michaels' experiment worth it? "Fuck, don't remind me!" Michaels laughs. "I blew a lot of money just to prove a point."

Today Michaels is philosophical, if a little revisionist, about the success of his Wollacticos. "Maybe I was pushing too hard to get names here to give more and more names and that's why I probably lost the plot a bit. [But] we were attracting the crowds. And the television ratings went up for SBS because I was involved."

Michaels' experiment in Wollongong did have one lasting impact on the NSL. He wasn't the first or last person to bring out big names, but he did succeed in changing perspectives about franchising. By the end of 1988 the NSL loosened the rules that enabled Footscray to be purchased (and renamed, regrettably, as "Melbourne City") and St George also went under the hammer.

APIA had already flirted with a form of private ownership that backfired on it badly, leading to court cases and irreparable bad will. Like so many football clubs the world over have found, private ownership done well allows clubs to balance the books with a bit of extra help from investors. Done poorly, and devastation awaits.

Footscray JUST for their sins didn't survive two seasons under private ownership and disappeared from existence.

Wollongong survived post Michaels and stayed in the NSL until the competition's dissolution in 2004. In fact, they thrived, winning back-to-back titles from 1999 to 2001 on the back of their young playmaker Scott Chipperfield. They survive today as an elite side in the top tier of NSW football.

But Harry Michaels'—as well as Alan Brazil's, Paul Mariner's and Trevor Francis's—involvement with the club seems more like a dream than a reality. Without doubt the Wollacticos in 1988 is one of the most unique seasons of NSL football ever, and will likely never be repeated.

Part 3 :
Rumours, Near Misses and Fevered Dreams

Rumours, Near Misses and Fevered Dreams

Australian football's fascination with the mainstream media TV coverage and front pages of the newspapers means the concept of a guest player is never far away. Over time the rumour mill and newspapers continue to focus on the possibility of a world-class superstar joining an Australian club for some limited cameo appearances.

While the men in this book added a piece of Australia to their legacies, there were others who flirted with, got close to, or were inches away from their own football excursions Down Under. What follows are credible, and incredible, rumours and near misses discovered in the research for this book (not mentioned elsewhere). Perhaps the most incredible aspect is so many were reported as "done deals", the player "was on the plane" or "he'll suit up this Saturday". But then they just never happened—without any follow-up from the media.

Sir Stanley Matthews: to Moreland City, 1962

The revered figure of Stanley Matthews led a touring Blackpool side to Australia in 1958 to take on the Joe Marston-led Socceroos. In the Socceroos team at the time was Moreland City player Frank Loughran who played in the 1956 Olympics for Australia alongside Moreland City teammate Ted Smith and would go on to feature in four games against Blackpool.

Loughran scored in the first game against the Tangerines and despite a heavy 7–0 loss at Olympic Park in Melbourne, he made such an impression on Matthews that he tried to persuade him to return to the UK with Blackpool and join their team.

Despite the flattering offer, Loughran remained in Melbourne and remained at Moreland City. According to the 2016 documentary *Moreland City FC 100 Years Strong – A real Australian Story*, in 1962 Moreland City had a written guarantee that Sir Stanley Matthews would come to Australia to play some guest games with them. Matthews main carrot was Moreland City's number one ticket holder Harry Hopman agreeing to provide tennis coaching to Matthews' son, Stanley Junior. Hopman was a journalist in Melbourne and the legendary captain-coach of 22 Australian Davis Cup teams, winning 15 as coach. Stanley Junior would go on to win the Wimbledon Boys title in 1962.

Moreland City's timing was terrible. It was in the middle of FIFA's ban on foreign players coming to Australia.

Eusebio: to Hakoah-Eastern Suburbs, 1977

A 35-year-old Eusebio was set to join the fledgling NSL with Hakoah-Eastern Suburbs in 1977. *Soccer Action* stated at the time he was to earn $3,000 for a one-off match against Footscray JUST, with the chance of second game away to Fitzroy-Alexander but only if they paid his match fee as they would get the gate. The Fitzroy-Alexander president retorted that they would be happy to pay his match fee, if he played for them.

Despite the efforts of Hakoah-Eastern Suburbs, Eusebio's availability scuppered the chance to play for them, and visa problems meant he never came to Australia during that time. The initiative of the fledgling NSL club was to be applauded, but the non-appearance of the 1966 World Cup superstar was seen as a gaffe.

Colin Bell: to Brisbane City, 1978 or 1979

Brisbane City, who had an unbroken run of 10 seasons in the NSL from its inception to 1986, was not an importing club by nature. Their greatest import was Jim Hermiston, who was ultimately pinched by local rivals the Brisbane Lions, before returning to play out his NSL career with City. Hardly the form of a club who would announce they had, in one swoop, signed Colin Bell, Pierino Prati and George Armstrong.

Of that lot, Bell was the real star. He'd played for England 48 times and is still considered a legend at Manchester City. Post war, only Sergio Aguero has scored more goals for the sky blues than Colin Bell. And yet, at the ripe age of 32 he was to join Brisbane City. In truth Bell's career was almost over. His knees were shot and he barely played after the report was published in *Soccer Action*, but he did go on to pick up a handful of games in the NASL so he was likely on the look-out for short-term contracts in less expansive leagues.

Neither Prati—a capped Italy international and a European Cup winner with AC Milan—or Armstrong—an Arsenal stalwart—arrived either.

Romeo Benetti: to Marconi, 1979

Romeo Benetti was a bulldog in the middle of pitch for both the Italian national team and a succession of Serie A clubs including Juve (twice), Sampdoria and AC Milan. He was a key figure in Italy's 1974 and 1978 World Cup squads, represented the Azzurri 55 times and was a multiple Serie A winner and serial Coppa Italia winner. He was a dark sorcerer of catenaccio. Italians loved him and opponents feared him.

At the tail end of his career, at the age of 34, having departed Juve for the second time, he was approached by Marconi to join Roberto Vieri on a Roman holiday. Marconi president Tony Labbozzetta said, "We have offered Benetti certain terms and conditions and we are waiting to see if he agrees." As it turned out he didn't, but it was a nice thought.

Alfie Conn Jnr: to South Melbourne, 1979 or 1980

Midfielder Alfie Conn Jnr, who had two international caps with Scotland in 1975, is better remembered as being a rare (and early) example of a player for both Rangers and Celtic. Like Mo Johnston a decade later, Conn had a spell in between the two Glasgow heavyweights, playing in England for Spurs where he famously sat on the ball at White Hart Lane after scoring the final goal in a 4–2 win over all-conquering Leeds. His debut at Rangers was at 16, coming on for Alex Ferguson. He was a maverick and an innovator and did things his own way and was, apparently, at the age of only 27, extremely open-minded to the NSL. So open that he had his agent approach South Melbourne Hellas with a "come and get me" plea—of sorts. Hellas said no at first, but was willing to give him a try the following season in 1980. That didn't happen. Conn returned to the UK from a jaunt to the NASL and played on with Hearts, Blackpool and Motherwell.

Archie Gemmill: to Wollongong City, 1981

Archie Gemmill was a hero in Scotland long before Trainspotting helped immortalise his most famous moment. In the 1978 World Cup Gemmill produced one of the finest individual goals of all time when he danced around a sea of hapless Dutch defenders before lifting it over the Dutch keeper. But in 1981, when he was still a spritely 34 years and Birmingham City captain, Gemmill was inches away from signing a guest contract with Wollongong City in the NSL. It was to be a three-match deal to kick-in when Birmingham City First Division season ended. The deal looked a certainty, with coach Ken Morton announcing the Gemmill deal at the time as practically done. Morton went so far as to add that Gemmill approached Wollongong.

Rene Houseman: to Sydney City-Hakoah, 1981

In 1981 it was Hakoah again looking to bring a big name to Australia. Now called Sydney City-Hakoah, they reached agreement for Rene Houseman to play in the NSL, which was then touted by *Soccer Action* as the most expensive contract in Australian football history. The deal also included his younger unknown brother Marcelo, aged 20.

Soccer Action on July 8th stated he was arriving the day of print and would be free to play on the weekend against Heidelberg, which was also their lead story. On July 15th *Soccer Action* confessed Rene was held up at Buenos Aires due to passport issues; it hadn't been renewed, but Marcelo had arrived. Two weeks later it was over. Whilst Marcelo was playing in Sydney City's youth team, Rene was due to arrive in Sydney on three separate occasions and never turned up, the whole episode deemed a farce. Little brother Marcelo never played a senior game with Sydney City Hakoah and ended up becoming a player agent, managing Nigerian talent and sending them to South America.

Martin O'Neill: to Heidelberg United, 1981

In the early 1980s Dunlop also had a practice of bringing big names to Australia as living billboards—Ian Callaghan and Bobby Charlton to name two—so this one might have merit. Dunlop were pumping money into football in the early NSL, including nearly $200,000 on sponsorship and some of that was used on imported stars. O'Neill was in town in 1980 with a Northern Ireland XI for friendlies against the Socceroos where he scored twice in three games, the perfect backdrop for a rumour of guest stint. Dunlop were going to make the deal a reality after the 1981 English season, which turned out to be O'Neill's last for Nottingham Forest. A 29-year-old pro with two European cups would have been a fine addition to any NSL club and for some reason Heidelberg was to be the lucky recipient.

Ilija Petkovic: to Footscray JUST, 1981

Ilija Petkovic was another revered member of the Yugoslav teams of the 1960s and 1970s, culminating in the final run in the 1968 European Championships where they knocked out England in the semi-final and pushed Italy into a replay in the final. But in 1981 he was being tempted with an offer to join the NSL side Footscray JUST. Footscray were holding up the table at that point in the season, and desperate for a lift. Petkovic was offered terms and the move seemed inevitable. But like so many Petkovic never landed in Australia and Footscray finished the season in 13th place.

Dragoslav Stepanovic: to Wollongong City, 1981

Curiously, when Gemmill was announced (before it fell through), Ken Morton mentioned that Yugoslav defender Dragoslav Stepanovic had also once been a realistic option. Stepanovic was capped 34 times for Yugoslavia and played for both OFK Belgrade and Red Star Belgrade before he was allowed to leave the Iron Curtain at the age of 28. His first stop on his world tour was at Eintracht Frankfurt, before joining a Bundesliga 2 side Wormatia Worms and then giving England a try with Manchester City. When he left City in 1981, a pit-stop in Wollongong beckoned but he instead embarked on a visit to the US.

Wynton Rufer: to Sydney City, 1982

Wynton Rufer is the best footballer New Zealand has ever produced and was awarded the Oceania Footballer of the 20th Century. In 1982 his star was on the rise; the 18-year-old scored four goals in New Zealand's final three World Cup Qualifiers that saw the All-Whites make the World Cup. *Soccer Action* reported that Sydney City had signed him on a 10-game guest stint, which would see him play in the NSL before heading back to Wellington to prepare for the tournament. Instead of Sydney City, it was Miramar Rangers in New Zealand which had Rufer for eight games before the tournament. Rufer went on to have a successful career in Switzerland and Germany in the 1980s and 1990s.

Frank Worthington: to anyone, 1985

At the end of the 1984/85 English season, Frank Worthington faced a dilemma. He was 36, was eager to leave Brighton & Hove Albion on a free transfer, and was getting calls from Manchester United manager Ron Atkinson to bring his showmanship to play back-up at Old Trafford. He was (allegedly) also eyeing off a run in the NSL after a successful tour of the Antipodes in 1984 with the 'World Soccer Series'. Ultimately, the "anti-establishment hellraiser" (as he was described in *National Soccer Monthly*) opted for Tranmere Rovers instead. Maybe he took a close look at the Australian establishment he'd be railing against (the NSL, the ASF, etc.) and thought he would need a tougher challenge.

John Fashanu: to Wollongong City, 1988

John Fashanu—younger brother of Adelaide City icon Justin—got the closest to that door without going through it. Reports suggest that he was extremely keen before his signing for Wollongong became impossible. He was with Wimbledon in 1988 when his hopes of playing for Wollongong were shattered by the Crazy Gang's inability to lose games in the FA Cup. They went on a "crazy" run, got to the final, beat Liverpool and by then the door to Wollongong had closed. Fashanu won the most improbable of FA Cups in 1988, but to miss out on playing a part in Wollongong's minor premiership in the NSL? It must represent a conspicuous gap on 'Fash the Bash's' cabinet.

Iain Ferguson: to Wollongong City, 1988

Unlike his countryman and namesake Ian Ferguson, Iain Ferguson (note the superfluous i) never played in the NSL. While Ian had a number of successful seasons with the Northern Spirit before making the great leap forward into the A-League with the Central Coast Mariners, Iain missed his chance in the northern summer of 1988, while he was visiting Sydney with his Australian wife. A striker with Dundee United,

Ferguson was Harry Michaels' last roll of the dice before he gave up on his 1988 vintage of the Wollacticos. It's unclear if Ferguson declined (he was in town anyway) or whether Michaels changed his mind (he wasn't in the same league as Francis, Mariner or Brazil). But Iain Ferguson never signed, which forced fans of Ian Ferguson's to wait 14 years to add the name to their autograph books.

Peter Reid and Mark Falco: to Wollongong City, 1989

Despite rumours that Michaels had walked away from the Wolves in 1988, he continued to flirt with his Wollactico concept (to some extent) in 1989. Like many names in 1988, midfielder and First Division champion with Everton, Peter Reid, then nearly 33 and with QPR, and fellow QPR pro, Mark Falco, were named in the press and signed, sealed, delivered and headed for the 'Gong. They were lined up to play in two matches, each—the same matches one imagines, in June of 1989. Except, of course, they didn't.

Norman Whiteside: to Heidelberg United, 1989

The NSL had a couple of bites at Norman Whiteside, who clearly wasn't in the habit of slamming the door in NSL Club faces. When announcing the Kosta Kouis signing, the 'Bergers also happened to throw in that they were optimistic Whiteside would join them. A tacked-on, throwaway remark at the end of another transfer announcement wouldn't be considered PR best practice today.

Giorgos Togias: to South Melbourne Hellas, 1989

Another in the signed-delivered-and-see-you-next-month-but-just-never happened category is Georgios Togias. He was booked for "up to" five guest games in 1989 with Hellas. At the time he was with Panionios, was 29, but had had a glittering seven-year career with Olympiacos which included caps for the national team. His motivation for choosing Hellas wasn't a wholly original one: he would be in Melbourne visiting family anyway.

Bruce Grobbelaar: to Northern Spirit, 1998

In an early, and gorgeously retained version of the Northern Spirit web fanzine, there is a piece from 20 February 1998 that claims the 41-year-old former Liverpool, Zimbabwe and then hired gun in England's lower leagues had approached the Spirit about setting shop in goal for the NSL newcomers. Spirit were keen too, apparently,

221

but had already offered Socceroo and Sydney United keeper Zeljko Kalac $400,000 over three years and were awaiting Kalac's answer. Ultimately neither move happened. Kalac moved back to Europe with Roda JC, and Grobbelaar continued to play in lower levels in England as well as South Africa.

It wasn't Grobbelaar's first nibble at a lamington. In 1983 a report in *Soccer Action* named him and Liverpool teammates (and West Adelaide's own) Graeme Souness as being keen to appear in the NSL for some sweet guest coin.

Eric Cantona: to Northern Spirit, 1998

To make a splash in their first season in the NSL, Spirit and their President Remo Nogarotto dug deep to find a big name to help put the team on the map. In 1998, few names were as big as Eric Cantona. Cantona was only 32 but had sensationally retired at the end of Manchester United's 1996/97 Premier League winning season. He had set the standard for cool (and violence) in the early years of the Premier League and when the seagulls from the Northern Spirit were looking for a trawler, he was the biggest in the ocean. "I would give my right arm to get him" said Nogarotto, who offered up a six-match guest contract, but in the end had to settle for Clayton Zane.

Paul Gascoigne: to Joondalup City, 2000

For a brief minute in the sun, Gazza was headed to Joondalup City. As the 2000 season wound to a close and Gazza was in the midst of "urgent talks" with his boss at Middlesbrough, Bryan Robson, rumours of a loan deal for the soon-to-be 33-year-old to the State League club in Perth started circulating. They circulated so far and wide that Bryan Robson—no stranger to rumours of an Australian stint himself—turned to the BBC to make an official statement. "It's just utter rubbish," Robson said.

To what extent Gazza was into the move is unknown. It was actually Joondalup making all the waves on the deal, with Geordie-born manager Paul Simmons "insisting" that the deal was "80% done".

"We're towards the end of negotiations," he said. "How big is this for Australian soccer?" Simmons gloated to *The Guardian*. As the rumour of Gazza to Joondalup intensified there was only one question on everyone's lips. Where?

What was in it for Gazza? Money? Australian business opportunities? No. It was fishing. Set on Lake Joondalup north of Perth, and a stone's throw away from the Indian Ocean, Joondalup is teeming with fish. It's an angler's paradise and Gazza, a keen angler, must have felt a little nibble on the worm in his heart.

Stan Collymore: to Newcastle Jets, 2006

After Northern Spirit folded with the NSL, Remo Nogarotto wasn't quite finished dangling his line in front of Premier League icons. In a new role with the A-League's Newcastle Jets, Nogarotto of 2006 asked his 1998 self to hold his beer while he tried to lure Stan Collymore out of retirement. Collymore had been retired for five years by this stage, and had barely played at all since leaving Aston Villa in 2000. He was a young retiree, at only 30, and had resisted other offers to return by Southend, Boston United and Wolves. By 2006 his most recent action was appearing in the 2005 film Basic Instinct 2 beside Sharon Stone.

But despite all logic and common sense, a four-game guest contract, the first of which was to occur in less than a month, seemed a done deal, until suddenly it wasn't. Nogarotto told the *Sydney Morning Herald* that Collymore "couldn't marry the two dates—the block of games we wanted, and his own availability".

Dexter Rosales: to Adelaide United, 2012

Rosales doesn't quite have the reputation as many of these other rumoured guests, but his pedigree is worth exploring. A junior with the USA, he played club football with River Plate in Argentina, Ajax Amsterdam in Holland and Valencia in Spain.

Australian FIFA agent Lou Nesci was approached and asked if Rosales could trial with Adelaide United. Offering to pay his own way to trial with Adelaide United, Adelaide football director Michael Petrillo was quoted as saying that Rosales had been recommended to them. When he didn't show, further digging saw that he did not even exist.

They weren't the only club to be offered the skills of Dexter Rosales to trial with the team, but they were the only club to announce it. Adelaide United put out a statement that both Rosales and former Chelsea player Fabio Ferreira would be heading to South Australia to trial.

Not all was lost for the Reds as the Portuguese Ferreira went on to play 51 times.

Louis Saha: to Caulfield United Cobras, 2015

The FFA Cup has been a godsend for lovers of fine improbable guest appearance rumours. And few rumours can hold a candle to Louis Saha to Caulfield United Cobras, of the Victorian State Third Division South East (or the sixth tier of Australia's disjointed pyramid). With a sixth round tie looming against state heavyweights Heidelberg United, Saha seemed the obvious choice for the Cobras. He hadn't played for a couple of years, was 36 at the time, and was last seen not scoring for either Sunderland or Lazio in 2013. Folklore has this deal as nailed on—shirts and merch were even printed for Saha—until the broadcast partner and bankroller Fox Football dropped their interest at the last minute.

Goran Pandev: to Western Sydney Wanderers, 2018

The exact reason why (arguably) Macedonia's greatest player Goran Pandev's deal to the A-League's Western Sydney Wanderers didn't happen isn't known, but the furore about it points to the FFA doubting Pandev's status as a "marquee". The FFA makes bonus, outside-the-salary-cap payments available to extraordinary players who suit up in the A-League to market it to new and wonderful places. At 33, with a reported two-year deal on the table, Pandev would have made a dream signing for the A-League. Longevity wasn't an issue and he certainly would have found willing idolisers in Australia with its large Macedonian communities across the country. He is his country's all-time top scorer in a record that will take some beating.

Peter Crouch: to Sydney FC, 2018

When Stoke City were relegated from the English Premier League, their 37-year-old, former England striker Peter Crouch still had a year to go on his contract when he was targeted by FFA as a marquee. Two-metre Peter was once asked what he would be if he wasn't a professional footballer and he famously quipped "a virgin". That type of character and hilarity would have been the perfect fit for the Australian mainstream media; however, once retired Crouch told *The World Game* website "I liked the idea of living in Australia but it (Sydney FC offer) never materialised."

Ivica Olic and Darijo Srna:
to Melbourne Knights, 2019

As the round of 32-match FFA Cup between Melbourne Knights and the A-League's Adelaide United approached, rumours of two remarkable signings started to emerge. The Knights, with their deep Croatian roots, were apparently in talks with Ivica Olic and Darijo Srna to join them as one-off guests in the Cup.

As the rumours went, Olic was the most progressed. Olic had been "talking" to the Knights for some time and, despite being 39 and two years retired, seemed keen. Srna was the more speculative of the two, mainly because he was more recently out of the game but had moved into an assistant coaching role with his long-time club Shakhtar Donetsk. Neither player signed, but the rumour was fun while it lasted.

Daniel Sturridge:
to 'several' A-League clubs, 2019

As Sturridge was on his way out of Liverpool after several mixed, injury-ravaged seasons, rumours started circulating about the 29-year-old finding his way down to the A-League. His star had faded since he was scoring goals in the 2014 World Cup for England, but while he was persona non-grata in England's transfer market, the question was being asked: just how far had he fallen from his peak? According to Fox Sports Executive producer Murray Shaw the answer was "this far". In the Fox Football Podcast Murray announced in April 2019 that Sturridge had been shopped around the A-League liberally. With Robbie Fowler confirmed as coach of Brisbane Roar, two and two were being put together all over the place.

"Finding a player is not hard but it's getting them here," Fowler told *Fox Sports*.

Bibliography and Related Sources

The book was compiled from a mixture of interviews with people involved with the players featured, including in some cases the players themselves, as well as other publications and research.

Quotes from individuals are typically cited, but there are anecdotes captured in this book that are provided uncited, in cases where the source preferred not to be named. These were always cross-checked with other primary and secondary sources.

The following books, newspapers, magazines and websites were used in our research.

Ardiles, Ossie, *Ossie's Dream*, Corgi Books, 2009

Ball, Alan, *Alan Ball: Playing Extra Time*, Sidgwick & Jackson, 2004

Batt, Peter, *Mick Channon: The Authorised Biography*, Highdown, 2004

Beardsley, Peter, *My life story*, HarperCollins, 1995

Best, George, *Blessed: The autobiography,* Random House, 2001

Best, George, *Blessed: The Autobiography*, Ebury Press, 2002

Bolt, Usain, *Faster than Lightning: My Autobiography*, HarperCollins, 2013

Brazil, Alan, *Both barrels from Brazil*, Racing Post Books, 2008

Brazil, Alan, *There's an awful lot of bubbly in Brazil*, Highdown, 2006

Brooking, Trevor, *My Life in Football*, Simon & Schuster, 2014

Callaghan, Ian, *The Ian Callaghan Story*, Quartet Books Limited, 1975

Case, Jimmy, *Hard Case*, John Blake Publishing, 2014

Channon, Mick, *The Authorised Biiography*, Highdown, 2004

Channon Jnr, Mick, *How's your Dad?,* Racing Post Books, 2016

Charlton, Sir Bobby, *My Manchester United Years*, Headline Publishing, 2007

Clough, Brian Howard, *Clough The Autobiography*, Corgi, 1995

Clough, Brian, *Cloughie Walking on Water*, Headline Book Publishing, 2002

Deans, Dixie, *There's only one Dixie Deans*, Birlinn, 2011

Del Piero, Alessandro, *Playing On*, Allen & Unwin, 2013

Dickinson, Matt, *Bobby Moore: The man in full*, Yellow Jersey Press, 2014

Docherty, Tommy, *The Doc: Hallowed Be Thy Game,*
Headline Publishing Group, 2006

Founten, Loukas, *A Decade United,* Loukas Founten, 2015

Fowler, Robbie, *My Life in Football,* Blink Publishing, 2019

Francis, Trevor, *One in a Million,* Pitch Publishing, 2019

Gatt, Ray, *The Rale Rasic Story,* New Holland Publishers, 2006

George, Charlie, *Charlie George:My Story,* Century, 2005

Goldsmith, Jason, *Surfing for England our lost Socceroos,* Fair Play Publishing, 2019

Gorman, Joe, *The Death & Life of Australian Soccer,*
University of Queensland Press, 2017

Hamilton, Duncan, *George Best Immortal: The Approved Biography,*
Windmill Books, 2014

Hamilton, Duncan, *Immortal: The Biography of George Best,* Windmill Books, 2014

Hay, Roy, *Games, Goals, Glory,* Hardie Grant, 2016

Heskey, Emile, *Even Heskey Scored,* Pitch Publishing, 2019

Howe, Andrew, *Encyclopedia of Socceroos,* Fair Play Publishing, 2018

James, Kieran, Walsh, Rex, Mustata, Razvan, Bonaci, Carmen
"The appropriation of migrant labor in Australian football" *Problems and Perspectives in Management,* LLC Consulting Publishing Company, 2012

Keegan, Kevin, *My Life in Football,* Macmillan, 2018

Kurn, Michael, *Life of a Saint,* Desire Dream Vision Ltd, 2020

Latchford, Bob, *A Different Road,* deCoubertin Books, 2015

Macdonald, Malcolm, *Super Mac: My Autobiography,* HIghdown, 2003

Macdougall, Ted, *Macdou-GOAL!:The Ted Macdougall Story,* Pitch Publishing, 2016

Mangan, Patrick, *Offsider,* Victory Books, 2010

Marinello, Peter, *Fallen Idle,* Headline Publishing Group, 2007

Read, Jim, *Justin Fashanu:The Biography,*
The Derby Books Publishing Company, 2012

Rush, Ian, *My Italian Diary,* Arthur Barker, 1989

Soccer Australia: 1999 Annual Report, Soccer Australia, 1999

Souness, Graeme, *Football: My Life, My Passion,* Headline Publishing Group, 2017

Stacey, Steve, *The Colour of Football,* Bristol Books, 2019

Warren, Johnny, *Sheila's, Wogs and Poofters,* Random House Australia, 2002

Whittell, Peter, *The life story of Doncaster Rovers legend Alick Jeffrey,*
Chronicle Publishing, 2003

Wilson, Jonathan, *Inverting the Pyramid,* Orion, 2008

Yorke, Dwight, *Born to score: the autobiography,* Pan Books, 2009

ABC News

Australian Financial Review

Australian Soccer Weekly

Belfast Telegraph

Canberra Times

Channel 10

Cherry Chimes (afcbchimes.blogspot.com)

Cornerflag.com.au

Dailymail.co.uk

David Jack's Blog: djcjack.com

Diatribe-column.blogsport.com

Everton Heritage Society

Football Nation Radio

Football United vs Soccer City podcast

Football Victoria podcast

Ftbl.com.au

Goal.com

Illawarra Mercury

Independent.co.uk

Kyabram Free Press

Kyabram Guardian

Lfchistory.net

Liverpoolfc.fandom.com

Manutd.com

Mcg.org.au

Meassociation.org.uk

Melbourneknights.com.au

Melbournesoccer.blogspot.com

Newcastle Herald

Ozfootball.net

Parkinson in Australia (Channel 10)

Peninsula Strikers Soccer Club

Platinum Awards

Punditarena.com

Readingfc.co.uk

Report of the NSL Task Force

Riverina Herald

Roy Morgan

SBS-TV

Scotsman.com

Smfc.com.au

Soccer Action

Soccer Federation of Western
    Australia Yearbook

Soccer International

Soccer News

Soccer World

Sportscene (Channel 7)

Sportstg.com

Star Soccer

Sydney Morning Herald

The Age

Theblizzard.co.uk

The Courier Mail

The Evening Times

The Guardian

TheWorldGame.sbs.com.au

Thin White Line

Walter Pless' Blog:
    walterplessonsoccer.blogspot.com

Western Suburbs Soccer Club (VIC)

Whitecapsfc.com

Wolvesheroes.com

Worldcup-2002.co.uk

Acknowledgements

These stories were put together after many interviews with coaches, teammates, fans, administrators, agents, promoters, journalists, commentators, historians and in some cases the players themselves.

Special thanks is reserved for the small band of heroic Australian football historians, most of whom work unaligned to any governing body, who have dedicated hours bent over scanners and spreadsheets for the love of the game. The history of Australian football is precious, unique, and represents the change in dynamics occurring in Australian society. To lose this history would be to lose a facet of our social history. Football historians who have rescued team sheets, scores, tables and stories from our past are now allowing this kind of book to be written, and more stories to be added to their foundations.

Shout outs to the people behind ozfootball.net: Andrew Howe, Tony Persoglia, John Punshon, Greg Stock and the work that Mark Boric does on melbournesoccer.blogsport.com. These resources are invaluable to the history of football in Australia. Also to David Jack, who's conversion of his video library from VHS to mp4 was a godsend.

Special thanks to the subjects themselves who made themselves available to speak with us. Mick Channon and his son Mick Channon Junior, Bob Latchford and Paul Mariner (may he rest in peace). Great thanks also to Bill McMurdo, George Best's long time manager and touring companion, and to Harry Michaels who was the protagonist in many stories.

It is always a pleasure to speak with Socceroos, so thanks to Rale Rasic (coach), Col Curran, Ante Milicic, Gary Marocchi, George Harris, Robbie Cornthwaite, Robbie Slater, Gary Van Egmond, Francis Awaritefe, Danny Moulis, Ted Smith, Frank Farina, Gary Cole, Jimmy Pearson, Adrian Alston, Paul Wade and Jeff Olver.

Thank you to the following people for their guidance, support and content in putting together *Be My Guest*.

Adam Peacock, Alex Alexandrou, Alf De Bono, Andrew Howe, Andy Paschalidis, Ann Odong, Ben McKay, Billy Millen, Bonita Mersiades, Brian Wheatley, Buddy Farah,

Tom Argyrou, Cliff Pointer, Cracovia FC, Dave Davutovic, David Jack, Dez Marton, Eric Marocchi, Evan Morgan Grahame, Floreat Athena, George Cotsanis, Grantlee Kieza, Greg Stock, Harry Bell, Henk Mollee, Iain Cook, James Corbett and the Everton Historical Society, Jim Butterfill, Joey Didulica, John Davidson, John Didulica, John Doropoulos, John O'Connell, John Pilkadaris, John Poleykett, John Sabetta, John Sigur, John Sydenham, Joshua Thomas, Keith Hughes, Keith Whelan, Kelmscott Soccer Club, Ken Boden, Ken Morton, Laurence Hall, Malcolm Rowney, Mark Boric, Michael Lynch, Micky Brock, Mike Mulvey, Mike Tetlow, Neil McGachey, Patrick Mangan, Patrick Skene, Paul Mavroudis, Pave Jusup, Peter Rowney, Philip Micallef, Ray Gatt, Rob Scanlon, Rockingham City FC, Ron More, Roy Hay, Shaun Mielekamp, Simon Hill, Simon Smales, Stan Pilkadaris, Stratos Tzanoudakis, Dom Stillitano, Tim Parker, Tony Persoglia, Tony Rallis, Travis Faulks, Vicky Morton, Walter Pless, West Adelaide, Western Pride.

Finally, we offer the largest thanks imaginable to our respective families, who forgave us late nights, missing weekends and constant chatter about topics barely relevant during a global pandemic. We hope that, on some level, information about the lineage of the Jack family and defunct celebrity bakeries provided some comfort or amusement.

Glossary

A-League	Australia's premier domestic national league competition which commenced in 2005
ASF	Australian Soccer Federation, one of the forerunners to the FFA (see below)
CAF	Confederation of African Football
CONCACAF	Confederation of North, Central America and Caribbean Football
FFA	Football Federation Australia (re-named Football Australia in 2021)
MLS	Major League Soccer, the national league competition in the USA
NPL	National Premier League, the state-based competition run in every state of Australia
NSL	National Soccer League, Australia's national league competition from 1977 to 2004

About the Authors

Jason and Lucas crossed paths whilst playing cricket together for Richmond City Cricket Club. Social media saw them understand they both shared a passion for the Socceroos and enjoyed the quirky history of Australian football.

Be My Guest was brainstormed together on the nine-hour drive from Melbourne to Jamberoo for the inaugural Australian Football Writers Festival in 2019. Jason is a football book nerd. Lucas is a spreadsheet nerd.

This is Jason's second book following 2019's *Surfing for England* (Fair Play Publishing), and is dedicated to his children Henry and Ivy.

For Lucas, this is his first book, after publishing longform articles for the *Football Pink* and covering the A-League for *The Roar*. Lucas dedicates this work to his wife Glentin and his daughters, Darby and Tully.

Jason Goldsmith   Lucas Gillard

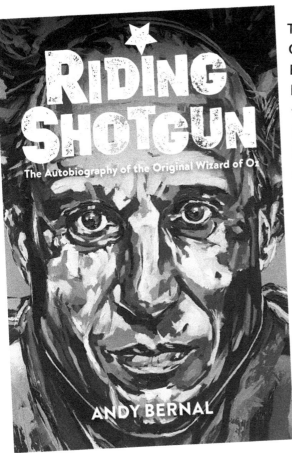

Really good football books

Code War$
The Battle for Fans, Dollars
and Survival
by Dr Hunter Fujak

The Australian Youth
Footballer Regulatory Guide
by Peter Paleologos
(Popcorn Press)

The Away Game
by Matthew Hall

Achieving the Impossible
- the Remarkable Story
of How Greece Won
EURO 2004
by George Tsitsonis

Whatever It Takes - The
Inside Story of the FIFA Way
by Bonita Mersiades
(Powderhouse Press)

Surfing for England
Our Lost Socceroos
by Jason Goldsmith

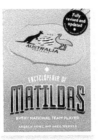

Encyclopedia of Matildas
Revised and Updated
by Andrew Howe
and Greg Werner

Encyclopedia of Socceroos
by Andrew Howe

'If I Started to Cry,
I Wouldn't Stop'
by Matthew Hall

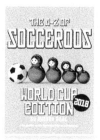

The A-Z of Socceroos -
World Cup Edition 2018
by Andrew Howe
(with Ray Gatt
and Bonita Mersiades)

Playing for Australia
The First Socceroos,
Asia and the World Game
by Trevor Thompson

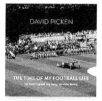

The Time of
My Football Life
by David Picken

The World Cup Chronicles 31
Days that Rocked Brazil by
Jorge Knijnik

Chronicles of Soccer
in Australia - The
Foundation Years 1859 to
1949 by Peter Kunz

The Aboriginal Soccer Tribe
by John Maynard

Support Your Local League,
A South-East Asian Football
Odyssey by Antony Sutton

Introducing Jarrod Black
by Texi Smith
(Popcorn Press)

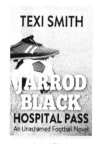

Jarrod Black
Hospital Pass
by Texi Smith
(Popcorn Press)

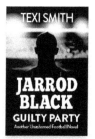

Jarrod Black
Guilty Party
by Texi Smith
(Popcorn Press)

Achieving the Impossible
- the Remarkable Story
of How Greece Won
EURO 2004
by George Tsitsonis

Available from

fairplaypublishing.com.au

and all

good bookstores

FAIRPLAY
PUBLISHING

FAIRPLAY
PUBLISHING

www.fairplaypublishing.com.au